Jesus: A Brief Hi

This series offers brief, accessible, and lively accounts of key topics within theology and religion. Each volume presents both academic and general readers with a selected history of topics which have had a profound effect on religious and cultural life. The word "history" is, therefore, understood in its broadest cultural and social sense. The volumes are based on serious scholarship but they are written engagingly and in terms readily understood by general readers.

Published

Heaven	Alister E. McGrath
Heresy	G. R. Evans
Islam	Tamara Sonn
Death	Douglas J. Davies
Saints	Lawrence S. Cunningham
Christianity	Carter Lindberg
Dante	Peter S. Hawkins
Spirituality	Philip Sheldrake
Cults and New Religions	Douglas E. Cowan and David G. Bromley
Love	Carter Lindberg
Christian Mission	Dana L. Robert
Christian Ethics	Michael Banner
Jesus	W. Barnes Tatum

Forthcoming

Reformation	Kenneth Appold
Monasticism	Dennis D. Martin
Apocalypse	Martha Himmelfarb
Shinto	John Breen and Mark Teeuwen
Sufism	Nile Green

Jesus

A Brief History

W. Barnes Tatum

WILEY-BLACKWELL

A John Wiley & Sons, Ltd., Publication

Contents

List of Figures

Preface and Acknowledgments

Much of my classroom teaching and most of my professional writing have been related to that historical figure named Jesus whose best-known title of honor "Christ" has often functioned in popular usage as his last name: Jesus Christ. The English word "Christ," of course, comes from the Greek *christos* and translates the Hebrew *mashiah*, or messiah (literally, "anointed one"). Within ancient Israel, the designation honored the reigning king as God's anointed, but after the Babylonian exile it could be used to honor any expected redeemer figure, whether royal or otherwise.

That Jesus would be remembered as the Christ represents something of an irony since the earliest written narratives about his life – the Gospels of Matthew, Mark, and Luke – often indicate Jesus' reluctance to use or to accept this complimentary designation. But it is this title of honor that underlies the name of the religion that traces its beginnings to Jesus: Christianity. This title also underlies the name of the adherents of this religion even today: Christians.

Recent decades have witnessed a phenomenal renewal of interest in the question of what Jesus was like as a historical figure. However, my "brief" history does not represent another biography about Jesus. It is not another attempt to reconstruct historically Jesus' life within its first-century setting. I am much more audacious and foolhardy than that! I envision this relatively small book to provide a readable account of how Jesus and his story have been received over the past two millennia – especially by those who confess him to be the Christ. This brief history constitutes in its own abbreviated, highly selective, way a "reception" history. I trace how Jesus, a Galilean Jew, born when ancient Rome ruled the Mediterranean world – including the Hellenized eastern sector – had come to be received as the Christ by more than 2 billion believers around the globe by the first decade of the twenty-first century. I situate my story of Jesus' reception within the framework of a brief prologue and a briefer epilogue, and I narrate the story in seven chapters.

The chapters themselves generally follow a chronological sequence. Chapter 1 surveys the diverse ways Jesus was viewed in the years of the Christian movement before Constantine (first to fourth centuries). Chapter 2 describes the debates about Jesus that resulted in his being defined as one person of the divine Trinity, with two natures, both divine and human – doctrines that remain foundational for Christian orthodoxy (fourth and fifth centuries). Chapter 3 highlights the many institutional and cultural expressions of this orthodox understanding of Jesus within Christianity during the Middle Ages (from the fifth to the fifteenth centuries). Chapter 4 delineates three cultural and ecclesiastical challenges to this orthodox understanding of Jesus – the Renaissance, the Reformation, and the Enlightenment (since the fifteenth century). Chapter 5 provides an overview of the new historical consciousness and the resulting quest for the historical Jesus (since the eighteenth century). Chapter 6 considers the diverse ways in which Jesus has been received as the Christ, and otherwise, in the modern and increasingly postmodern world – with a focus on recent special-interest theologies (since the eighteenth century). Chapter 7 identifies the ongoing relationship of Jesus to other religions of the world (since the first century).

The recurring questions presupposed by my version of the Jesus story are those of traditional theology: Who was he (Christology)? What did he do (soteriology)? But the answers to these questions are grounded in a response to a third question: Whose was he (contextualization)? Where appropriate, consideration of Jesus' reception will be supported not only by ancient texts, creeds, and theological treatises, but by liturgy and practice and by the arts – visual and dramatic.

I am indebted to the staff of Blackwell Publishing, now Wiley-Blackwell, who guided this project into print. I am especially grateful to Andrew Humphries, who first approached me about my undertaking mission impossible and who later met with me during the Society of Biblical Literature (SBL) meetings in Edinburgh, in Washington, DC, in San Diego, California, and – along the way – over lunch with Linda and myself near Carfax in Oxford. Other contributors to the production process have included Annette Abel, Charlotte Frost, and Janet Moth.

As a faculty member in a Methodist-affiliated, liberal arts college in the United States, I have had opportunities both to teach a broad range of courses in religion and to teach collaboratively with faculty from other academic disciplines. My presentation herein has been strengthened by my participation with students and faculty in these settings, whether apparent or not. I also wish to thank others at Greensboro College for their continued professional support. These include Craven E. Williams, President; Paul L. Leslie, Vice-President for Academic Affairs and Dean of the Faculty; Michael Simmons and Virginia R. Hunt, Reference Librarians; Cathy Vail, Proctor Hall Secretary; Daniel Chambers, Information Technology Assistant; and The Royce and Jane Reynolds Endowment Fund for Faculty Development.

I am appreciative of encouragement and support from fellow academics who have been involved in the development and the refinement of this writing exercise. These include Mahlon Smith, a long-time friend and fellow participant in the Jesus Seminar now actively retired from the faculty at Rutgers University; Chris Frilingos, a once-upon-a-time student in my classes at Greensboro College and now a member of the religious studies faculty at Michigan State University; and Richard Ascough of the religious studies faculty at Queen's University in Kingston, Ontario, who graciously agreed to have at least a three-time go at my emerging manuscript. April L. Najjaj of the history faculty at Greensboro College also read portions of the manuscript.

Once again, my colleagues Rhonda Burnette-Bletsch, of the Greensboro College religion faculty, and Walter Beale, of the English faculty at our neighboring institution, the University of North Carolina Greensboro, have provided helpful comments by reading chapters of the manuscript in progress. As I like to say, GC is the older institution (chartered 1838); but UNCG is the larger of the two (current enrollment around 17,000).

I also wish to acknowledge my having reworked material for Chapters 5 and 6 in this volume that originally appeared in my *In Quest of Jesus*, published in a revised and expanded edition by Abingdon Press (1999), and in the two editions of my *Jesus at the Movies* published by Polebridge Press (1997 and 2004).

Then, above all, and especially in this undertaking, Linda my spousal partner has been supportive in ways that defy explanation. Her considerable theological sensitivity and literary acumen are evident in all that I have written well.

W. Barnes Tatum
Jefferson-Pilot Professor of Religion and Philosophy
Greensboro College
Greensboro, North Carolina, USA

Prologue

Jesus, a Jew from Galilee

Jesus was a Jew. He hailed from that northern area of the land of Israel known as Galilee. This claim about Jesus' identity and place appears obvious from even the most casual and uncritical reading of the earliest written narratives about his life – the familiar gospels of Matthew, Mark, Luke, and John.

These four gospels identify Jesus as a Galilean and point to Nazareth as his home village, although Matthew and Luke place his birth in Bethlehem of Judea. Matthew and Luke also provide Jesus with family genealogies indicating descent from King David; and the author of Luke further underscores Jesus' Jewishness by including a notation of his circumcision on the eighth day.

The gospels of Matthew, Mark, and Luke have come to be known as the "Synoptic" Gospels because they together ("syn-") view ("optic") the ministry and message of Jesus. When Jesus in these gospels becomes a public figure, after his baptism and his calling of twelve disciples, he confines his "kingdom" activities of teaching in parables and healing the sick primarily to Galilee. Only occasionally do Jesus and his disciples undertake forays beyond Galilee – northwestward toward Tyre and Sidon, northward into the environs of Caesarea Philippi, and eastward beyond the Sea of Galilee These three gospels describe only one journey of Jesus – from Galilee to Judea and the holy city of Jerusalem.

However, the Gospel of John identifies several journeys of Jesus from Galilee to Jerusalem over at least a three-year period (based on the number of Passovers cited). In the Fourth Gospel, Jesus' message does not center on the "kingdom of God" nor does he speak in parables. Instead, Jesus himself constitutes the center of his own message as he punctuates long discourses with striking self-referential sayings introduced by the turn of phrase used by God in the Jewish scriptures, "I am ..." (compare "I am the LORD your God," Exod. 20:2, with "I am the resurrection and the life," John 11:25).

All four of these narrative gospels conclude with accounts introduced by Jesus' entry into Jerusalem on an ass, although Matthew has him riding two animals. The following sequence of events encompasses Jesus' final meal with his followers, his subsequent arrest, his legal hearings before the Jewish authorities and the Roman prefect Pontius Pilate, his execution by crucifixion, and his burial in a tomb. And so this Jew from Galilee dies on a Roman cross in Judea outside Jerusalem. But the gospel accounts themselves end with stories about an empty tomb and about Jesus' after-death appearances – stories about Israel's God having resurrected Jesus from death.

Historians today usually circumscribe the life of Jesus with such dates as 4 BC–AD 30 (or 4 BCE–30 CE). This method of numbering years from the date of Jesus' birth originated in the sixth century with a Scythian monk who lived and wrote in Rome: Dionysius Exiguus, or Dennis the Little. Thus our contemporary calendar itself serves as a reminder of the influence this Galilean Jew has had on emerging western culture and increasingly on world culture, wherever this calendar is used. But the contradiction of having Jesus born in 4 BC or 4 BCE, four years before his birth, stems from Dennis' miscalculation by at least four years.

What was the world like into which Jesus was born? The Mediterranean world of Jesus' day was culturally complex and represented three principal strata: Jewish, Greek, and Roman.

The Jews traced their descent from antiquity, from Abraham, Isaac, and Jacob and the events centered around the later figure of Moses. The Judaism of Jesus' day, often referred to as Second Temple Judaism, had emerged following the Babylonian exile, 587–539 BCE, after the ruler Cyrus the Persian decreed that the displaced Judeans, or Jews, could return to their homeland and rebuild the temple in Jerusalem dedicated to their God, Yahweh. Many Jews did return, but others did not. The Jewish *diaspora* (literally, "scattering") had begun. The temple was rebuilt and established itself as a focal point for Jewish identity at home and abroad – with a hereditary priesthood, the growing importance of the high priest, and a regularized pattern of sacrifices on behalf of God's people.

Within a century, the priest and scribe named Ezra had returned to the homeland with what would become the Torah, the five books of Moses, written in Hebrew, the ancient language of the Israelite people. Now, with the Torah, a scribal class and synagogues would appear. The Torah was soon complemented by other writings, and Judaism's scriptures eventually became threefold: Torah (Law); Nebi'im (Prophets); Kethubim (Writings). Thus Israel's experience of exile and return served as the catalyst for transforming the religion of pre-exilic Israel into post-exilic Judaism.

In 334–333 BCE, Alexander the Great crossed over from Greece into Asia Minor and swiftly conquered the entire Persian empire. Along with Alexander came the Hellenization of the eastern Mediterranean world – the bringing of the Greek language, literature, philosophy, and the arts to the peoples of his subjugated territories. After Alexander's untimely death in 323 BCE, his empire was divided among his generals, with the Jewish homeland first falling under the aegis of the Ptolemaic dynasty of Egypt and then under the Seleucid dynasty of Syria.

In the third century BCE, the Torah and other writings of the Jews began to be translated from Hebrew into Greek, probably in Egypt, in Alexandria. But a major crisis occurred when the Seleucid king Antiochus IV, in 167 BCE, adopted a policy aimed at eliminating Judaism: an altar to Zeus was set up in the temple; copies of the Torah were burned; the practice of circumcision was forbidden. In response, a priest, Mattathias the Hasmonean, initiated armed resistance to the Seleucids, and his son Judas (called Maccabeus, "the hammer") led his people to improbable victories and joyously rededicated the temple to Yahweh in 164 BCE. Judas became the first of the Hasmoneans or Maccabeans to briefly give his people an independent Jewish state in the land of Israel, in 164–163 BCE. This period of Hasmonean rule saw the appearance among the people of Israel of various Jewish sects – including the Sadducees, the Pharisees, and the Essenes. Ironically, the Hasmoneans precipitated the next major culture shift by establishing a friendship treaty with the ambitious Romans, and eventually invited Roman intervention to settle a dynasty dispute among themselves.

In 63 BCE the Roman general Pompey entered Jerusalem with his legions and profaned the temple itself by allegedly riding his horse into its sacred precincts. Thus began Roman political domination of the Jewish homeland. Rome, in transition from republic to empire, soon replaced the Hasmoneans with a client ruler and dynasty of their own choosing. Herod was named king (40–4 BCE) to be succeeded by his sons, among whom his kingdom was divided three ways. Archelaus became ethnarch over Judea and Samaria (4 BCE–6 CE) with Herod Antipas as tetrarch over Galilee and Perea (4 BCE–39 CE) and with Philip as tetrarch over the territories to the northeast (4 BCE–34 CE). Between the affirmation of Herod the Great as king by the Roman Senate (40 BCE) and the outbreak of the first Jewish revolt against Rome (66–70 CE [some would extend the end date to the fall of Masada in 74 CE]), the Romans had effected a transition from governing the Jews through local vassals to ruling them by Roman administrators. The best-known of these bureaucrats was Pontius Pilate (26–36 CE).

In Rome's political expansion to the east, Rome herself had been Hellenized so that the hyphenated expression Greco-Roman seems quite accurate at the broad cultural level. Although Latin was the language of Rome, Rome used the Greek language administratively in the provinces and territories of the eastern Mediterranean. Rome not only imitated Greek architecture, art, and literature, but adopted and renamed the gods of the Greek pantheon, admired Greek philosophy and literature, and began making claims of divinity for the emperors, recalling a precedent established by Alexander.

Because of the rise of sects within Judaism during the second century BCE, and their continued presence in the first century CE, first-century Judaism has often been described in the plural as Judaisms. Nonetheless, there was a core of beliefs and behaviors that provided Jews with a common identity in contradistinction to non-Jews, or Gentiles. Jews believed in the oneness of God, as affirmed by the *Shema* ("Hear O Israel ...," Deut. 6:4–5). Jews had a strong sense of identity as a people chosen by Yahweh and separated from the nations, as recognized by such practices as male circumcision (Gen. 17:11), sabbath observance (Exod. 20:8 and Deut. 5:12), and dietary restrictions (Lev. 11:1–47). In summary, Jews lived in accordance with God's commandments mediated through Moses. In the Greco-Roman world, Jews were often called *atheoi* ("atheists") because of their refusal to honor publicly the Roman gods, and "people haters" (*misanthrōpoi*) because of their ethnocentric practices.

Such was the first-century world inhabited by Jesus, the Galilean Jew, from the village of Nazareth. The recognition of Jesus' Jewishness can be reinforced by noting three occasions of silence in the four gospels, although arguments from silence can be less than compelling. First, the four gospels report incidental contact of Jesus with Gentiles in the course of his travels, but they contain no references to Jesus' association with the two major cities of Galilee both of which had been built or rebuilt by Herod Antipas following Hellenistic models: Sepphoris, located only four or so miles from Nazareth, and Tiberias, on the southwestern shore of the Sea of Galilee. Secondly, the four gospels contain no polemic by Jesus against Greco-Roman gods. His proclamation and teaching of "the kingdom of God," pervasive in the Synoptic Gospels, presupposes a characteristically Jewish monotheism. The *Shema* itself appears on his lips in Mark (12:29–30). Thirdly, there are no references to Jesus' belonging to one of the Jewish sects contemporary with him. He was not a Sadducee, not a Pharisee, not an Essene. In this, Jesus differs from Paul, the diaspora Jew, who two decades later identifies himself as a Pharisee in his own words (Phil. 3:5).

We now turn to the story of how Jesus the Galilean Jew has been received over the centuries. We begin with the beginnings – Jesus and Christian beginnings, the period from his life and death to the peace of Constantine in the fourth century.

Chapter 1

Jesus and Christian Beginnings
(First to Fourth Centuries)

There is no evidence that either Jesus or his disciples wrote anything about him and their shared activities during his lifetime. Even if Jesus' followers had written something, they could not have composed those Jesus books called "gospels." As confessional documents, the four earliest gospels presuppose a "faith perception" that even Jesus' closest associates seemingly lacked until their professed experiences of the living Jesus after his crucifixion and resurrection. Only then did they receive Jesus with conviction as "the messiah" and "the Son of God" and confer on him many other honorific names, and begin proclaiming the message of what God had accomplished through his life, death, and resurrection.[1]

Jesus the Jew belonged to no sect. But after his life, death and resurrection, his movement became a Jewish sect alongside such groups as the Sadducees, the Pharisees, and the Essenes. What distinguished this new community, centered in but probably not confined to Jerusalem, was its commitment to Jesus as God's messiah in fulfillment of promises made of old to Israel. But forty years would pass before Jesus' followers began writing narratives about him, sometime ca. 70 CE. By then, the story of Jesus was no longer confined to the land of Israel. The oral tradition of Jesus' words and deeds was no longer passed on solely in Aramaic, but had been translated into Greek. Just as Jesus came to be called "Christ" so the tellers of his story came to be called "Christians." This first occurred in Syrian Antioch, according to one source

(Acts 11:26). However, the gospels, which narrate Jesus' story, would not represent the earliest writings of the Christian movement.[2]

A Strange Case: Paul and his Letters

Paul, a Jew from the diaspora, possibly from Tarsus in Cilicia, had in all probability not known Jesus during the latter's lifetime. How strange! In fact, Paul had become a persecutor of "the church of God" when he experienced from God a transcendent "revelation of Jesus Christ" and received God's call to announce "good news," not to his own people the Jews but as "an apostle," to the Gentiles (Gal. 1:11–17). There followed three decades of Paul's itinerant activity around the northeastern region of the Mediterranean – from Damascus to Antioch, from Ephesus to Corinth, and finally to Rome, where he was most likely executed during the rule of Nero (mid-60s CE).

Paul's success in creating small communities of believers among the Gentiles necessitated his continuing oversight of these groups, which he exercised through revisits and an extensive correspondence. Thirteen letters attributed to him eventually found their way into the New Testament – nearly half of the writings in the twenty-seven-book collection. Biblical scholarship today considers a core of seven letters, all written in the decade of the 50s CE, as being undisputedly from Paul (Romans, 1 and 2 Corinthians, Galatians, 1 Thessalonians, Philippians, and Philemon). Three letters are often disputed (2 Thessalonians, Ephesians, Colossians). Three are nearly universally considered not to be by Paul (1 and 2 Timothy, Titus). However, all thirteen can be plotted along a "Pauline trajectory" extending from the 50s CE into the second century. My comments on the letters are here confined primarily to the undisputed seven.

Paul's letters were not written as missionary tracts for unbelievers but as pastoral directives to his own struggling communities, although his letter to the Romans was addressed to a congregation he had neither founded nor yet visited. As a letter of self-introduction, Romans represents the longest, most systematic, and for later generations theologically the most influential of all his letters. Along the way, many future Christians would be introduced to Jesus through the words of Paul.

Although Paul's correspondence reflects the traditional literary form of Greco-Roman letters, he adapted the form for his apostolic purposes. Paul characteristically greets his recipients with: "Grace to you and peace from God our Father and the Lord Jesus Christ." He concludes his letters with benedictions that, in one letter, are expressed in a threefold formula: "The grace of the Lord Jesus Christ and the love of God and the communion of the Holy Spirit be with all of you" (2 Cor. 13:14). Paul's most frequently used titles for Jesus are "Christ" and "Lord." His identification of God as "Father" also serves notice that he understood Jesus to be God's "Son," although he uses this title less frequently (Gal. 1:16). These brief excerpts make the point: Paul does not grapple with the specific issues related to the later debates that resulted in the doctrine of the Trinity, but he certainly has the theological vocabulary: Father, Son, and Holy Spirit.

Paul's claimed apostolic authority came from the resurrected Christ (Gal. 1:1). His preaching centered on the crucified Jesus (1 Cor. 2:2). His letters presuppose and invoke the crucified and living Christ until he returns (1 Thess. 4:13–18; 1 Cor. 15:51–8). However, Paul learned details about Jesus as a historical figure from others, including Peter, whether in Jerusalem or elsewhere. Jesus was human and a Jew (Rom. 5:15, 9:5). Jesus had been born of a woman under the law (Gal. 4:4). Jesus also had brothers, one of whom was named James (1 Cor. 9:5; Gal. 1:19). Presumably, Jesus had twelve disciples (1 Cor. 15:5). On three occasions, Paul indicates knowledge of Jesus' teachings by citing sayings without directly quoting them (1 Cor. 7:10–11, 9:14; 1 Thess. 4:15–17). Paul also reports Jesus' words at the Last Supper over bread and wine – the earliest written account of the communal ritual later known as the Eucharist (1 Cor. 11:23–6).

Within Paul's letters are also various expressions of presumably pre-Pauline traditions related to other liturgical practices of the early church. First, there is an invocation in Aramaic, which has been transliterated into Greek letters: *marana tha* "Our Lord, come!" (1 Cor. 16:22) Secondly, there is a confessional formula in

Greek: *kyrios Iēsous*, "Jesus [is] Lord" (1 Cor. 12:3; Rom. 10:9). Thirdly, there is an ancient hymn about Jesus' humiliation and exaltation, in six stanzas of three lines each, into which Paul has probably inserted at the end of the third stanza these words: "even death on a cross" (Phil. 2:6–11). Fourthly, there is a creedal formula that Paul had received, expanded, and passed on to the Corinthians identifying what was to him of utmost importance: "that Christ died ... that he was buried ... that he was raised ... that he appeared ..." (1 Cor. 15:3–5).

Paul's letters give explicit confirmation that he was the authority over the congregations he had called together as "the body of Christ" (1 Cor. 12:27). Women play significant roles (Rom. 16:1, 3, 6, etc.). Paul can, and does, order the expulsion of a man for immorality from the community at Corinth (1 Cor. 5:1–8). However, the authority within his congregations appears to be based on a charismatic model of personal gifts rather than on a hierarchical model of specific offices (1 Cor. 12–14). But he does address one letter to "all the saints in Christ Jesus ... with the bishops and deacons" (Phil. 1:1). By the mid-second century, when the three pseudonymous letters of 1 Timothy, 2 Timothy, and Titus were probably written, churches had offices designated as bishops, elders, and deacons with women expressly subordinated (1 Tim. 2:8–3:16; Titus 1:5–9).

Anonymous Narratives: Three Gospels and One Sequel

As we have seen, Paul's letters grew out of his mission to preach the "good news" about what God the Father was doing through the Lord Jesus Christ. The salvation offered first to the Jews was now available to the Gentiles – to all who receive Jesus Christ by faith. Paul's mission and message presupposed a Jesus story. But in his occasional writings there are only glimpses of a back story to Jesus' crucifixion and resurrection.

However, with the gospels included in the New Testament, we finally get narratives about Jesus and his story – or stories. Each author uses available tradition, some oral and some written, to fashion a Jesus story appropriate for the interests and needs of that community. By contrast to the letters of Paul, the canonical gospels are anonymous documents. Not one writer identifies himself by name. The titles by which they are known today were added in the second century when they were collected together, to distinguish them from one another ("according to Mark," etc.). The chronological parameters of their composition are 65 to 100 CE. Furthermore, the specific places and circumstances of composition are not divulged. These are indeed Jesus-books, with Jesus himself front and center. Implicit in these narrative gospels is the recognition that Jesus beckons the reader through his words and his deeds to journey with him. Nonetheless, like the letters of Paul, the gospels themselves are theological statements. They are narrative theologies. The structure and the content communicate the Christological distinctiveness of each narrative. Structure and content also provide clues about those for whom each gospel was first written.

The Gospel of Mark, the shortest and earliest of the four (according to the dominant view of modern biblical scholarship) focuses on Jesus' activity as an adult. After baptism and testing, Jesus begins proclaiming the coming kingdom of God and performing mighty works in Galilee (chs. 1–9), followed by a brief journey (ch. 10) that takes him to Jerusalem, where he experiences crucifixion (chs. 11–15). Along the way, there is a discourse of parables in Galilee (ch. 4) and in Jerusalem a discourse of sayings about the end-time (ch. 13). Throughout the gospel, there is an enigmatic secrecy about Jesus' messianic identity involving his presumed self-designation as "the Son of Man" that extends to the brief resurrection account, which originally ended abruptly with an empty tomb to which post-resurrection appearances were subsequently added (16:1–8, 9–20). Increasingly, Jesus becomes alienated and rejected by family and foe; and he begins talking cryptically to his disciples about his impending death and resurrection (8:31, 9:31, 10:32–4). As Jesus hangs dying on the cross, he cries to God with an exclamation of abandonment (15:34, cf. Ps. 22:1) to which the Roman centurion responds, "Truly, this man was the Son of God" (25:39). As this soldier recognizes, Mark's Jesus is indeed the Christ, the crucified Christ, the Son of God. In Mark's Gospel, Jesus' divine sonship is defined in terms of his obedient suffering and death. Theologically, the Jesus in Mark's narrative presentation corresponds closely to the Jesus of Paul's letters, given their shared focus on the crucifixion and resurrection.

On the horizon for the readers of this gospel appear the desecration of the Jerusalem temple (13:14) and the imminence of Jesus' eschatological coming as the "Son of Man" (13:26, cf. Dan. 7:13). This gospel represents a call for its community to follow Jesus unto death with the attendant promise that faithfulness will bring salvation (13:13). The emphasis in the gospel on suffering messiahship and suffering discipleship suggests a work having originated out of a situation of suffering such as occurred during the first Jewish revolt against the Romans and the persecution of Christian believers in the city of Rome by the Emperor Nero during the decade of the 60s.

The Gospel of Matthew derives its narrative framework for the Jesus story from Mark, and Jesus again undertakes only one journey from Galilee to Jerusalem (chs. 19–20). However, there are significant literary additions and modifications. The author of Matthew begins his gospel with a genealogy and infancy stories (chs. 1–2) and concludes his gospel with stories related to the resurrection of Jesus (ch. 28). On a mountain in Galilee, Jesus affirms the divine authority given to him, commissions his eleven surviving disciples to make disciples of all nations by baptizing them and by teaching them, and finally promises to be with them until the close of the age (28:16–20). Interestingly, the baptism is to be performed with a three-part formula: "in the name of the Father and of the Son and of the Holy Spirit." This was the formula that became associated with the baptismal rite by which initiates received Christ. Equally interesting is the subject of the teaching: "all that I have commanded you." The body of the gospel itself has been organized into five blocks of Jesus' teachings, reminiscent of the five books of the Jewish Torah, each with its own theme: the higher righteousness (chs. 5–7); discipleship (ch. 10); secrets of the kingdom (ch. 13; cf. Mark 4); the church (ch. 18); and the end of the age (chs. 24–5; cf. Mark 13). These teachings, especially the so-called Sermon on the Mount (chs. 5–7), became of abiding importance as followers of Jesus acted out their reception of him as the Christ by imitating him – the theme of the *imitatio Christi*.

The Gospel of Matthew recalls Jewish manuals intended for instruction, such as the Manual of Discipline, among the Dead Sea Scrolls from Qumran, or the rabbinic Mishnah, promulgated several decades after the second Jewish revolt against Rome during the reign of the Emperor Hadrian (132–5). I view the Gospel of Matthew as a similar guidebook that gives instruction in Jesus' own words. Themes and emphases in Matthew suggest that this Jesus book was written for a community of Jewish believers in Jesus as the Christ, the teaching Christ, who is also the crucified Son of God (Matt 27:45–54).

The Gospel of Luke also uses the Gospel of Mark as the literary source for its narrative framework and perhaps acknowledges this in the formal prologue (1:1–4). In Luke, Jesus also takes one journey from Galilee to Jerusalem; but it seems that he will never arrive because of the greatly expanded travel narrative (chs. 9–19), seemingly through the territory of Samaria (9:51–6,10:28–37, 17:11–19). Like Matthew, Luke has also prefaced his story with infancy accounts, although very different traditions (chs. 1–2). Also like Matthew, he has augmented his narrative with resurrection-appearance stories – but with different stories located in and around Jerusalem, not Galilee (ch. 24). Throughout the gospel appear stories and sayings – particularly parables – that indicate Jesus' concern for representatives of the diverse society of his day: not just outcasts (poor people, women, tax collectors, Samaritans), but also insiders (Pharisees) and outsiders (Gentiles). In Luke, Jesus appears as the universal Christ of God (9:20) who has been crucified as an innocent man (23:15–16, 22, 47).

However, this writer does not stop there. Where the first volume ends the second volume begins – with the ascension of Jesus into heaven outside Jerusalem (Luke 24:50–2; Acts 1:1–11). The book of Acts narrates the story of Jesus' subsequent reception, as the proclamation of him as Christ and Lord was carried from the center of the Jewish world to the center of the Gentile world, from Jerusalem (ch. 1) and eventually to Rome (ch. 28). The mission to the Gentiles is anchored in the leadership of the twelve apostles, with Peter running the first leg (chs. 1–12) and Paul receiving the baton for the final, more difficult, leg (chs. 13–28). That which empowers the outreach to Gentiles is that which provides thematic unity throughout Luke and Acts: the Holy Spirit. (Luke 1:15, 35, 67, 2:26, 3:16, 22, 4:1, 14, 18, 9:20, 23:46; Acts 1:8, 2:4, 10:44, 11:16, 19:6, 28:25). In Acts, the outpouring of the Holy Spirit and the gift of tongues provide evidence that the recipients have indeed received Jesus.

Both the Gospel of Luke and the book of Acts are addressed to one bearing the Greek name Theophilus ("God-lover") – whether an individual or any "God-lover," Jew or Gentile. I view the context of both works to be the Christian mission to Gentiles. They also reflect a political apologetic on behalf of Jesus' innocence before the governmental authorities and take a swipe at the Jews who harass Paul every step of the way.

Unlike Paul's writings, these books are not letters. However, within their narratives about Jesus also appears the language evident in the letters of Paul that would be used years later to formulate the doctrine of the Trinity: Father, Son, and Holy Spirit.

An Author Called John: A Fourth Gospel, More Letters, and an Apocalypse

Among the four gospels, the Gospel of John was the last to be written and is the odd gospel out. I have already sketched differences between the earlier Synoptic Gospels and the Fourth Gospel. Now I will elaborate more on the distinctiveness of John's story of Jesus.

First, there is the distinctiveness of John's theological and chronological framing of the Jesus story. John opens with a prologue whose words recall the opening of the book of Genesis: "In the beginning was the Word ... And the Word became flesh ..." (1:1–18). The pre-existent Word has become incarnate as a human in Jesus; and confirmation that Jesus as a human has died comes from the piercing of his side and the resulting flow of blood and water as he hangs on the cross (19:34). The story of Jesus' public activity extends over three years insofar as three Passovers are mentioned (2:12, 6:4, 12:1), and Jesus makes at least four trips from Galilee to Jerusalem (chs. 2, 5, 7, 12).

Secondly, John's characterization of Jesus is distinctive. As the incarnate Word, Jesus talks both publicly and privately about himself through a series of sayings that begin with "I am ..." (6:35, 48, 8:12, 9:5, 10:7, 11, 14, 11:25, 14:6, 15:1), much like God talks in the Jewish scriptures (Isa. 40–55). These sayings are woven into larger discourses, and the central theme becomes "eternal life" (3:16) or simply "life," as expressed in the gospel's statement of purpose (20:30–1). Also, as the incarnate Word, Jesus punctuates his talk with references to God as Father, to himself as the Son, and – in the so-called farewell discourses (chs. 13–17) – to the Holy Spirit as the Paraclete (variously translated into English as "Comforter," "Counselor," "Advocate"). Jesus also promises that after his return to the Father, the Holy Spirit will come, which does occur on the evening of the resurrection (20:19–23). By contrast to the eschatological perspectives in the authentic letters of Paul and in the Synoptics, the Gospel of John does not anticipate a future coming of the Lord Jesus Christ.

The distinctiveness of John's characterization of Jesus is further thrown into relief with the observation that the Jesus figure in John's Gospel talks more like the author(s) of the three letters attributed to John, especially 1 John, than he talks like the Jesus of the Synoptics. Furthermore, in spite of great differences between the Gospel of John and the Revelation to John, the latter contains one of the best-known "I am" sayings. Both God and the exalted Jesus declare, "I am the Alpha and the Omega" (Rev. 1:8 and 22:13). Perhaps the Fourth Gospel, by contrast to the three Synoptics, originated out of the experiences of a charismatic community to whom Jesus as the Word become flesh continued to speak after his exaltation through Christian prophets in the first person just as, in the past, God had spoken through prophets to Israel: "I am ... ." John's community seems to live at a juncture between its synagogue past (John 9:22, 12:42, 16:2) and the threat of those who deny Jesus' having come in flesh and blood (1 John 4:2–3, 5:6).

The New Testament today includes five writings which bear the name of John: the gospel, three letters, and the book that concludes not only the New Testament but the entire Bible. The book at the end appears to be all about the end: Revelation is the only apocalyptic book in the New Testament. Its author has drunk deeply from the well of apocalyptic imagery and symbolism, especially from the books of Daniel and Ezekiel. The book of Revelation itself reflects a well-delineated literary structure: an introduction (ch. 1); the body (2:1–22:5) and a conclusion (22:6–21).

The introduction (ch. 1) immediately establishes the imminence of the events to be revealed by God through Jesus Christ and his angel with such words as "soon" and "near." Up front, Jesus Christ is described as a "faithful witness" (Greek, *martyr*). Details follow about the book's socio-historical origin: written by a man named John, but not identified as the disciple son of Zebedee; written for seven churches in the Roman province of Asia; written on the isle of Patmos, where John himself was suffering exile; and written to exhort its readers and hearers to remain faithful through their present and coming sufferings.

The conclusion (22:6–21) reiterates the imminence of the events outlined in the book with a litany of declarations and invocations: "soon," "soon," "near," "soon," "come," "come," "come" "soon," "Amen. Come, Lord Jesus!" That this book was intended for its first-century readers is made certain by the words spoken to John: "Do not seal up the words of the prophecy of this book, for the time is near" (22:10).

The body (2:1–22:5) opens with personalized letters from the exalted Jesus addressed to each of the seven churches, which assess the spiritual state of each particular church. There follows a long series of dramatic visions, which assess the state of the world at large. As the story unfolds, the visualization cuts back and forth from heaven to earth. Transcendent figures appear in heaven: God, seated on a throne; Jesus, standing as a slain lamb; the Spirit, having transported John to heaven. Three awful beasts dominate the earth: a great red dragon identified as the Devil, Satan, and ancient serpent; a beast from the sea that defies any known zoological category, which functions politically; and a beast from the land with two horns like a lamb and a voice like a dragon, which functions religiously. At last, a reckoning occurs that includes a first resurrection of martyrs, a stated thousand-year period (the millennium), and a second resurrection of all the dead for final judgment. Along the way, all the dominators and their legions are defeated. A new heaven and a new earth appear. God and the Lamb, martyrs and other faithful ones, are triumphant. Go(o)d wins. (D)evil loses. Christ reigns.

Although I have not commented on all twenty-seven writings in the New Testament, I have considered those most prominent in the reception of Jesus over the subsequent 2,000 years. The letters of Paul will be of greatest interest to those wanting to understand the meaning of Jesus' death. The Synoptic Gospels will be of greatest interest to those whose focus is the shape and events of Jesus' life. The Fourth Gospel will be of greatest interest to those sorting out both the relationship of the pre-existent Word to God and the inter-relationship among God the Father, Jesus the Son, and the Holy Spirit. The book of Revelation, of course, will beckon those concerned about the threat and the promise of Jesus' future coming.

Christianity's Earliest Writings: Literary Diversity, Theological Unity

The twenty-seven writings ultimately included in the New Testament represent several literary genres. In part because of this literary diversity, these writings represent a variety of perspectives on how Jesus was received and portrayed in the earliest Christian literature. However, beneath this diversity lies a basic theological unity: Jesus as the Christ, the Son of God.

But more than this, the letters of Paul, the four gospels of Mark, Matthew, Luke, and John, the book of Acts, and the book of Revelation share two basic assumptions: first, that Jesus as the Christ was the fulfillment of promises made by the God of Israel as attested in the Jewish scriptures; and secondly, that Jesus as the Christ of God was a human being who died by crucifixion and was resurrected by God from the dead. These points of unity may sound commonplace, but their significance appears when they are compared to other ancient writings that also testify to Jesus as one from God.

Christianity's Transformation: From a Jewish Sect to a Gentile Religion

The movement initiated by Jesus the Jew during his lifetime continued after his death as a Jewish sect alongside other Jewish groups such as the Sadducees, the Pharisees, and the Essenes. But within a few years of Jesus' death, the Jesus movement – with its missionary mandate – had established itself in the broader Greco-Roman world beyond the Jewish homeland. The diaspora Jew named Paul became the most important figure in taking the "gospel" about the Lord Jesus Christ to Gentiles. His letters, as well as all the earliest Christian writings, so far as we know, were written in the common Greek language of the eastern Mediterranean region.

By the end of the first century, Christianity was well on its way toward a separation from Judaism as an overwhelmingly Gentile religion within the Roman empire. Two events facilitated this transformation of the Jesus movement from being a Jewish sect toward becoming a world religion. The first event happened within the movement. The second involved the world at large.

The first event, occurring ca. 49 CE, involved Paul and leaders of the Jerusalem church, including Peter: the so-called "Jerusalem conference" (Gal. 2 and Acts 15). Although the two written accounts differ in their details, both agree on the central question discussed and the answer given. The question: must Gentile converts be circumcised? Or, more profoundly: must Gentiles become Jews in order to become people of God through Jesus Christ? The answer: No! With a handshake, the theological basis for the independence of the Gentile churches from Judaism had already been established.

The second event, in 70 CE, was the fall of Jerusalem and the destruction of the Second Temple to the Roman legions under Titus, which effectively ended the first Jewish revolt. In later decades, there followed an uprising of Jews in the diaspora centered in Alexandria in Egypt (115–17), and a second revolt of Jews in Judea under the leadership of the messianic claimant Simon Bar Kochba (132–5). Judaism had been forever changed.

The transition had begun from Second Temple Judaism, with priesthood and sacrifice, toward a rabbinic Judaism centered in Torah that resulted in the codification of the Mishnah and the development of the Talmud, the one Palestinian, the other Babylonian. After the Roman destruction of the Jerusalem temple, the Sadducean and the Essene sects soon passed from the pages of history. The former had been closely associated with the priesthood and had obvious ties to the temple. The latter, presumably represented by those who lived at Qumran in the Judean wilderness, had experienced the destruction of their settlement after depositing their scrolls in the caves of the Judean wilderness. The Jesus community itself, once located in Jerusalem, was increasingly marginalized among their fellow Jews and fled from that city. The future of Judaism rested with the Pharisees and their scribes. The future of Christianity lay with the churches among the Gentiles.

However, Jewish Christianity itself did not immediately disappear. Christian writers of the second to the fifth centuries refer on occasion to gospels used by Jews who considered themselves to be Christians. These Jewish-Christian gospels are identified by name as the Gospel of the Hebrews, the Gospel of the Ebionites, and the Gospel of the Nazoreans.[3] However, no extant copies exist, so it is difficult to understand precisely how Jesus was presented in these works, although snippets of some texts correspond to stories or sayings known from other gospels. These Jewish-Christian gospels repeatedly mention John the Baptist; and two describe the scene of Jesus' baptism where the Holy Spirit descends upon him and a voice declares him to be God's "Son." Other episodes involve the call of disciples beside the Sea of Tiberias, the healing of a man with a crippled hand, and the story of a rich man commanded to sell all and give to the poor. The most distinctive theme occurs in the fragments from the Gospel of the Hebrews, where the Holy Spirit is repeatedly described by Jesus as "my mother."

The earliest references to Christianity and Jesus from outside Christian circles appear near the end of the first and at the beginning of the second century. The earliest reference from a Jew comes from the historian Flavius Josephus (37–100). He was writing from Rome under the patronage of the Flavian emperors: Vespasian (69–79), Titus (79–81), and Domitian (81–96). Josephus himself had participated in the first Jewish revolt against Rome by leading Jewish forces in Galilee. He defected and became an interpreter for the Roman general Titus, the son and successor of Vespasian, during the siege and subsequent destruction of Jerusalem (70 CE).

After the war, Josephus settled in Rome and wrote two important histories explaining Jews and Judaism to Greco-Roman audiences: *The Jewish War* and the *Antiquities of the Jews*. The latter work, a sweeping chronicle of the Jewish people, contains two passages that seemingly mention Jesus. I say "seemingly" because Josephus' writings were preserved by Christian scribes, who probably inserted or modified the two references to Jesus, who is acknowledged to be the Christ (*Antiquities* 18:63–4 and 20:200). The first passage reads like a miniature gospel insofar as Jesus is described as a "wise man" and "a teacher," who performed wondrous deeds. Jesus is also identified by the narrator as "the Christ," who was condemned to crucifixion by Pilate at the instigation of the Jewish leaders, but subsequently was raised from the dead. In the second passage, the narrator describes and deplores how the Jewish leaders had killed "James ... the brother of Jesus, who was called Christ."[4]

The earliest perspectives on how Romans themselves viewed Christians and Jesus come from three writers who had served emperors in various capacities: Suetonius (d. ca. 122), Tacitus (d. ca. 117), and Pliny the Younger (d. ca. 113).

In his history of *The Twelve Caesars*, Suetonius comments on the reign of the Emperor Claudius (41–54) and notes how Claudius had expelled Jews from Rome because of disturbances involving "Chrestus," probably a Latin variant of *Christos*.[5] In his *Annals*, Tacitus demonstrates the cruelty of the Emperor Nero (54–68) by graphically describing how Christians, blamed for the great fire in Rome, had been fed to the dogs, or crucified, or torched alive. Although Tacitus acknowledges the guilt of Christians, he matter-of-factly connects them with a Jesus who had been executed during Tiberius' reign by Pontius Pilate the governor of Judea).[6]

A third Roman voice is heard through a letter from Pliny the Younger to the Emperor Trajan (98–117). While governor of the province of Pontus and Bithynia, in what is now northern Turkey, Pliny wrote to Trajan asking for advice on how to deal with Christians who refused to participate in the public honors accorded the emperor, but who customarily came together to "share a meal" and "to sing a hymn to Christ as if to a god."[7] Here, through the eyes of a Roman official, we see what we have already learned about Christian worship from its earliest beginnings. A meal was integral to worship (1 Cor. 11:17–26). Hymns were also sung celebrating Jesus as a mediator between heaven and earth (cf. Phil. 2:6–11 and Col. 1:15–20).

All three Roman writers describe Christianity as a *superstitio* (superstition) – a group whose beliefs and practices were considered by the Romans to be alien and strange. Since Christians lived throughout the empire as "the Other," here was trouble waiting to happen. Like the Jews before them, Gentile Christians set themselves apart from their neighbors and were accused of being "human-haters" (Greek: *misanthrōpoi*). Also like Jews, Christians professed an exclusive belief in the oneness of God, so they were also called "atheists" (Greek: *atheoi*) for not supporting the public piety of Rome by honoring emperors and the traditional pagan deities. Christians also had their own peculiar public relations problems, facing accusations of practicing magic, cannibalism, and sexual immorality.[8]

Two of the most penetrating and far-ranging intellectual challenges to Christians and Christianity in the second and third centuries came from the writings of Celsus and Porphyry. Both were philosophers in the Platonic tradition. Both were familiar with Christian literature, including the scriptures.

Celsus wrote his critique, *The True Word* or the *True Doctrine*, sometime in the 170s CE.[9] This work itself has not survived; however, much has been reconstructed based on the expansive rebuttal titled *Against Celsus* by the theologian and scholar Origen (185–ca. 254). At the center of Celsus' characterization of Jesus lies the claim that Jesus himself concocted the tale of his virgin birth to cover up his illegitimacy, and that he fled to Egypt, where he learned the magical arts; upon his return, he declared himself to be "Son of God." But in fact, Jesus was "a magician" whose followers continued practicing magic after his death. By contrast, Porphyry (233–304) – known for his polemical treatise *Against the Christians* – reached a more appreciative assessment of Jesus himself.[10] He characterized Jesus as one of those "pious" men who encouraged his followers to worship the supreme One. It was Jesus' followers who later claimed that Jesus was the "Son of God" and the "Word" through whom all things were made (cf. John 1).

Emerging Christianity: A "Catholic" Church

As Christianity established itself in the wider Greco-Roman world, the diversity evident in the first century became even greater. Both the expansion and diversification resulted in an "explosion" of literature. However, Gentile Christians continued to define themselves in relation to Judaism and to address concerns raised by the encounter with pagan religion and culture.

In relation to Judaism, Christian writers increasingly expressed a theological anti-Judaism that prepared the way for a de-Judaizing of Jesus. Collections of texts from the Jewish scriptures were used both to support the Christological claims about Jesus as the fulfillment of God's promises and to establish that the Jews, responsible for the death of Jesus, had always been a "stiff-necked people" (Exod. 33:5). This so-called *adversus Judaeos* tradition, anticipated in the gospels themselves, expressed itself through the epistle of Barnabas and the writings of such theologians as Justin Martyr (ca. 100–65) and Tertullian (ca. 160–240), and continued virtually unabated into later generations.[11]

At the same time, Christians began to speak to power in defense of Christianity – even to Roman emperors. Justin Martyr and Tertullian were also among these apologists.[12] Justin, who was a native of Neapolis in Samaria and became at mid-century a resident of Rome, addressed his *First Apology* to the emperor Antoninus Pius (138–61). Therein he expounds on the divine Word (Logos) incarnate in Jesus and defends the virgin birth, the death, the resurrection, and the ascension of Jesus Christ. Tertullian was born in Carthage in North Africa, and studied the law in Rome before returning to Carthage. He has been called the "father of Latin theology," as the first prominent thinker to write in Latin rather than Greek. He receives credit for being the first writer to use the word *trinitas* for the triune God and for introducing the concept of *persona*, or person, into Trinitarian thought. His *Apology*, which appeared around the year 197, addresses the rulers of the Roman empire and refutes in biting language many of the usual charges directed at Christians. He counter-attacks by pointing out that all persons are allowed to worship whatever gods they choose, except Christians, who worship the one true God.

However, Christianity did not only define itself in relation to the Jews and the pagans. Christians also began to define themselves in relation to each other. Many Christian authors characteristically described themselves as constituting a "catholic" church (from the Greek, meaning "universal"). This use of this term to identify the church appears for the first time in the writings of Ignatius, bishop of Antioch (d. ca. 117).

The means by which the emerging Catholic Church defined itself and thereby facilitated the transmission and reception of Jesus as the Christ, the Son of God, involved the development of institutional polity, community scriptures, and summary statements of belief. To put it bluntly: bishop, canon, and creed

First, bishops. Within earliest Christianity there had been impulses toward a more egalitarian order that included women in leadership roles. But by the second century a hierarchical polity with bishops, elders, and deacons was establishing itself, with a delineation between those with priestly privileges and the laity. The authority of the bishops, grounded in the apostles of the first generation, came to appeal to the legitimating principle of apostolic succession. One of the themes in the *Ecclesiastical History* of Eusebius, the bishop of Caesarea (ca. 263–339) – dating from the early fourth century – was his tracing the succession of bishops in the sees of Jerusalem, Antioch, Rome, and Alexandria.[13]

Secondly, canon. Of particular interest for the ongoing reception of Jesus was the process by which the disparate writings produced by the earliest first-century Christians eventually comprised a new collection of authoritative writings – a New Testament.

The word "canon" (from the Greek word for a "reed," which could be cut and used as a measuring stick), came to designate a rule or a standard. By extension "canon" has come to mean any body of writings considered authoritative by a particular social group. Thus the New Testament represents the foundational written authority for believers in Jesus as the Christ. By the mid-second century, all the books eventually included in the new Christian scriptures, including the originally anonymous gospels, bore the names of specific apostles or persons closely associated with the apostles, such as Matthew, Mark, Luke, John, Paul, Peter, James, and Jude. Dozens of other writings were also circulating with attributions to these and other apostles, such as Thomas and Philip.

But how did the twenty-seven-book canon come to be? I prefer to say that these books "canonized" themselves, meaning that they earned the respect of believers, through their "apostolicity," their "catholicity," and their "orthodoxy." In fact, the role of the bishops, who themselves represented Christ through a line of succession from the apostles, became determinative for which writings could be used by the gathered community in its worship. In responding to the question of how the twenty-seven-book canon came to be, we will note a few markers along the canonization trail, generally following the path of Bruce M. Metzger.[14]

The earliest followers of Jesus, like their Jewish contemporaries, had scriptures – at least the scrolls identified in Hebrew as the "the Law (*Torah*) and the Prophets (*Nebi'im*)." No doubt the letters of Paul, the four gospels, and the writings we surveyed earlier would have been considered authoritative, in some sense, by the communities who originally received them. The letter now known as 2 Peter, considered by many scholars to be the last New Testament book written (as late as the 140s) refers to multiple letters of Paul, suggesting that a gathering of his letters had already occurred (2 Peter 3:14–16). The Church Fathers, such as Ignatius, disclose in their writings varying levels of familiarity with some of the letters and the gospels.

In Rome, at mid-first century, Justin Martyr knew at least the three Synoptic Gospels and collectively refers to them in several of his writings as "Memoirs of the Apostles." Given his exposition on the divine Word (Logos), mentioned earlier, it seems likely that Justin also knew the Fourth Gospel. More importantly, Justin discloses the importance of the gospels for the life of his church. During Sunday (not sabbath!) services, he reports, the memoirs were read alongside the prophets. The leader used the readings as the basis for instruction and exhortation. Thus if the gospels were used in worship in a manner comparable to the prophets, then the gospels were approaching canonical status, at least for that community.

The person often credited with defining the first Christian canon is Marcion (ca. 110–60), who had also established himself in Rome as a generous benefactor of one of the congregations there, although he was a native of Sinope, a seaport on the Black Sea. In 144 his ideas resulted in his being excommunicated from that community. Marcion had adopted for his "Bible" ten of Paul's letters and the Gospel of Luke. His sparse selection of writings cannot be called a New Testament because there was no Old Testament. He totally rejected the Jewish scriptures.

Underlying Marcion's proposal was his reading of the Jewish scriptures and his understanding of Paul, whom he considered to be the only apostle to have correctly understood the gospel. Marcion juxtaposed the creator God as a jealous deity of justice over against the transcendental alien deity of love. It was the God of love who was revealed through Jesus Christ in order to liberate humankind from the domination of the creator God. Therefore, there are two Gods. But Marcion's distinction between the lesser God of justice and the supreme God of love probably comes not from mythological speculation but from a common-sense reading of human experience and Paul's antithetical message of "law" and "gospel." Therefore, although Marcion has often been identified as a "Gnostic" (based on a Greek word meaning "knowledge"), he probably was not a Gnostic insofar as he affirmed salvation by faith not by knowledge. However, Marcion did advocate a Christology that was "docetic" (based on a Greek word meaning "to appear," or "seem") and claimed that Jesus Christ only appeared or seemed to be human (cf. Roman 8:3).[15] Marcion's major work, appropriately called *Antitheses*, has not survived. Nonetheless, much of his thought is recoverable from the writings of his opponents, such as Tertullian, who wrote an extensive rebuttal *Against Marcion*.[16]

A contemporary of Marcion, who had studied in Rome with Justin Martyr, was a man from Mesopotamia named Tatian (d. ca. 185). Tatian approached the gospels quite differently than had Marcion. He took Matthew, Mark, Luke, John and wove them together into one consecutive narrative of the Jesus story. This act provides evidence that these four gospels had already been gathered together. Tatian's harmonized version was called the *Diatessaron* (in Greek, "four-in-one").

Given Marcion's appropriation of the ten letters of Paul and Tatian's use of the four gospels, it is clear that by the middle of the second century the basis for a two-part canon of gospels and letters had already been established. Perhaps Marcion's preference for one gospel and Tatian's harmonization of the four gospels into one gospel prompted Irenaeus, bishop of Lyon (ca. 120–202), to declare that the Word had given the gospel in fourfold form, but united by the one Spirit: the gospels of Matthew, Mark, Luke, and John.[17] Just as the emerging canon would have multiple letters, so the canon would also have multiple gospels.

Fast forward to the early fourth century: and consider again Eusebius, the bishop of Caesarea, and his completed masterwork, *Ecclesiastical History* – from the incarnation of Jesus to the peace of the church under Constantine. Another theme that runs through his work is his judicious review and evaluation of the many so-called apostolic writings with regard to their acceptance or non-acceptance throughout the church. The approval list, as reported by Eusebius, included: the four gospels of Matthew, Mark, Luke, and John; the book of Acts; the thirteen letters of Paul; the letters of 1 John and 1 Peter; and (possibly) the book of Revelation.[18] By this reckoning, at the beginning of the fourth century, the list included twenty-one or twenty-two of the twenty-seven writings eventually comprising the New Testament. The first enumeration of exactly twenty-seven New Testament writings appears in the year 367, in an Easter letter from Bishop Athanasius of Alexandria to his priests in Egypt, which identified those writings considered approved for liturgical reading.[19] But even then the canon was not "closed."

Now for the third dimension involved in the self-definition of the church in the second and third centuries: creed. The expansive ecumenical creeds of the fourth century were preceded by more succinct formulations of doctrine intended to communicate to even the least members of the church the essential teaching of the community and to establish doctrinal boundaries. These brief doctrinal summaries constituted what in the second century were identified as "the rule of faith."

Already we have seen how the Gospel of Matthew concluded with the risen Jesus' command that his followers baptize "in the name of the Father and of the Son and of the Holy Spirit" (Matt 28:19). Just as the baptismal formula in Matthew contains Trinitarian talk of Father, Son, and Holy Spirit, so does a somewhat expanded "rule of faith" (approximately a hundred words in length) set forth by Irenaeus that includes these words: "in one God, the Father Almighty, the creator of heaven, and earth ... and in one Christ Jesus, the Son of God ... and in the Holy Spirit ... ."[20] Trinitarian talk runs through the varied writings of theologians in the beginning centuries of Christianity: from Justin to Irenaeus, from Tertullian to Origen.[21]

But it is the meaning of the Trinitarian talk that matters. Already among the theologians of the second and third centuries had emerged the Christological issues that would dominate the theological agendas for the subsequent 200 years.

"Gnosticism": The Nag Hammadi Library

Those early church leaders who described the church as being catholic or universal, also defined the church as representing "orthodoxy" (from Greek, "right opinion") in contradistinction to "heresy" (again from the Greek, with a derived meaning of "deviancy"). Paul himself uses the Greek word "heresies" to describe factions quarreling among themselves in Corinth (1 Cor. 11:19).

However, in the second century, theologians created a literary form that catalogued and analyzed various expressions of false belief and improper behavior by those individuals and groups who professed to be followers of Jesus Christ. These vigilant writers earned for themselves the designation of heresiologists. Although not alone in his condemnation of heretics, Irenaeus the bishop of Lyon, in Gaul, certainly became the best known in the second and third centuries through his detailed five-book diatribe *Against Heresies*. He condemned both Marcion and Tatian, among others.

One of the most interesting developments in recent decades has been the growing recognition that the theological and institutional diversity evident in twenty-first-century Christianity also characterized Christianity during its opening centuries. The titles of books by Bart Ehrman[22] and Richard Valantasis[23] have even announced the rediscovery of ancient Christianities that had been "lost" or had "vanished." Perhaps an observation is appropriate here. These Christianities were never completely lost nor did they absolutely vanish, since the beliefs and practices have been known through the writings of those theologians – such as Irenaeus – who opposed these versions of Christianity.

The recognition that earliest Christianity was quite diverse has also led to the designation of the theological-ecclesiastical traditions represented by the orthodox catholic church before Constantine as "proto-orthodox," not yet the ecclesiastically established "orthodoxy." Perhaps another observation is also appropriate here. The categories of "catholic," "orthodoxy" and "heresy" were already being used by the "proto-orthodox" leaders before Constantine. The war of words was vicious and slanderous from both sides, much like the venom often spewed forth in our own day – whatever the ideology, whatever the topic.

Gnosticism, as a worldview, identifies a particular way of understanding reality. Scholars continue to discuss the complex origin of Gnosticism. They have identified a number of factors and several possible sources, including Persian-Iranian religion, Jewish teaching, Greek philosophy, and Christianity itself. Scholars also despair of the possibility of defining the phenomenon.[24] The variety of texts and persons purported to represent it do not lend themselves to a simple definition. Nonetheless, I suggest that Gnosticism foundationally represents a dualistic worldview that sharply distinguishes between the realm of spirit and the realm of matter, between the individual soul and the physical body, and that judges the spiritual realm to be the source of good and the material realm to be the occasion for evil. Consequently, this definition brings with it several corollaries: this world must be the work not of the one supreme God but of some lesser being. The human problem can be described as ignorance derived from the individual soul's entrapment in the material world. Salvation comes through realizing the knowledge (or "gnosis") of one's predicament and how to escape – a knowledge often mediated by a redeemer figure.

When the Christian – or Judeo-Christian – story was interpreted through the lens of this worldview, that story often involved the recognition that the God who sent Jesus into the world as savior had not created this world. Furthermore, Jesus as the emissary from the supreme God was not fully human but only seemed to be human ("docetism"). Resurrection, the transition from death to life, occurred when the knowledge imparted through Jesus was realized, not after physical death.

For centuries, knowledge about Gnostics and the teaching of Gnosticism was derived primarily from the polemical writings of the heresiologists. However, in 1945 all this changed with the discovery in Upper Egypt, near the town of Nag Hammadi, of a buried jar containing thirteen codices of fifty-two texts written on papyrus in the Coptic language but translated from Greek. These texts were published in English translation as *The Nag Hammadi Library* under the general editorship of James M. Robinson.[25] The evidence indicates that the collection was buried sometime in the fourth century, perhaps to hide it from church authorities after Christianity received recognition as a licit religion within the Roman empire. Most of the documents were not previously available in manuscript form, but they give indication of having been written by Christians with Gnostic sensibilities. Since we are interested in the library for the light it might shed on how Jesus was received and perceived by these believers, what can we say?

More than thirty of the writings from the Nag Hammadi trove make mention of Jesus by personal name and/or by honorific addresses such as "Christ," "Savior," and "Lord." Several of the tractates have been identified as writings associated with Valentinus (ca. 100–75), a philosopher from Alexandria, who in the mid-130s moved to Rome and participated in the churches there until he relocated to Cyprus around 160.[26] Irenaeus attributes to Valentinus a complicated myth of origin that leads to the birth of Jesus; but he also mentions The Gospel of Truth, one of the Nag Hammadi texts that represents a mystical meditation on the meaning of Jesus' coming, as one through whom those devoted to him realize knowledge about themselves. In one passage, this document uses the traditional language of Father, Son, and Holy Spirit, but with a gnosticizing twist.

Perhaps the best known of the Nag Hammadi tractates today is the Gospel of Thomas, introduced as "the secret sayings which the living Jesus spoke and which Didymos Judas Thomas wrote down." The contents consist of 114 sayings, many enigmatic and peculiar to this gospel but others strikingly similar to sayings in what became the canonical gospels of Matthew, Mark, Luke, and John. But the collection contains no narrative gospels comparable to these four.

Several writings are what might be called Jesus books that take the form of a dialogue between Jesus and his disciples, which – like the Gospel of Thomas – takes place after his resurrection. These include: the Apocryphon of James, the Apocryphon of John, the Book of Thomas the Contender, Eugnostos the Blessed, the Sophia of Jesus Christ, the Dialogue of the Savior, and the Letter of Peter to Philip. This use of a dialogue format projects Jesus as a teacher of esoteric wisdom, appropriate for Gnostic gospels and Gnostic communities.

Although these gospels from Nag Hammadi are not narratives, we find scattered throughout the Christian writings in this long-lost collection references to familiar names and events mentioned in the canonical gospels. We find mention of Jesus' birth, his transfiguration, his crucifixion, and his resurrection. We discover on Jesus' lips the phrases "the kingdom of God" and "the kingdom of heaven." There is an occasional parable and references to his healings. His disciples are identified collectively as being both eleven and twelve in number. Among those named individually are Peter, Andrew, James, John, Levi, Matthew, Thomas, Philip, and Judas. We also find the names of Elizabeth, the mother of John the Baptist; Mary his mother; Mary Magdalene, his companion; and his brother James. Simon (of Cyrene) is also mentioned.

The Gospel of Philip contains sayings of Jesus that, in Gnostic fashion, challenge traditional Christian beliefs in the virgin birth and bodily resurrection. But the most memorable characterization of Jesus appears in the Apocalypse of Peter, where, again in Gnostic fashion, he laughs as his captors crucify him by nailing him to the tree. He laughs because they think he suffers but, in reality, he feels no pain. He is a docetic redeemer figure. This has resulted in the characterization of the Gnostic Jesus as "the laughing Savior."[27]

Two other Gnostic gospels, neither of which was discovered at Nag Hammadi deserve brief comment because of more recent publicity. The Gospel of Mary describes Mary Magdalene as being loved by Jesus more than the other disciples, and she demonstrates one-upwomanship against Peter who, of course, indeed became the rock on which Rome built its church.[28] The Gospel of Judas presents Judas the betrayer as the one disciple who "gets it" and complies with Jesus' request to surrender him to the authorities. Gnostic Christians know the old, old story of Jesus but they plumb the depths of its meaning.[29]

Living as Christians in the Roman Empire: The Threat of Persecution

Persecution and martyrdom were woven into the story of early Christianity. Stephen has been remembered as the first "Christian" martyr, on which occasion Saul, or Paul, was present. Like Jesus in the Gospel of Luke, Stephen in the book of Acts offers up his spirit and asks forgiveness for his killers – only now Stephen directs his petition to the "Lord Jesus" (Luke 23:45; Acts 7:59).

The Gospel of Mark and the book of Revelation have often been understood to have been composed in persecution situations, perhaps during the imperial reigns of Nero and Domitian. However, contrary to a common view on the persecution of Christians by imperial Rome, any persecutions aimed at Christians during the reigns of these two emperors would have been local and episodic, not empire-wide.

Nonetheless, Christians themselves began to produce a growing body of writings about those who had remained faithful unto death. These martyrologies, or stories of martyrdoms, circulated among the churches. Martyrs came to be venerated as exemplars of faithfulness and holiness – as saints. But the martyrs themselves are identified as the imitators of Christ.[30]

Around the time that Pliny was writing to the Emperor Trajan, Ignatius, the bishop of Antioch, wrote seven letters to different churches while en route to Rome under guard for trial. In his *Letter to the Romans*, Ignatius asks that the believers there not interfere with what he fervently desired – to be torn apart by wild animals for Christ's sake and thus to "imitate the Passion of my God."

Midway through the second century, there appeared *The Martyrdom of Polycarp*, apparently a first-hand account of events related to the execution by fire of the beloved and aged bishop of Smyrna, sent by the church at Smyrna to the church at Philomelium. When the flames would not consume Polycarp's body he was stabbed, and his blood extinguished the flames. The structure and details of this narrative recall the passion of Jesus.

Still later there appears a lengthy letter from the churches of Vienne and Lyon to fellow believers in Asia and Phrygia about the horrific spiral of violence that happened in these towns in 177. What began as the social ostracism of Christians in public places escalated first to physical abuse by mobs and then to proceedings before the local civil authorities, followed by days of blood-sport – all during the reign of Marcus Aurelius (161–80). These events ended days later when the burned remains of the martyrs were mockingly swept into the river Rhone.

Not until the rule of the emperor Decius (249–51) was there an edict that required all inhabitants of the empire, including Christians, to sacrifice to the traditional pagan gods and to receive a certificate validating the required act. After Decius' death in battle against the Goths, his near-successor Valerian (253–60) reaffirmed the policy targeting especially bishops, clergy, and others of high standing, which continued until his capture by the Persians.

The next wave of persecution – the so-called Great Persecution – was initiated during the latter years of the reign of the reforming emperor Diocletian (284–305), who established a tetrarchy of emperors: an Augustus and a Caesar in the east and an Augustus and a Caesar in the west, although he remained the senior emperor among the four. In 303, for whatever reason, Diocletian abandoned a policy of toleration toward Christians and issued edicts requiring the destruction of Christian scriptures and church buildings, and also forbidding Christians to assemble for worship. The enforcement of these edicts varied greatly throughout the empire: it was severe in many locales, but lightest in Gaul and

Britain, where Constantius served as the Augustus. Thus, in a convoluted, ironic way, these anti-Christian edicts prepared the way for Constantius' succession by his son Constantine. After Constantius' death, by natural causes, in the summer of 306, Constantine was proclaimed emperor in what is now known as the city of York – where Constantine today sits proudly cast in bronze outside the great cathedral of York Minster.

Christianizing the Roman Empire: Constantine the Great

With the death of Constantius and the succession of Constantine in the west, the tetrarchy collapsed, with several claimants vying for imperial positions. Decisive moments in Constantine's consolidation of his own power occurred in the years 312 and 313.[31]

In 312 Constantine brought his army into Italy bound for Rome, where he encountered and defeated the larger army of Maxentius at the battle of the Milvian Bridge, which resulted in the death of Maxentius and in Constantine becoming sole ruler of the empire in the west. It was before this military engagement that Constantine experienced his famous vision of the cross in the sky, reported in various accounts. According to this story, after Constantine had called upon the highest God for help he saw in the sky a cross arising from the sun with some such words of assurance or exhortation as "By this sign, conquer." So Constantine, according to tradition, had the monogram for Christ – the transversed *chi* (X) and *rho* (P) – placed on his military standards and the shields of his men. Constantine had previously expressed devotion to solar deities such as Apollo, Sol Invictus, and Mithras. Although Constantine may have attributed his victory before the city of Rome to the God of the Christians, his own transition from paganism to Christian monotheism probably occurred over a longer period of time.

Subsequently, in 313, Constantine and Licinius – his counterpart in the east – issued the so-called Edict of Milan, which proclaimed toleration throughout the Roman empire for Christians and all others to worship and observe their religious obligations unhindered. Furthermore, Christians were to have restored the property previously taken from them, whether it was individually owned or corporate property such as churches. Whatever the reason Constantine – and his father – had for not hounding Christians during the recent persecutions, he was becoming one of them and a generous patron of Christianity and the Church. The Roman empire was being transformed into a "Christian" empire.

But in 312 and 313 much still lay ahead. Constantine would not become the one and only ruler of the entire empire until a decade of skirmishes between him and Licinius had resulted in Lucinius' defeat and eventual death in 324. By then, Constantine was already thinking about moving the capital of the empire eastward from Rome. But before that geographical move, there would occur an event that would forever shape the Christianity adopted by him – the Council of Nicaea in 325. But, before going forward, we must look back to consider how the reception of Jesus as the Christ created the demand for scribal rewriting of his story, and how Jesus was becoming publicly ever more visible through images of him and buildings dedicated to him.

Material Culture: Manuscripts, Architecture, and the Visual Arts

With Constantine early Christianity experienced a sudden reversal of fortune. The one-time Jewish sect and later persecuted minority in the Greco-Roman world had suddenly found favor with a Roman emperor. It is understandable, therefore, that material remains from the Christian movement would be scarce before the fourth century. Nonetheless, physical evidence for Jesus' reception does appear in the areas of manuscripts, architecture, and the visual arts.

Although the twenty-seven documents later incorporated into the New Testament were originally written in Greek in the latter half of the first century, none of the original manuscripts exists today. What is considered to be the oldest fragment of any New Testament book, containing only a few lines from John 18, dates from ca. 125. Known as P^{52}, with the "P" indicating papyrus as the writing material, it is preserved in the library of the University

Figure 1   Graffito of a crucified donkey man discovered scratched on a wall on the Palatine hill in Rome (possibly second century). *Photo: AKG Images*

of Manchester. Among the earliest collections of subdivisions of the New Testament, probably from the third century, are the papyri housed in the Chester Beatty Library in Dublin: P[45], four gospels and book of Acts; P[46], Pauline letters; and P[47], the book of Revelation. Not until the fourth century are there manuscripts which bind between the same covers subdivisions of a New Testament together with the Greek version of the Old Testament known as the Septuagint (LXX).[32]

The Greek word translated "church" in the New Testament is *ekklesia* (Latin, ecclesia), from which the English adjective "ecclesiastical" is derived. The word *ekklesia* appears only twice in the New Testament gospels, both times in the Gospel of Matthew, both times on the lips of Jesus (Matt. 16:18, 18:17). The first passage represents what later became known as the "investiture of Peter" that has been used to support the authority of the bishop of Rome, the Pope: "You are Peter [*Petros*] and on this rock [*petra*] I will build my church" (Matt 16:18; also 18:17). However, the word *ekklesia* has the etymological meaning of "being called out from" and in the Greco-Roman world was used was to designate human assemblies of various kinds (Acts 19:32, 39, 41). Thus there was "church" before there were "church" buildings.

As is evident in Paul's letters, his churches gathered together in the houses of members. The head of household where the community gathered would have served as host and patron. Paul identifies some hosts, or patrons, by name: Stephanas (1 Cor. 1:16, 16:15), the couple Prisca and Aquila (1 Cor. 16:10; Rom. 16:3); Gaius (Rom. 16:23); and Philemon (Philem. 1:2). This arrangement would have necessitated meetings in the houses of more prosperous members of the community with adequate space. The letter called 1 Corinthians provides insight into the order, or disorders, of worship in such a house church. One can imagine a diverse group gathered around a common table in the dining area where a meal is shared, perhaps bracketed by the breaking of bread and sharing the cup (1 Cor. 11:23–6). Therefore the private house – or domicile – represents the earliest communal gathering-place for the early Christians in the first century, and it continued to provide such into the second century.

However, the Edict of Milan, which in 313 granted toleration of worship and reparations for property seized or destroyed in the recent persecutions, presupposed that Christians owned places of assemblage. Furthermore, as we shall explore later, Constantine immediately and aggressively undertook building programs in Rome, and elsewhere, through which he transformed the urban landscape by constructing churches of monumental size following the architectural design of the Greco-Roman basilica.

But how did Christianity get from the house church to the basilica?[33] In recent years, developmental architectural models have presented themselves, which begin with the "house church." By definition, this structure is a house being used for assemblies "as is" without architectural changes. The next step of development would be what has been called a *domus ecclesiae* (literally, "house of a church"), which means a house that has been architecturally adapted for use as a church. Still another step of development would be an *aula ecclesiae* ("hall of a church"), which identifies a building constructed as a place of assembly. The final step would be the basilica itself, such as those ordered by Constantine, a building on a grand scale intended to be used for worship.

What has enabled the conceptualization of this developmental model was the discovery, beginning in the 1920s, of the buried remains of the Roman garrison town of Dura-Europos situated on the Syrian frontier. The town was destroyed, along with a Jewish synagogue and a Christian church, by the Sassanian Persians in 256. This church building represents the only certain surviving example of a *domus ecclesiae* – between the period of Paul's missionary movement and Constantine's basilica-building campaign. Architectural adaptations of the house for Christian use included the enlargement of the dining room to create a rectangular assembly hall by removing a wall. Also, one of the rooms was transformed into a baptistery richly displaying images appropriate for its intended use. Among the subjects of the frescoes are the good shepherd, the walking on the water, the stilling of the storm, the woman at the well, the healing of the paralyzed man, and (apparently) three women approaching a tomb. Here the confession of Jesus as the Christ by his followers along the Euphrates river informed the shaping of the material world – architecturally and visually.

Dura-Europos has also contributed to an understanding of the origins of the Christian appropriation of the visual arts by providing evidence that early Christian artistic expression was not confined to a funereal setting. Nonetheless, much of the evidence for Christian art and other artifacts before Constantine come out of the catacombs of Rome.

The catacombs began as a burial place, not as a hiding place. Early in the second century, people began using the underground network to bury their dead. Toward the turn of the next century, the Roman church appointed a pensioner named Callistus, who had served time as a Christian in the mines of Sardinia, to supervise the Christian cemetery. Later the catacomb he supervised came to called, and is known today as, the catacomb of St. Callistus.[34]

From the St. Callistus catacomb, companion catacombs in Rome, and other sites – including the baptistery at Dura-Europos – come a number of pictorial representations deemed to be pre-Constantinian in date. These representations appear in four media: frescoes, murals, sarcophagi, and statues.[35]

An inventory of the subject matter by Graydon Snyder lists thirty-one different biblical scenes that occur a total of 181 times. Since our principal focus centers on Jesus as the Christ, I comment here specifically on how Jesus fares in the cemetery competition. Of the thirty-one biblical scenes, fifteen relate to the Jesus story. As I tabulate the results, the baptism of Jesus receives six votes with the raising of Lazarus a close runner-up with five. But taken together, minus the raising of Lazarus, scenes depicting Jesus' healing someone of some malady takes in seven votes. This commentary on the inventory is descriptive, not analytical. But it does suggest that Jesus Christ appears as a savior who delivers his own through acts of healing. Notably absent from the art prior to the fourth century is any depiction of Jesus fixed to a cross – that, is, a crucifix.

However, there is the graffito of what has been described as "the crucified donkey man."[36] Discovered in 1856 in the servants' quarters of the imperial palace on the Palatine Hill in Rome, this drawing depicts a person with the head of a donkey fixed to a cross. Another man points upward toward the so-called donkey man with an inscription in awkward Greek that can be translated, "Alexamenos worship(s) God." Perhaps material evidence of this kind of derision against Christians helps explain the avoidance of representations of the crucified Son of God by Christians. After all, a publicly visual reminder that the subject of Christian devotion had been executed by the Roman state immediately casts suspicion upon all those who identify themselves as "Christians." Perhaps this also explains the apparent popularity, based upon material evidence, among Christians in the second and third centuries of such symbols as the anchor, the boat with a mast, the fish, and the fish-related acrostic ΙΧΘΥΣ ("Jesus Christ, God's Son, Savior").

Notes

1 L. Michael White provides a detailed account of Christian beginnings, as he sees them, through the end of the second century: *From Jesus to Christianity: How Four Generations of Visionaries and Storytellers Created the New Testament and Christian Faith* (HarperSanFrancisco, 2004).

2 For further information on the New Testament writings within their socio-historical setting consult standard introductions, such as Bart D. Ehrman, *A Brief Introduction to the New Testament* (Oxford: Oxford University Press, 2004), or Stephen L. Harris, *The New Testament: A Student's Introduction*, 6th edn. (Boston: McGraw-Hill, 2009).

3 Robert J. Miller, ed., *The Complete Gospels: Annotated Scholars Version*, revised and expanded edn. (Santa Rosa, CA: Polebridge, 1994), 225–46.

4 Josephus, *Jewish Antiquities*, trans, Louis H. Feldman, 9 vols., Loeb Classical Library (Cambridge, MA: Harvard University Press, 1926, 1965), 9:49–51 and 495–7.

5 "Claudius" 25.4; see Suetonius, *Lives of the Caesars*, trans. J. C. Rolfe, 2 vols., Loeb Classical Library (Cambridge, MA: Harvard University Press, 1914, 1959), 2:52.

6 *Annales* 15.44; see Tacitus, *Annals*, trans. John Jackson, 4 vols., Loeb Classical Library (Cambridge, MA: Harvard University Press, 1937, 1962), 4:283–4.

7 *Epistulae ad Trajanus* 96; Pliny the Younger, *Letters*, trans. William Melmoth, 4 vols., Loeb Classical Library (Cambridge, MA: Harvard University Press, 1935, 1963), 2:401–5.

8 Stephen Benko, *Pagan Rome and the Early Christians* (Bloomington: Indiana University Press, 1986), 54–78, 103–39.

9 Robert L. Wilken, *The Christians as the Romans Saw Them* (New Haven: Yale University Press, 1984), 108–12.

10 Wilken, *Christians*, 159–60.

11 Rosemary Radford Ruether wrote a seminal study on the *adversus Judaeos* tradition that focuses especially on the Church Fathers: *Faith and Fratricide: The Theological Roots of Anti-Semitism* (Minneapolis: Seabury, 1974), 117–82.

12 Bart D. Ehrman has gathered into one volume an informative collection of writings that represent the diverse dimensions of earliest Christianity, which counts Justin Martyr and Tertullian among the apologists: *After the New Testament: A Reader in Early Christianity* (Oxford: Oxford University Press, 1999), 57–65, 75–82.

13   Eusebius, *Ecclesiastical History*, trans. Kirsopp Lake and J. E. L. Oulton, 2 vols., Loeb Classical Library (Cambridge, MA: Harvard University Press, 1959).

14   Bruce M. Metzger, *The Canon of the New Testament: Its Origin, Development, and Significance* (Oxford: Clarendon Press 1988). For a more recent proposal on the canon issue, see David Dungan, *Constantine's Bible: Politics and the Making of the New Testament* (Minneapolis: Fortress, 2007).

15   The non-Gnostic view of Marcion's program has been advocated by R. Joseph Hoffmann, *Marcion on the Restitution of Christianity: An Essay on the Development of Radical Paulinism in the Second Century* (Chico, CA: Scholars Press, 1984), 155–84.

16   Tertullian, *Against Marcion* The Ante-Nicene Fathers, ed. Alexander Roberts and James Donaldson (Grand Rapids, MI: Wm. B. Eerdmans, repr. 1993), 3:269–475.

17   Irenaeus, *Against Heresies*, The Ante-Nicene Fathers, ed. Alexander Roberts and James Donaldson (Grand Rapids, MI: Wm. B. Eerdmans, 1996), 3.11.8.

18   Eusebius, *Ecclesiastical History*, 1:3.25.1–7.

19   Metzger, *Canon*, 211.

20   Irenaeus, *Against Heresies*, 1.10.1

21   For developments before Nicaea, see Bernard Lonergan, *The Way to Nicea: The Dialectical Development in Trinitarian Theology*, trans. Conn O'Donovan (Philadelphia: Westminster Press, 1976).

22   Bart D. Ehrman, *Lost Christianities: The Battle for Scripture and the Faiths We Never Knew* (Oxford: Oxford University Press, 2003).

23   Richard Valantasis, *The Beliefnet Guide to Gnosticism and Other Vanished Christianities* (New York: Doubleday, 2006).

24   Karen King, *What Is Gnosticism?* (Cambridge, MA: Belknap Press of Harvard University Press, 2003).

25   James M. Robinson, gen, ed., *The Nag Hammadi Library in English* (New York: Harper & Row, 1977). Elaine Pagels was among the first scholars to gain public attention about these finds with her *The Gnostic Gospels* (New York: Random House, 1979).

26   Bentley Layton has reconstructed the "family" relationships among the Nag Hammadi texts, distinguishing between the Valentinians and other groups, in his *The Gnostic Scriptures: Ancient Wisdom for the New Age*, Anchor Bible Reference Library (New York: Doubleday, 1987), chart, p. xvi.

27   John Dart, *Laughing Savior: The Discovery and Significance of the Nag Hammadi Gnostic Library* (New York: Harper & Row, 1976).

28 Karen King, *The Gospel of Mary of Magdala: Jesus and the First Woman Apostle* (Santa Rosa, CA: Polebridge, 2003).

29 James M. Robinson, *The Secrets of Judas: The Story of the Misunderstood Disciple and his Lost Gospel* (HarperSanFrancisco, 2007).

30 The ancient texts, which report the martyrdoms epitomized in the narrative, are found in Ehrman, *After the New Testament*, 28–30, 30–5, 35–41.

31 A major secondary source for understanding the Constantinian era is the study by Charles Mason Odahl, *Constantine and the Christian Empire* (London: Routledge, 2004).

32 Bruce M. Metzger and Bart D. Ehrman, *The Text of the New Testament: Its Transmission, Corruption, and Restoration*, 4th edn. (New York: Oxford University Press, 2005), 52–92. Also see Larry W. Hurtado, *The Earliest Christian Artifacts: Manuscripts and Christian Origins* (Grand Rapids, MI: William B. Eerdmans, 2006).

33 L. Michael White, *Building God's House in the Roman World: Architectural Adaptation among Pagans, Jews, and Christians*, ASOR Library of Bible and Near Eastern Archaeology (Baltimore: Johns Hopkins University Press, 1990).

34 Graydon F. Snyder, *Ante-Pacem: Archaeological Evidence of Church Life Before Constantine* (Macon, GA: Mercer University Press, 2003), 87.

35 Fabrizio Mancinelli, *Catacombs and Basilicas: The Early Christians in Rome* (Florence: Scala Books, 1981).

36 G. M. A. Hanfmann, "The Crucified Donkey Man," in Günter Kopke and Mary B. Moore, eds. *Studies in Classical Art and Archaeology: A Tribute to Peter Heinrich von Blanckenhagen* (Locust Valley, NJ: J. J. Augustin, 1979): 205–7.

Chapter 2

Jesus and the Triumph
of Christian Orthodoxy
(Fourth and Fifth Centuries)

Christianity became a recognized religion within the Roman empire in 313 with the proclamation of the Edict of Milan by Constantine, the western emperor, and Licinius, the eastern emperor. Constantine himself made his own reception and approval of the religion of Jesus Christ immediately visible by authorizing an extravagant building program in the city of Rome itself.

Upon entering Rome in the year prior to the Edict of Milan, Constantine had given to Miltiades, the bishop of Rome (311–14), the Lateran Palace as a permanent residence for the presiding bishop. He also commissioned the construction of a large basilica for worship next to the palace just inside the eastern city wall. There followed the construction of a series of Christian basilicas ringing the city outside the walls, thereby avoiding the city center and unduly offending the pagan populace. After Sylvester became the bishop of Rome (314–35), Constantine also undertook the ambitious building of a basilica over the traditional site of Peter's burial to the west of the city walls in the area known as the Vatican Hill. This first St. Peter's basilica stood until superseded in the sixteenth century by the St. Peter's known today.

Rome was not the only beneficiary of Constantine's building campaign. His efforts to provide Christians with suitable, and even ostentatious, places of worship became central to his policy of Christianizing the Roman empire. Churches built with imperial patronage signaled the changed status of Christianity in the

empire. By their very presence, church buildings invited the populace to receive Jesus and the salvation offered through him.

Constantine even decided to relocate the center of his emerging "Christian" empire from Rome to a site in the east. As his
"New Rome," he chose the town of Byzantium located on a peninsula protruding into the waters separating the Sea of Marmora
and the Bosporus Strait. The formal dedication of Constantine's
city – with its palace, forum, chariot stadium, and three imposing
churches – occurred in the spring of 330. The most prominent of
the churches, in the city to be renamed Constantinople, was the
cathedral consecrated to Christ as the "Holy Wisdom" (*Hagia
Sophia*) of God.

Through his aging mother Helena, Constantine also involved
himself in marking sites in the "Holy Land" associated with the
life of Jesus. In 326 Helena arrived at the port of Caesarea, accompanied by her imperial entourage, on her fabled pilgrimage to the
Holy Land. She received assistance from Bishop Eusebius, the
church historian and later biographer of Constantine himself.
Helena evidently walked in the footsteps of Jesus from Galilee to
Judea – to Bethlehem and to Jerusalem. She visited sites, whether
discovered by her or previously identified by others, where –
according to tradition – had occurred Jesus' birth, his crucifixion
and resurrection, and his ascension. Where Helena walked arose
churches of the Nativity, the Holy Sepulcher, and the Ascension.
Although the church buildings today bearing the names of the
Nativity in Bethlehem and the Holy Sepulcher in Jerusalem do
not date back to Constantine, the sites for these earlier structures
have not changed. Helena even returned home with the rem-
nants of what became known as the "True Cross" – the relics and
legends of which would become scattered across Europe.
Constantine honored his mother and her endeavors by renaming
a town after her: Helenopolis. Like mother, like son!

With the proclamation of the Edict of Milan and the inauguration of Constantine's building campaign, however, the Christianizing of the Roman empire had just begun. The principal opposition
to Constantine eventually came from his fellow emperor Licinius,
who adopted Olympian Jupiter as his patron deity and encouraged a pagan revival in his eastern territories. He even began

persecuting Christians through various measures both restrictive and life-threatening. Constantine ended Licinius' religious as well as political threat by defeating him militarily in the summer of 324. The battles had the trappings of a holy war. Constantine and his troops displayed Christian symbols such as the chi-rho on helmets, shields, and banners, whereas Licinius and his army displayed comparable pagan symbols and were accompanied by priests who sought divine help through traditional pagan rites and sacrifices.

Having at last achieved leadership over the entire Roman empire, Constantine immediately addressed a letter to the inhabitants of the empire's eastern regions. He assured his peoples that Christianity remained a favored religion, that churches and Christians should receive restitution for possessions lost, and that he considered himself to be serving the one true God.

Constantine's battlefield skirmishes with Licinius were but a foreshadowing of the theological conflicts that awaited him and his successors for the next two centuries. During this period, Roman emperors summoned four great councils for the purpose of having bishops discuss and resolve issues confronting the entire church. Church synods involving bishops from particular regions met with some regularity. But these councils have been designated as ecumenical (Greek: *oikoumenē*, "the inhabited world") because they acted on behalf of the world-wide church – meaning, of course, the world of the Roman empire. These four ecumenical councils hammered out creedal statements that became the orthodox Christian doctrines about the nature of God and the meaning of the incarnation of God in Jesus Christ: the Council of Nicaea I (325); the Council of Constantinople I (381); the Council of Ephesus (431); and the Council of Chalcedon I (451).[1]

The Council of Nicaea I (325): The Relation of the Son to God the Father

The theological debates of the second and third centuries involved serious disputes between those Christians claiming to represent the orthodox views of the one catholic church and those believers of more heterodox persuasions whose views and actions were later considered to be deviant or heretical. At the beginning of the fourth century, a church wrangle erupted that engulfed the emerging "Christian" empire, especially in the eastern sector of the Mediterranean world.

The uproar began as a dispute between Bishop Alexander of Alexandria, in Egypt, and a presbyter in a local church named Arius (ca. 256–336). The dispute involved Arius' views on the relationship between God and Jesus, or Jesus and God. This issue had been present since the beginnings of the Jesus movement and had been addressed in various ways within emerging Christianity. Although vilified by many contemporaries and certainly by later generations, Arius was grappling philosophically and biblically with Christianity's foundational theological issue.

Arius believed that God as God was one, eternal, unbegotten, without source, without beginning, and thus the cause of all things. By contrast, the Son was neither eternal nor unbegotten. God the Father had created the Son as the "Word" through whom all things were subsequently created (John 1:1–3). Although the Son was pre-existent and "only-begotten" (John 1:18), the Son was a created being – a creature. He was the "first-born of all creation" (Col. 1:15). Thus God the Father was the source of the Son and the Son had a beginning. As Arius and his followers declared, "There was a time when the Son was not."

This theological view suggested that Jesus was neither truly God nor truly human. This view jeopardized both the revelation of God the Father through Jesus the Son and the salvation of humankind through Jesus the Son. Thus the counter-claim by Arius' opponents: "There was never a time when the Son was not."

Around 318, in a synod convened by Bishop Alexander, Arius' views were condemned, and he was expelled. Arias sought refuge with sympathizers. A flurry of communications circulated among church leaders. Considerable ecclesiastical unrest resulted in the eastern empire at the time when Constantine was engaged in his showdown with his rival Licinius. Early in 325, another synod of bishops met in Antioch intending to condemn Arius' teaching. At this point, Constantine intervened as a conciliator between the disputing parties and called for a general meeting of bishops to resolve the matter. Although Ancyra was the announced site, it was later moved to Nicaea in Bithynia.

With Constantine serving as the imperial host, the Council of Nicaea convened in June of 325.[2] No official record of the proceedings exists, but events can be reconstructed based on documents by those in attendance. The number of bishops in attendance, according to tradition, was 311. Most of the bishops attending came from the east. Bishop Sylvester of Rome was absent, although he was represented by two designated priests.

The Emperor Constantine made an opening call for peace and reconciliation. He remained in attendance throughout the deliberations and participated in the debate. Constantine's religious advisor, Bishop Ossius of Cordova, probably presided over the meetings. Among those in attendance were Bishop Eusebius of Caesarea and Athanasius, a young deacon from Alexandria. The latter would become the chief antagonist of the opponents of the Nicene settlement for fifty years. Different views were expressed and proposals entertained before an alternative statement to the proposals being considered was developed and presented. As a resolution of the theological issues raised by Arius and his sympathizers, the proposed creedal statement bound together the Father and the Son by the Greek word *homoousios*, meaning the "same essence" or the "same substance." The relevant portion of what has become known as the Nicene Creed reads: "We believe ... in one Lord Jesus Christ, the Son of God, begotten from the Father, only-begotten, that is, from the substance of the Father, God from God, light from light, true God from true God, of one substance [*homoousios*] with the Father." Thus the Son of God was no mere creature but fully divine with God the Father and co-eternal with God the Father. Although formally a Trinitarian declaration, the creed itself ends abruptly: "And in the Holy Spirit."[3]

Some in attendance at the council, and certainly many thereafter, raised questions about the appropriateness of the "same substance" word. Some pointed out that the expression was non-biblical. Others suggested that the expression sounded too materialistic. Still others complained that no written interpretation of the language accompanied the creed. Nonetheless, with Constantine's expressed wish that those present endorse the statement, the body did so overwhelmingly, although not unanimously. Two of the bishops, longtime friends of Arius, refused to sign on to the statement. They lost their episcopal sees and joined their friend in exile.

The theological issue was not the only item on the agenda. The council also endorsed, this time unanimously, the proposal by the emperor that the annual day celebrating Easter – the feast-day of Jesus' resurrection – be made uniform. In most regions, Christians had already turned away from following the Jewish calendar, with its movable date for Passover, and adopted an alternative formula of calculating the annual date for Easter: the first Sunday after the first full moon after the spring equinox. But some churches in Syria and Palestine had continued to link the celebration with the Jewish month of Nisan.

The Council of Nicaea was the church's first experience with a Roman emperor's participation in ecclesiastical politics. Not only was Constantine transforming the Roman empire into a Christian empire, he was laying the foundation for Christendom, where for more than a thousand years the heads of state and church leaders would compete and struggle with each other.

The Council of Constantinople I (381): God as Trinity, One Substance, Three Persons

The leading principals in the Arian controversy soon died: Alexander in 328, Arius in 336, and Constantine in 337. However, the controversy over the right understanding of Jesus the Son's relationship to God the Father lived on during the period when Constantine's three sons succeeded their father and shared rule with each other: Constantine II (d. 340); Constans (d. 350); and Constantius II (d. 361).

Advocates of Arianism and those who viewed the "same substance" (*homoousios*) language as unwarranted continued to attack the Nicene settlement. Proponents of a semi-Arian point of view defined the Son in relation to the Father as "like substance" (*homoiousios*). Calls also went forth for the elimination of the "substance" (*ousios*) word. For decades, the questions raised by the Nicene Creed were discussed in dozens of synods, and numerous rival creeds were formulated. The Emperor Constantius II himself harbored semi-Arian views. If this were not confusing enough, he was briefly succeeded by Julian, the emperor remembered as "the Apostate" because this nephew of Constantine attempted a revival of paganism during his brief reign (361–3).

Athanasius, now the long-time patriarch of Alexandria, had tenaciously championed the Nicene settlement since his own his days at the Council in Nicaea. He articulated his own understanding of the unity of and the distinction between the Son and the Father by affirming that what is said of the Father is also to be said of the Son, except that Son is Son, and not Father. Athanasius paid dearly for his tenaciousness by being exiled from Alexandria on five different occasions before his death in 373.

In spite of decades of theological posturing and wrangling among parties with differing viewpoints, the Nicene settlement had not been settled – at least not in the Greek-speaking east. In addition to Athanasius, there were three other remarkable theologians who clarified how Christians can think about God as one, but as three in one. These three hailed from Cappadocia in central Asia Minor: Basil of Caesarea (330–79), Gregory of Nazianzus (330–89), and Gregory of Nyssa (335–94).

Since Tertullian, Latin-speaking Christianity had the categories with which to define the Christian understanding of God as Trinity: one divine substance, but in three persons, Father, Son, and Spirit. However, in Greek-speaking Christianity, the Cappadocians were the first to correlate, in Greek, the word *ousia* (as in *homoousios*) as the broad category for divinity with the narrower category of *hypostasis* for the distinctive qualities of the Father, the Son, and the Holy Spirit. So in this and other areas, the Cappadocians moved theological understanding toward what has become commonplace Christian God-talk: God as a Trinity, Father, Son, and Holy Spirit; one substance (*homoousios*), but three persons (*hypostaseis*).

In 380 another church council was called by the Emperor Gratian (375–85), who ruled the western empire, and the recently appointed Emperor Theodosius I (379–95), who ruled the religiously troublesome eastern empire. Theodosius, in particular, was committed to the Nicene settlement. Thus the purpose of this council of 150 bishops was to reaffirm the creed adopted at Nicaea and to condemn those holding heretical theological positions. Among the latter continued to be those with Arian and Arian-related viewpoints such as denying the divinity of the Holy Spirit.

This council convened in Constantinople in the spring of 381.[4] No written record of the proceedings remains. However, a letter – written the next year – from bishops who had been present in Constantinople to bishops gathered in Rome for a synod there sets forth the doctrinal decisions of what became known as the second ecumenical council. The council reaffirmed and clarified the Nicene-Constantinopolitan Creed, which soon established itself as the baptismal creed in the eastern churches and later found its way into the eucharistic liturgy in the eastern and the western churches. Today, this belief statement is known simply as the Nicene Creed:

> We believe in one God, the Father, almighty, maker of heaven and earth, of all things visible and invisible;
> And in one Lord Jesus Christ, the only-begotten Son of God, begotten from the Father before all ages, God of God, light from light, true God from true God; begotten not made, of one substance [*homoousios*] with the Father; through Whom all things came into existence, Who because of us men and because of our salvation came down from heaven and was incarnate from the Holy Spirit and the Virgin Mary, and became man, and was crucified for us under Pontius Pilate, and suffered and was buried, and rose again, on the third day according to the Scriptures and ascended to heaven, and sits on the right hand of the Father, and will come again with glory, to judge living and dead, of Whose kingdom there will be no end;
> And in the Holy Spirit, the Lord and life-giver, Who proceeds from the Father, Who with the Father and the Son is together worshipped and together glorified; Who spoke through the prophets; in one holy Catholic and apostolic church. We confess one baptism to the remission of sins; we look forward to the resurrection of the dead and the life of the world to come. Amen.[5]

The Nicene Creed retains the *homoousios* expression introduced at Nicaea. This reiterates belief in the divinity of Jesus. The Nicene

Creed also expands the brief reference to the Holy Spirit in the confessional statement adopted at Nicaea. However, the expansion does not incorporate the *homoousios* word but acknowledges the divinity of the Holy Spirit by using biblical and liturgical turns of phrase. Thus the council reaffirmed and clarified the creed adopted at Nicaea and also condemned by name ten heresies inconsistent with the revised statement, including the Arians.

From 392 to 395 Theodosius was the last emperor to serve over both halves of the Roman empire. During his rule he completed the "Christian" revolution initiated by Constantine. Through imperial edicts, Christianity was declared to be the only licit religion of the Roman empire. The edicts also called upon all subjects to believe "in the one Deity of the Father, Son, and Holy Spirit, in equal majesty and in holy Trinity."[6]

Transition: From the Trinity to the Incarnation

While the second ecumenical council was meeting in Constantinople in 381, a young man named Augustine (354–430) was teaching rhetoric in the North African city of Carthage. Augustine had not yet found his way to God. But after a long internal struggle and an intentional search for the truth that carried him to Rome and to Milan, he experienced a transforming experience in 386 that led to his baptism in 387, his ordination in 391, and his elevation to the episcopacy as the bishop of Hippo in 396, where he served until his death. A prolific writer, Augustine became one of the most influential theologians in the history of Christianity. In our setting, he serves as a transitional figure between the conciliar decisions about the Trinity and the definition regarding the Incarnation.

Augustine is widely known for his spiritual autobiography – perhaps the very first of its genre – titled simply *The Confessions*. Written ca. 400, the work contains these familiar words addressed by Augustine to God: "Thou hast formed us for Thyself, and our hearts are restless till they find rest in Thee."[7] From the safe place of having found his rest in God, he proceeds to lay bare his own life – from his earliest days through his conversion. In his reflections, he periodically breaks forth in language that recalls the doctrine of the Trinity as formulated in the Nicene Creed and also anticipates the doctrine of the Incarnation as defined later at Chalcedon. He confesses that in his sinfulness he needed someone to reconcile him to God: "But a mediator between God and man must have something like unto God, something like unto man; lest being in both like unto man, he should be far from God; or if in both like unto God, he should be far from man; and so should not be a mediator." He continues: "that Mediator between God and man, the Man Christ Jesus, appeared between mortal sinners and the immortal Just One."[8]

Here Augustine, also borrowing from 1 Timothy 2:5, identifies Jesus as "the Mediator" – a title that also indicates what Jesus has accomplished. What Jesus did for Augustine corresponded to Augustine's greatest desire and need as explored throughout *The Confessions*.

Some years later, Augustine wrote a more expansive and exquisite treatise focused specifically *On the Trinity*. As suggested, Augustine was quite familiar with the metaphysical ponderings and theological give and take over the doctrine of the Trinity that resulted in the Nicene Creed. He presupposed the church's doctrine in his own explorations and emphasized throughout his treatise the equality of all three persons, each of whom possessed the whole substance of the Godhead. Therefore, Augustine's greatest contribution to Trinitarian reflection probably comes not from a philosophical refinement of the doctrine but from his discovering within the human self comparisons or analogues to the divine Trinity. This turn inward might be expected from the author of *The Confessions*. The first analogue involves human love that has three dimensions: the lover, the one loved, and love. The second analogue involves the human mind that has three dimensions: memory, understanding, and will. And so God is one in three persons, Father, Son, and Holy Spirit.[9]

Of particular interest as Augustine moves beyond the analogues is his recognition that the scriptures declare, "God is love" (1 John 4:8, 16). His exegesis leads to the conclusion that the immediate reference is to the Holy Spirit as love because the Holy Spirit kindles in humans the love of God and love of neighbor – as Jesus commanded (Matt. 22:34–40).

To discontinue our discussion of Augustine with so much unsaid appears inadequate; but our principal concern is with the reception of Jesus as the Son in relation to the Father and the Holy Spirit as one of the three persons of the distinctly Christian Trinitarian understanding of God.

The Council of Ephesus (431): The Incarnate Son, One Person, Not Divided

The Nicene Creed had affirmed the Lord Jesus Christ to be "true God from true God" and also acknowledged that "he became man." Now that the Godness of Jesus, at best implicit in the confessions of the earliest church, had been explicitly declared, attention turned to consider how the divinity and the humanity were related in the incarnate Jesus. Theology gave way to Christology – thinking about the Son of God, the Lord Jesus Christ.

The Nicene Creed itself includes no details of Jesus' public activity on earth, such as his baptism, his words, and his deeds; however, this creed frames Jesus' life between his conception through the Holy Spirit by his virgin mother Mary *and* his crucifixion, suffering, and burial under Pontius Pilate, followed by his resurrection from the dead. Thus the Nicene Creed has a "missing" center – the human life of Jesus. The preoccupation in recent centuries with Jesus as a historical figure was seemingly of little concern in the "Christian" empire inaugurated by the first Christian emperor, Constantine.

Early in the third century, Tertullian – the pioneering figure in Latin Christianity – had identified language appropriate for articulating the doctrine of the Trinity that contributed to the orthodox definition at Nicaea: God as one substance, three persons. Tertullian also anticipated the doctrine of the Incarnation by describing Jesus as one person but two natures, one divine and the other human. Again, however, the Greek-speaking east was playing conceptual catch-up with the west.

Like the theological debates over the Trinity in the fourth century, so the fifth-century discussions about how God the co-eternal Son became incarnate as the human Jesus involved more than critical thinking. There were also the inevitable rivalries among the patriarchal churches. This involved not just the Roman church in relation to churches in the east, but also competition among eastern centers of Christian thought and practice: Constantinople as the "New Rome"; and the older centers of ecclesiastical authority and theological education, such as Antioch in Syria and Alexandria in Egypt. In addition to institutional conflict, there were personalities with various degrees of contentiousness.

In the opening decades of the fifth century Cyril, the patriarch of Alexandria (d. ca. 444), squared off against Nestorius, the patriarch of Constantinople (d. ca. 451). From an Alexandrian family, Cyril succeeded an uncle as patriarch of that city in 412 and continued the theological tradition established by Athanasius, another patriarchal predecessor. Nestorius, a native of Syria and representative of the school of Antioch, had been living as priest and monk in Antioch when was appointed patriarch of Constantinople. His tenure was brief: 428–31.

The flashpoint of the controversy that resulted in Nestorius' early departure was his preaching against the time-honored designation of the Virgin Mary as *Theotokos*, "mother of God" (Greek; literally, "God-bearer"). Nestorius claimed it was inappropriate to refer to Mary in this way because she was not "Mother of God," but more accurately "Mother of Christ." Perhaps the negative responses to Nestorius locally were viewed by Cyril as an opportunity to embarrass simultaneously the patriarchate of Constantinople and the school of Antioch. Cyril and Nestorius exchanged letters in which Cyril claimed that Nestorius had divided the *one* Lord Jesus Christ as though he were *two sons*, the one divine and the other human. Cyril reminded Nestorius how the names of honor bestowed upon the Lord Jesus Christ in the gospels, such as "the Son of God" and "the Son of Man," refer to Jesus as one person and are not to be divided in accordance with his divine and his human natures. "The Son of God" honors Jesus' person, not just his divine nature. Likewise, "The Son of Man" honors Jesus' person, not just his human nature. Thus the recognition of the Virgin Mary as *Theotokos* appropriately affirms the unity of Jesus' person.

As a result of Nestorius' correspondence with Cyril, Nestorius appealed to Pope Celestine I (422–32); but a Roman synod sided with Cyril and asked Nestorius to either recant or stand condemned. Nestorius then requested Emperor Theodosius II to call a council to hear his case; but Theodosius II called for such a council in concert with his fellow Emperor Valentinian III and also with the consent of Pope Celestine I. The outcome of the council was inevitable.

In June of 431, the third ecumenical council convened in Ephesus with some two hundred or so bishops in attendance, including Cyril, but not Nestorius.[10] The basic question asked of the body was whether or not the contents of letters exchanged by Cyril and Nestorius were doctrinally in conformity with the Nicene Creed. The judgments were affirmative for Cyril and negative for Nestorius. The patriarch of Constantinople was removed from his ecclesiastical office and banished from the priesthood.

The Council of Chalcedon I (451): The Incarnate Son, One Person, Two Natures

The years between the Council of Ephesus (431) and the Council of Chalcedon I (451) were years of continued acrimony between the Antiochian and the Alexandrian approaches to the personhood of Jesus. The Antiochian emphasis on the humanity of Jesus seemed to threaten the integrity of Jesus' personhood by dividing him in two. This was the accusation leveled against Nestorius that led to his removal from his episcopal office and his loss of priestly status.

Whereas Nestorians were accused of so distinguishing between the human nature and the divine nature in Jesus Christ that he appeared to be not just two natures but two persons, the Alexandrians so emphasized the divinity of the Word that became flesh that the humanity seemed to be swallowed up by the divinity. Even Cyril of Alexandria made comments on occasion that seemed to present Jesus Christ as being of "one nature" (Greek: *mia physis*). The view that Jesus possessed one nature came to be known as monophysitism, and it played an important role in the events leading up to and subsequent to the fourth ecumenical council that convened in Chalcedon in 451.[11]

Among the first to level charges against Nestorius had been a monk named Eutyches, from a monastery in Constantinople. But years later Eutyches found himself charged with heresy for his monophysite claim: "I confess that our Lord was of two natures before the union [between the divine and the human natures at the Incarnation], but I confess one [divine] nature after the union."

Flavian, a successor to Nestorius as patriarch of Constantinople, convened a local synod in 448 that condemned Eutyches. Both Eutyches and Flavian presented their respective cases to Pope Leo I (440–61), who agreed with Flavian. However, the very next year – 449 – Eutyches was rehabilitated at a council called for Ephesus by Emperor Theodosius II. Soon thereafter Theodosius II died and was succeeded by Emperor Marcian. Out of this imperial and ecclesiastical confusion, the Emperor Valentinan III and the Emperor Marcian summoned the Council of Chalcedon to meet in the year 451.

Pope Leo I was not personally present in Chalcedon, but he was well represented. He also sent a doctrinal letter about Eutyches to Flavian, the patriarch of Constantinople. This document earned for itself the label "Leo's tome," presumably because of its great length and its weighty theology. Pope Leo I forthrightly declares the importance of Jesus Christ's having not one but two natures, divine and human. In language similar to the definition later adopted by the council, he affirms that Jesus Christ is "true God and true man." He cites scripture: "Every Spirit that confesses that Jesus Christ came in the flesh is from God, and every spirit which puts Jesus asunder is not from God, and this is *Antichrist*" (1 John 4:2).

The Council of Chalcedon did condemn Eutyches and his Christology that mixed the two natures of Christ. The decisions taken by the previous three ecumenical councils were reaffirmed, including the Nicene Creed. But of greatest importance for later

Christian history and for the later church was the definition of the unity of Christ and the relationship between his divine nature and his human nature:

> Therefore, following the holy fathers, all of us unanimously teach that everyone must confess that our Lord Jesus Christ is the one and the same Son, who is perfect according to divinity and perfect according to humanity, truly God and truly human, composed of a rational soul and a body, of one substance [*homoousios*] with the Father according to divinity and of one substance [*homoousios*] with us according to humanity, completely like us except for sin; he was begotten by the Father before all ages according to his divinity and, in these latter days, he was born for us and for our salvation of Mary the Virgin, the God-bearer [*Theotokos*], according to his humanity; the one and the same Christ, Son, Lord, only-begotten, acknowledged in two natures, without confusion, without change, without division, without separation; the difference of natures is in no way suppressed by their union, but rather the properties of each are retained and united in one single person [*prosōpon*] and single hypostasis; but he is neither separated nor divided in two persons, but he is the one and the same only-begotten Son, God the Word, the Lord Jesus Christ, such as he was announced formerly by the prophets, such as he himself, the Lord Jesus Christ, has taught us about himself and such as the creed of the fathers has transmitted to us.[12]

A careful reading discloses how this statement positions itself between the alleged Nestorian division of Christ into two persons, on the one hand, and the Eutychian – or monophysite – mixing of the two natures, divine and human, into a single nature.

As might be expected, like the Nicene Creed that preceded it, the definition of Chalcedon left many questions unanswered and raised many more questions. Perhaps it is helpful for us to consider that creeds may be more important for what they intend to deny than for what they affirm.

Nonetheless, that proto-orthodox theological tradition that had struggled for centuries was finally triumphant toward the conclusion of the fifth century. Christianity had become a world religion.

The one, catholic, and orthodox church had – with imperial patronage – established a doctrinal umbrella over its belief system: the doctrine of a Triune God, one substance, in three persons; and the doctrine of the Incarnation, the Lord Jesus Christ, the Son of God, in two natures, divine and human. These doctrines provide the framework for discussions about God and Jesus Christ that continue into the twenty-first century. Presupposed by and central to both doctrines is the person of Jesus, whose reception had already begun transforming in his name the lands and culture around the Mediterranean.

The world of Christianity was expanding. Peoples were afoot on the borders of the Roman empire: Celts, Goths, Vandals, Franks, Huns, among others. Already by the fourth century, among the Goths was Bishop Ulfila, who had become theologically an Arian and had initiated a mission to his peoples. He was the first to translate the New Testament into Gothic.

After the Council of Ephesus in 431 and the condemnation of Nestorius, his followers relocated eastward, first to Persia and from there onward to India and China. The migration evidently led to the introduction of Christianity into the culture of eastern Asia as early as the seventh century. Recent years have seen the publication of the so-called *Jesus Sutras* – writings that possibly cast Jesus in the role of a Christian-Taoist redeemer figure. Today Christian tradition is represented in the Middle East by the Assyrian Church of the East, with members in Iraq, Iran, Syria, and Lebanon.

After the Council of Chalcedon in 451 and the condemnation of monophysitism, churches in Egypt refused to accept the Christological definition of Jesus as one person with two natures, human and divine. They came to be identified as monophysite churches or, more recently, to identify themselves as non-Chalcedonian Orthodox churches. Besides the Coptic church, they include the Armenian, Syrian, Ethiopian, and Malankara Syrian churches.

Early Monasticism: From Martyr to Monk

Paul in his letters centers on Jesus' death as the crucial moment in Jesus' life for the lives of his followers and for later generations.

The gospels of Matthew, Mark, Luke, and John amplify that moment into passion narratives of Jesus' final days. The book of Revelation extols Jesus as that faithful "witness" (Greek: *martyr*) whose blood frees the faithful from sin. Thus Jesus' suffering unto death in the earliest Christian literature provided a template for the stories of Christians who themselves had experienced persecution and martyrdom prior to the legalization of Christianity in the Roman empire under Constantine.

Central to the fourth- and fifth-century debates over the doctrines of the Trinity and the Incarnation that resulted in the Nicene Creed of 381 and the definition of Chalcedon of 451 was the presentation of Jesus in the Gospel of John as the pre-existent Word become flesh. As we have observed, the Creed itself affirms the conception and the death of Jesus with no reference to events between.

However, the fourth and fifth centuries also saw the emergence of Christian monasticism as a movement in which men and women were called by Jesus through his example and his teachings to turn away from the world. These monks (from the Greek *monos*, solitary), particularly laypeople, began intentionally seeking solitude in order to pursue more disciplined lives of righteousness and holiness.

Much has been written about factors contributing to the appearance of Christian monasticism in the fourth century. Certainly monasticism presupposed ascetic practices common both without and within the church – practices of spiritual self-denial and self-discipline, such as fasting and prayer, akin to athletes preparing themselves for athletic competition. But another factor involved the changing status of Christianity in the empire from a persecuted minority to a favored religion and then to the only recognized religion. Whereas the "witnesses" to the Christian life in the age of persecution had been those who had followed Jesus unto death, now the "witnesses" to the Christian life were those who devoted themselves wholly to following Jesus in their living. The former have been described as "red" martyrs; the latter as "white" martyrs.[13]

If the Jesus of the Fourth Gospel was central to the issues and formulations of the ecumenical councils, then the Jesus of the Synoptic Gospels was paramount for the emergence of the monastic movement. Prior to Jesus' public activity of preaching and healing in all three Synoptics, he withdraws into the desert for forty days, where he encounters the Devil. Periodically Jesus also withdraws, sometimes with his disciples, to pray. His teachings and his example support the later counsels of poverty, chastity, and obedience.

The monastic movement itself began in the deserts of Egypt. Two names are usually associated with its beginning. They also represent respectively the two principal forms of monasticism: Antony (251–356), solitary or eremitic monasticism; and Pachomius (290–346), communal or coenobitic monasticism. Both men became influential in the development of monasticism in both the east and the west.

Antony's influence came through a fourth-century work titled the *Life of Antony*, attributed to Athanasius.[14] The story opens with an account of how Antony came to renounce the world. Accordingly, he went to church thinking about how Jesus' disciples had forsaken everything to follow him. During the service, as the gospel was being read, he heard Jesus say to the rich man, "If you would be perfect, go, sell what you possess and give to the poor, and you will have treasure in heaven" (Matt. 19:21). This Antony did. He disposed of his possessions and eventually withdrew into the desert, where he spent years in isolation praying and combating demons. The rest is history. Soon translated from Greek into Latin, the *Life of Antony* became widely read and emulated throughout the Mediterranean world. When Augustine – in his *Confessions* – tells of his own conversion experience, he recalls how Antony had been grasped in church by the reading of the gospel. Thus Augustine himself opened the book of the apostle Paul, which was lying at hand, and was transformed by the first words on which he eyes fell, "Put on the Lord Jesus Christ" (Rom. 13:13–14).

Pachomius' influence came primarily through the circulation of the so-called *Pachomian Rules* developed over time for the governance of the network of monasteries responsible to him. His own language was Coptic, but his *Rules* were eventually translated into Greek and from the Greek into Latin. Born of pagan parents in Thebes, Pachomius as a young man had been inducted into the Roman army and had received gestures of care and food from Christians. Subsequently, he became a Christian himself.

He began living as a hermit in close proximity to the cells of others, but soon began creating a communal structure whereby monastics, male or female, shared lives and possessions together under the leadership of an abbot or abbess. Pachomius himself had been called "Abba," meaning Father. When he died, he reportedly had nine male and two female monasteries under his authority with more than 3,000 monastics having been under his supervision.

Pachomius and the *Pachomian Rules* influenced eastern monasticism through Basil of Caesarea. Intending himself to establish a monastery, Basil had visited monastic sites in Egypt, Palestine, Syria, and Mesopotamia. He favored the communal approach of Pachomius, and the *Rule of St. Basil* was drawn up for the monastery founded by him in Cappadocia, ca. 356. From Cappadocia, the use of Basil's rule spread throughout the Greek-speaking east.

Both Antony and Pachomius influenced Benedict of Nursia (480–543), who has become the most important single figure in the history of western monasticism. Benedict grew up and went to school in Rome before deciding to pursue the life set forth in the example and teachings of Jesus. He withdrew to the mountains, where for three years he lived as a hermit in a cave. Later he founded the famous monastery of Monte Cassino in central Italy. Sometime around 530 he drew up the so-called *Rule of St. Benedict* to govern those who commit themselves to the monastic life. The prologue calls upon followers of Jesus – in a familial way – to be obedient and to renounce their own will "with the intention of fighting for the true King, Christ the Lord."[15] The battling Benedictines also became famous for their hospitality, in which they were to receive visitors as though they were Christ (Matt. 25:31–46).

In the fifth century, monasticism found its way into the westernmost territory that had never been invaded by the Romans nor incorporated into the Roman empire: the land of Ireland.[16] The reception of Christianity by the Irish is attributed to the missionary bishop Patrick (ca. 390–460). Patrick evidently came from a Romanized British family which was Christian. As a young man, he had been kidnapped by Irish adventurers and forced into slavery in the western part of Ireland for several years, only to escape and return to Britain. He experienced a call by God to return to his former captors in obedience to the missionary command of Jesus in the gospels. He became a priest and returned to Ireland, where he spent the remainder of his life bringing the message of Christ to the people.

Whether monasticism itself first entered Ireland through Patrick or other channels remains unclear. But it did establish itself, and Irish Christianity expressed itself in distinctive ways with an artistic richness, a scholarly intensity, and a spiritual depth. The Celtic cross, distinguished by the circle at the top, remains the most recognizable symbol of early Irish Christianity.

As missionaries themselves, the Irish monks and their successors returned to Britain and then the continent, from where Christ had been brought to them. The Irish monk Columba (d. 597) established a community on the island of Iona off the west coast of Scotland, and this community engaged in a mission to the Picts. The monk Aidan (d. 651) undertook a mission to the Anglo-Saxons and relocated to the island of Lindisfarne off the northeast coast of England. Lindisfarne became the home of the English monk Cuthbert (d. 687), who moved among the poor, became a hermit, and reluctantly accepted leadership as bishop. The monk remembered as the Venerable Bede (d. 735) lived and labored in a scriptorium at the double monasteries of Wearmouth and Jarrow on the river Tyne. Here he translated portions of the Bible into Old English and wrote his monumental *Ecclesiastical History of the English People*.[17]

Bede's history discusses the Synod of Whitby (664) where the Irish church and the Roman church were finally reconciled over the issues of how monks should cut their hair and how to calculate the day for Easter. Since the Easter issue had been addressed much earlier at the Council of Nicaea in 325, this three-century time-lag indicates how the Irish church had maintained its independence from Rome.

Material Culture: Manuscripts, Architecture, and the Visual Arts

The Christianization of the Roman empire under Constantine and his successors resulted in dramatic changes in Christianity's

Figure 2 Portrait of Christ with a beard and a halo, framed by the Greek letters alpha and omega (based on Revelation 1:8, 22:13), from the catacomb of Commodilla in Rome (fourth century). *Photo: AKG Images/ Pirozzi*

– and thus Jesus' – impact upon culture in terms of the production of manuscripts, the developments in church architecture, and the proliferation of the visual arts.

Monasteries became sites for the writing, copying, and preservation of literature – especially biblical manuscripts. Monks became practitioners of the scribal arts and thus received and transmitted the Jesus story by pen. By the fourth century significant changes were occurring in terms of the kind of writing material in use. Papyrus was being replaced by parchment, or animal hides. The ancient scroll form of the book was also being supplanted by the codex, the form like the modern book in which leaves are bound together between covers.

The earliest extant Greek manuscript of the entire Bible, which contained all twenty-seven books of the New Testament, dates from the fourth century. This manuscript is called Codex Sinaiticus because of its book form and its place of discovery. Codex Sinaiticus was found in the 1840s at St. Catharine's monastery on Mount Sinai by a German scholar, Constantin von Tischendorf, who was in the region looking for ancient biblical manuscripts. Today this manuscript resides in the British Library in London. The only other comparable Greek manuscript from the fourth century is Codex Vaticanus, which originally also contained the entire Bible, although the preserved manuscript breaks off in the middle of the New Testament book of Hebrews. This manuscript has been in the Vatican Library in Rome since at least the fifteenth century. Both Codex Sinaiticus and Codex Vaticanus are old enough to have been among the fifty manuscripts of the Bible commissioned by Constantine, around the year 331, to be produced on parchment by professional scribes for use in churches in Constantinople, but this has been questioned and has never been conclusively established.

By the end of the fourth century, the New Testament or portions thereof had been translated from Greek into several languages, including Syriac, Armenian, and Coptic in the east and Gothic and Latin in the west. The great variety in textual readings among the Latin manuscripts led Pope Damasus (d. 384) to commission a scholarly priest named Jerome to undertake a uniform revision of the Latin Bible. Jerome first translated the gospels, and eventually translated the entire Bible from the original languages of Hebrew and Greek into the common (or "vulgar") Latin. Jerome's Latin Vulgate translation became the Bible of the Latin-speaking church for over a thousand years.

Manuscripts not only disseminated the Jesus story through text but came to interpret the story visually through pictures, or illuminations, showing the image of Jesus and moments in his life. The Celtic-Irish monasteries at Iona and at Lindisfarne received and celebrated Jesus by producing two remarkably beautiful gospel books based on a Latin text in the seventh and eighth centuries: the Lindisfarne Gospels, now in the British Library, London, and the Book of Kells, on display in the Trinity College Library, Dublin. The intricate and colorful artwork in both books originally contained figures of the four evangelists identified by their traditional symbols: Matthew, a human; Mark, a lion; Luke, an ox; and John, an eagle (symbols based on Revelation 4:7). However, the Book of Kells also contains a number of images related to Jesus and his story, including a Madonna and child, the temptation of Jesus, the arrest of Jesus, and the enthronement of Jesus. The enthroned Jesus confronts the viewer with eyes wide open, at full body length, through a frame with an intertwined design and squared corners. Enrobed in mellow reddish orange, he has long, wavy blond hair and a red beard. The paleness of his face and feet are noticeable, as is the paleness of his right hand, which holds an unidentified book close to his heart.

The reception of Jesus by Christians required not only biblical texts but the physical settings where Christians could gather regularly for the reading and exposition of the scriptures, the performance of the liturgy, and the administration of the sacraments. As I have already observed, the development from church as community to church as building developed in overlapping stages over the first three centuries of Christianity: from the domestic house church, to the house modified for use as a church, to the meeting-hall church, and finally – with Constantine – to the basilica.

The word *basilica* (Latin from the Greek for "royal") designated a large building intended to accommodate crowds for a variety of activities, including commercial transactions and legal proceedings. In the imperial period, palaces featured the basilica as a hall where the emperor could meet and address large audiences.

Architecturally, the basilica was a spacious, roofed hall, with a rectangular floor plan, a flat ceiling, and a triangular-shaped roof. The building usually had interior colonnades that divided the space, with aisles down each side, but with a longer hall down the center, at the end of which was a rounded extension, or apse, with a raised platform or dais. The longer hall, or nave, was characteristically of greater height than the side aisles in order to allow light through the upper-level, or clerestory, windows.

The basilica design lent itself well to adoption as ecclesiastical architecture. The building could accommodate a sizable number of congregants. The apse and raised dais could be used as the focal point for worship. Here the chair (*cathedra*) of the bishop would be located, with other officiants seated in a semicircle around him. The sermon would be delivered by the bishop from the chair. Thus bishops' churches came to be known as cathedrals. Other ecclesiastical furniture needed would be a lectern for reading the scriptures and an altar for the celebration of the Eucharist.

Although Constantine was engaged in Christianizing the Roman empire, the adoption of the basilica reciprocally facilitated the Romanization of Christianity. The major churches authorized by Constantine in Rome, the Holy Land, and Constantinople early in the fourth century reflected the basilican style. However, none of these buildings constructed under his patronage has survived.

Nonetheless, if manuscripts provided a vehicle for the reception of the Jesus story not only verbally but also visually, how much more did church buildings provide space and surface for interpreting the Jesus story through the visual arts? With Constantine's acceptance of Christianity, Christian art moved out of the catacombs and into the light. The settings for Christian iconography became more numerous and more varied. For example, Christian basilicas were often associated with free-standing baptisteries with a centered design containing a font, or bath, into which candidates would step for baptism. With the increase in the number and variety of settings, the inventory of Christian images also expanded considerably.

Many of the most popular narrative-based representations of Jesus from the pre-Constantinian period continued to appear in the fourth century and beyond. These scenes from the gospels included Jesus' baptism, his healing of the paralyzed man, his multiplying the loaves and the fishes, his encounter with the woman at the well, and his raising of Lazarus. Additional narrative-based representations included Jesus' temptation, his changing water into wine, his healing the man born blind, his raising either the widow of Nain's son or Jairus' daughter, his arrest, his trial, and his enthronement.

But in the fourth century there also appeared what Robin Margaret Jensen has called a "new category" in representations of Jesus – the portrait.[18] Although personal portraits had become commonplace in the Greco-Roman world, not until the fourth century did there appear portraits of Jesus. By portrait is meant a frontal image, from the waist up, without indication of narrative context. One of the earliest of these portraits appears in Rome in the burial chamber of the catacomb of Commodilla. With dark beard and hair, Jesus gazes forlornly. His head is framed by a halo with the Greek letter A (*alpha*) to the viewer's left and an Ω (*omega*) to the right (based on Revelation 1:8 and 22:13). The significance of the portrait is its potential for bringing the viewer into the presence of the one portrayed. Correspondingly, the importance of portraits of Jesus lies in their invitation to the viewer to enter into the presence of the sacred. These portraits anticipated the devotional use of icons (or images of the sacred) in the eastern church tradition.

The fourth and fifth centuries were also the years when Christianity, through the four ecumenical councils, defined what became the orthodox doctrines of the Trinity and the Incarnation. Unless Christian theology and Christian art represent two altogether different kinds of human engagement, then there must be some relationship between the two.

Although the ecclesiastical buildings authorized by Constantine in Rome, the Holy Land, and Constantinople no longer stand as built, the Italian city of Ravenna has a significant concentration of well-preserved Christian buildings from a century or two later.[19] Located on the Adriatic Sea, across the peninsula from Rome, Ravenna had been the capital of the western Roman empire when it fell to Germanic tribes in 476 and later served as the capital of the Ostrogothic kingdom (489–553) founded by King Theodoric, who like his fellow Ostrogoths was a Christian, but an Arian Christian. Because of the number and variety of ecclesiastical structures and the rich panoply of artwork, especially mosaics, that can be found there, Ravenna provides a "laboratory setting" in which to explore possible iconographic reflections of the theological controversies that precipitated the four ecumenical councils in 325, 381, 431, and 451.

For our purposes, we are interested in the interiors of three buildings: first, the baptistery of Neon, which was built when Ravenna was under orthodox rule before the establishment of the Ostrogothic kingdom in 489; secondly, an Arian baptistery, which was built after 489 by Theodoric, the Arian king; and, thirdly, an Arian cathedral also built after 489 by Theodoric and dedicated to Christ the Savior – although the name of the latter church was changed to the basilica of Sant' Apollinare Nuovo, when in 553 the city reverted to the rule of the Byzantine empire through the conquests of the orthodox Emperor Justinian (527–65).

Justinian also contributed to the construction in Ravenna of the basilica of Sant' Apollinare in Classe and the basilica of San Vitale as orthodox churches. In the latter basilica, Jesus dominates the apse from on high as ruler of the universe while Emperor Justinian, Empress Theodora, and their courtiers appear below on each side of the apse dressed in all their opulence.

The Arian baptistery has a mosaic that has been viewed by some to be a non-figurative representation of the Trinity: a cross mounted on a throne between the figures of Peter and Paul. This interpretation does not seem convincing, especially in an Arian setting, insofar as Arians did not traditionally affirm belief in the Triune God.

More convincing is seeing – as suggested by Robin Margaret Jensen – intended Christological differences between the contrasting representations of an older, bearded, Jesus in the orthodox baptistery of Neon and the youthful, beardless, Jesus in the later Arian baptistery, as though the latter image might be intended to "erase" the earlier. This could suggest that Arian Christology, which viewed Jesus as creature, recognized that Jesus' creatureliness involved aging.

This interpretation receives support from the mosaic program in the Arian cathedral, which has panels of mosaics down each side of the nave. The Jesus in the panels on the left, which includes scenes from his ministry, appears beardless with light-colored hair. The Jesus in the panels on the right, which includes scenes from Passion Week, appears with a dark beard that appears to grow longer as he moves toward crucifixion – although no crucifixion scene itself is included. Here within the Arian cathedral, Jesus does appear to age over the course of his ministry. Surely the visual subtlety involved in the contrasting images of Jesus in Ravenna would be no greater than the verbal subtlety between *homoouios* and *homoiousios* in the Christological debates of the fourth century.

The observation that the iconographic program in the sixth-century Arian cathedral in Ravenna displays a series of events from Passion Week, but omits the crucifixion before concluding with the empty tomb and post-resurrection appearances, leads to a final comment similar to the comment at the end of the preceding chapter. Given the centrality of the crucifixion in the earliest Christian writings, the letters of Paul and the four gospels, the lateness with which Jesus crucified enters the visual language of the church remains surprising. The earliest known representations of Jesus on the cross do not appear until the fifth century and crucifixes do not become common until even later.

Notes

1 For a chronological overview of the issues and conclusions related to the doctrine of the Trinity, both pre-Nicaea and post-Nicaea, consult William J. LaDue, *The Trinity Guide to the Trinity* (Harrisburg, PA: Trinity Press International, 2003).

2 "First Council of Nicaea – 325 AD", <http://www.piar.hu/councils/ecum01.htm>, *Decrees of the Ecumenical Councils*, trans. Norman P. Tanner.

3 J. N. D. Kelly, *Early Christian Creeds*, 3rd edn. (New York: David McKay, 1972), 215–16.

4 "First Council of Constantinople – 381 AD", <http://www.piar.hu/councils/ecum02.htm>, *Decrees of the Ecumenical Councils*, trans. Norman P. Tanner.

5 Kelly, *Early Christian Creeds*, 297–8.

6 Theodosian Code 16.1.2; see Henry Bettenson, ed., *Documents of the Christian Church* (London: Oxford University Press, 1943), 31.

7 *Confessions* 1.1; see *The Confessions of Saint Augustine*, in *Basic Writings of Saint Augustine*, ed. Whitney J. Oates, 2 vols. (New York: Random House, 1948), 1:3.

8 *Confessions* 10.42–3, in *Basic Writings*, 1:42–3.

9 Augustine, *On the Trinity* 8.10.14 and 10.10.16, in *Basic Writings*, 2:787–8, 804–5.

10 "The Council of Ephesus – 431 AD", <http://www.piar.hu/councils/ecum03.htm>, *Decrees of the Ecumenical Councils*, trans. Norman P. Tanner.

11 "The Council of Chalcedon – 451 AD", <http//www.piar.hu/coun
    cils/ecum04.htm>, *Decrees of the Ecumenical Councils*, trans. Norman
    P. Tanner.
12 My English translation of the definition of Chalcedon is based on
    the Greek text of Philip Schaff, *The Creeds of Christendom with a History
    and Critical Notes*, 3 vols. (1st published Harper & Row, 1877; revised
    and repr. Grand Rapids, MI: Baker Book House, 1919), 2:62–5.
13 Philip Sheldrake, *A Brief History of Spirituality* (Oxford: Blackwell
    Publishing, 2007), 40–72.
14 *The Life of Antony and the Letter to Marcellinus*, trans. and introd. Robert
    C. Gregg, Classics of Western Spirituality (New York: Paulist Press,
    1980), 30–99.
15 *Rule of St. Benedict*, trans. Carolinne White (London: Penguin,
    2008), 7.
16 Graydon F. Snyder, *Irish Jesus, Roman Jesus: The Formation of Early
    Irish Christianity* (Harrisburg, PA: Trinity Press International, 2002),
    129–39.
17 Bede, *Ecclesiastical History of the English People with Bede's Letter to
    Egbert and Cuthbert's Letter on the Death of Bede*, revised edn., trans.
    Leo Sherley-Price, rev. R. E. Latham; minor works trans.
    D. H. Farmer (London: Penguin, 1990).
18 Robin Margaret Jensen, *Face to Face: Portraits of the Divine in Early
    Christianity* (Minneapolis: Fortress Press, 2005), 30–4.
19 Jensen, *Face to Face*, 159–65.

Chapter 3

Jesus and Medieval Orthodoxy
(Fifth to Fifteenth Centuries)

With the sixth century, the world of antiquity was changing. The sprawling Roman empire, centered in the city of Rome, had been ruled by an emperor from the reign of Augustus (27 BCE–14 CE) through the reign of Diocletian (284). It was Diocletian who first divided the empire geographically into the two regions that became the western Roman empire and the eastern Roman empire. Instead of a single emperor, there was for a brief period the tetrarchy – an arrangement of four emperors, with a senior Augustus and a junior Caesar in the west and a comparable Augustus and Caesar in the east.

Constantine consolidated his rule and reunified the western and the eastern halves of the Roman empire (324–37), but after his death the empire once again became a western empire and an eastern empire. Although there were brief periods of single-emperor rule, customarily there were two rulers. This political arrangement was apparent when we considered how the ecumenical councils of Constantinople I (381), Ephesus (431), and Chalcedon I (451) had often been summoned by both emperors acting together.

The capture of Ravenna by Germanic tribes in 476 and the related abdication of the western Roman emperor Romulus Augustus serve as convenient markers for the end of the Roman empire. The eastern empire carried on as the Byzantine empire centered in Constantinople and reasserted itself under the vigorous leadership of the Emperor Justinian (527–65). The so-called

Middle Ages had begun, bracketed by the Dark Ages on the far side and on the near side by the Enlightenment.

The Middle Ages, or the medieval period, span the thousand or so years characterized by the growing dominance of Rome and the papacy in western Europe and the eventual division – in 1054 – of the one, catholic, and orthodox church into the Roman Catholic Church and the Eastern Orthodox family of churches. In spite of differences in polity and practice, both Roman Catholicism and Eastern Orthodoxy shared the hard-won doctrinal formulations of the Trinity and the Incarnation: God as triune, one substance, in three persons, the Father, the Son, and the Holy Spirit; and Jesus Christ, the incarnate Son, with two natures, divine and human. The Roman Catholic Church and Eastern Orthodoxy also made sure that those inhabitants of the lands in Europe beyond the boundaries of the old Roman empire became hearers and recipients of the message about Jesus as they extended their influence through missionary expansion.

The medieval period was the time of Christendom when "Christ ruled" – through state and church, through kings and bishops, with the relationship between the two an ongoing issue. This was the time of that hierarchical social order known as the "feudal system." Power flowed downward from kings and bishops to knights and priests, and ultimately to the laity or common folk who served their lords, under that one Lord – Jesus as the Christ. This was also the time when the papacy through the Inquisition began to seek out "heretics" or deviants in belief or behavior, although the Jews constituted the more obvious "Other" within Christendom. And this was the time when Christendom was first threatened by Islam. After the death of the Prophet Muhammad in 632, Muslims became "the Other" from without, as their warriors swept out of Arabia, into neighboring Asia, then across North Africa, and into southern Europe. The Christian patriarchal cities of Jerusalem, Antioch, and Alexandria were swallowed up under the charging hoofbeats of Islamic armies, leaving only Constantinople barely beyond their reach – for the time being. Christian Crusaders sought to retake the Holy Land from the Muslims. But eventually Constantinople and the Byzantine empire were conquered in 1453 by the Ottoman Turks, who were themselves Muslims.

Rome, the Papacy, and the Eastern Church: A Church Dividing

Christianity had been forged in the one world that was the Roman empire. But that one world already represented two linguistic and cultural spheres that not even the Roman admiration and imitation of the Greeks could eliminate – the Latin-speaking west and the Greek-speaking east. All roads did lead to the city of Rome, whether by land or by sea; and both Paul and Peter as apostles of the Lord Jesus Christ followed those roads, but by different paths. Along the way, Paul and Peter crossed that imaginary linguistic line that separated the east from the west. In Rome they were put to death when Nero was emperor. In Rome, their places of martyrdom and burial were memorialized by the early Christians, providing the church of Rome with prestige not only for being located in the capital city of the empire but also for erecting shrines to these two foundational apostles.

By the time Constantine became sole ruler of the Roman empire in 324 four churches had become recognized as the most important sees of the Christian church: Rome, Antioch, Alexandria, and Jerusalem. In his *Ecclesiastical History* Eusebius provided lines of apostolic succession for the bishops of these four churches. Rome was the only church among the four in the Latin west. The other three were situated in the Greek east. Therefore, Rome was not only separated linguistically but also geographically from the other patriarchal churches, as they came to be known.

After becoming the sole emperor, Constantine announced plans to relocate his capital to his adopted city of Constantinople, the "New Rome." The church and its bishop in "Old Rome" could now develop free of immediate imperial oversight. Although the move to Constantinople occurred after the Council of Nicaea (325), both the Council of Constantinople I (381) and later the Council of Chalcedon I (451) adopted resolutions calling for the bishop of Constantinople to be granted privilege and honor second only to the bishop of Rome. The latter resolution, however, was rejected by Pope Leo I, although he later endorsed the council's Christological definition of Jesus Christ that he had earlier helped formulate through his letter to Flavian the patriarch of Constantinople.

The first four ecumenical councils give evidence of complications in the relationship between the Roman church and churches in the east to which differences in language and geography probably contributed. All four councils met at sites in the Greek-speaking east. Not one pope was physically present at any of these four councils nor for the next three, which convened in subsequent centuries. But popes often involved themselves in the work of the councils through their appointed representatives and even through written communications.

Nonetheless Pope Leo I's rejection of the recommendation regarding prerogatives and honors for the see of Constantinople anticipated more serious disagreements between the Latin church in the west and the Greek church in the east. The papacy increasingly claimed jurisdiction over and responsibility for the catholic, or universal, church. Pope Leo I, later known as the Great, was among the first popes to appeal to Jesus' words in Matthew 16:18 to support the primacy of the pope and the authority of the papacy over the entire church. "And I tell you, you are Peter, and on this rock I will build my church, and the gates of Hades shall not prevail against it." This simple pronouncement attributed to Jesus, with its engaging word-play, preserved in a single gospel, and received by the bishops of Rome, became the foundation stone beneath the Roman church. Jesus' supplementary words in Matthew 16:19 further spelled out the transcendent authority bestowed upon Peter and his successors: "I will give you the keys of the kingdom of heaven, and whatever you bind on earth will be bound in heaven, and whatever you loose on earth will be loosed in heaven." This pronouncement gave those who occupy the chair of St. Peter the symbol for their office: the crossed keys of the kingdom of heaven. Pope Leo I was not only positioning the Roman church in relation to the eastern churches but also anticipating the changing circumstances within the Roman empire.

After the collapse of the western Roman empire in 476 and the transformation of the eastern Roman empire into the Byzantine empire, there was no emperor in the west until Christmas Day in the year 800. On that occasion, Pope Leo III (795–816) began the resuscitation of the western Roman empire by crowning the king of the Franks, Charlemagne (d. 814), as "emperor of the Romans." Charlemagne retained his capital at Aachen, now in western Germany; and his empire morphed into the Holy Roman Empire that lasted in various configurations until the nineteenth century. Charlemagne and his imperial successors were Christians in a "Christian" empire, but often pitted in a power struggle with Leo and his papal successors.

The Iconoclastic Controversy: Can Images of Jesus be Created and Venerated?

The four ecumenical councils of the fourth and fifth centuries had established and defined the foundational Christian doctrines of the Trinity and the Incarnation. However, debate continued over related issues; and three subsequent councils were convened to deal with them.

The fifth ecumenical council, Constantinople II (553) was called by Byzantine Emperor Justinian and Pope Vigilius (537–55).[1] The council reviewed, defended, and reaffirmed the actions of the four previous councils related to the doctrines of the Trinity and the Incarnation. The teachings of Arius, Nestorius, and Eutyches among others were once again condemned as heretical.

The sixth ecumenical council, Constantinople III (680–1), was called by the Byzantine Emperor Constantine IV (652–85), in consultation with Pope Donus (676–8) and his successor Pope Agatho (678–81).[2] This council met in response to a claim being made about the incarnate Jesus – that Jesus Christ had only one will, a view described as monothelitism (Greek, "one will"). This council also reaffirmed the actions of all previous councils and condemned monothelitism, which was viewed as a form of mono-physitism – and thus a subversion of the definition of Chalcedon I that Jesus, as the Incarnate Son, was one person with two natures, one divine, the other human.

The seventh ecumenical council, Nicaea II (787), occurred in the midst of a long and sometimes violent dispute over the place of sacred images in the life of the church and in the lives of believers.[3] As we have seen, the visual arts had become an increasingly important means within Christianity for receiving and transmitting Jesus and his story, which included not only images of Jesus but of his mother Mary and other saints. Sacred images had come to play a central role in Christian belief and practice. Now the Christological question assumed a form more explicitly related to Christian worship and devotion: Can images of Jesus be created and venerated?[4]

What has become known as the iconoclastic controversy erupted in the Byzantine empire and the eastern church in the eighth and ninth centuries, and fell into two distinct phases. Each phase was precipitated by a Byzantine emperor and was concluded through the intervention of a Byzantine empress. The controversy pitted those who wished to eliminate images against those who traditionally supported their devotional use – iconoclasts (Greek, "image-destroyers") against iconodules (Greek, "image-venerators"). Some have suggested that the controversy over images came to the fore now because of Christianity's new religious rival in the region, which was itself iconoclastic – Islam.

Emperor Leo III (717–41), for whatever reasons, precipitated the first phase of the controversy when he ordered the removal of an image of Jesus from above the gate to his palace in Constantinople and its replacement by a cross. Subsequently, a synod of bishops in 753 adopted decrees supporting iconoclastic views, appealing both to the biblical injunctions against idolatry and to the actions of previous councils that the incarnate Jesus possessed divine and human natures. It was said by iconoclasts that an icon could only portray Jesus' humanity – his physicality – and not his divinity; therefore, icons separated Jesus' humanity from his divinity.

The chief defender of the veneration of images was John of Damascus (ca. 675–749), a monk, priest, and theologian who was located at Mar Saba monastery near the then Muslim city of Jerusalem. John also appealed to the doctrine of the Incarnation in support of the veneration of icons. He claimed that the biblical injunctions against idolatry had been superseded by God's becoming incarnate in Jesus, who as the second person of the Trinity became material flesh.

After years of conflict, the Council of Nicaea II convened at the initiative of the Empress Irene, who was serving as regent for her young son Constantine VI (780–97). A letter from these two informed Pope Adrian I (772–95) about the coming general council and urged him either to attend or to send legates. Adrian gave his approval for the gathering, but did not attend personally, sending representatives instead. The announced purpose was to respond to the decrees approved by the synod of bishops years earlier. The council brought to a close the first phase of the iconoclastic controversy.

The council reaffirmed the decisions of the six previous councils and then declared the church's position with regard to icons – both the production of representational art and the distinction between veneration and adoration. Like figures of the cross, it said, images may be painted, may consist of mosaic or some other suitable material, and may be displayed in churches, on sacred instruments and vestments, on walls and panels, and in homes and by public ways. The subject of images may be Jesus Christ, Mary the God-bearer, revered angels, and the saints. Although full adoration was reserved for the Triune God and the divine nature of Jesus the Son, veneration could be expressed in the same ways in which honor was shown to the cross, the gospels, and other sacred objects – namely, with incense and lights.

The second phase of the iconoclastic controversy was precipitated in 815 with an attack on icons and on iconodules by Emperor Leo V (813–20). This phase was ended by actions of a synod in Constantinople initiated by Empress Theodora in 843, on the first Sunday in Lent, when icons were restored to churches. Thereafter the first Sunday in Lent came to be commemorated annually in the Orthodox liturgical calendar as the "Triumph of Orthodoxy" or "Orthodox Sunday."

The Filioque Controversy: Does the Holy Spirit also Proceed from the Son?

The doctrines of the Trinity and the Incarnation, and related issues such as the veneration of icons, had been addressed by the first seven ecumenical councils. But there was another issue that had not yet made its way to their agendas. This issue involved one of the co-equal, co-eternal persons of the Trinity – the Holy Spirit.

With hindsight, the Holy Spirit seems to have been the overlooked member of the triune family: the Father, the Son, and the Holy Spirit. The initial Creed adopted at the Council of Nicaea I in 325, which was formally Trinitarian, had concluded abruptly: "And in the Holy Spirit." The Council of Constantinople I of 381 enlarged upon that pithy statement: "And in the Holy Spirit, the Lord and life giver, who proceeds from the Father, who with the Father and Son is together worshipped and together glorified ..."

No other council among the seven made modifications to the Nicene Creed. In fact, the Council of Ephesus (431) and the Council of Chalcedon I (451) explicitly prohibited the formulation of any other confession of faith. The Council of Constantinople III (680–1) not only disallowed the making of other creedal statements but warned against introducing words into the Creed that distorted the meaning. The Council of Nicaea II in 787 expressed responsibility for neither subtracting from nor adding to but rather for guarding the church's tradition as expressed in the actions of the previous six councils.

Nonetheless, before the end of the sixth century, a modification had been made in the Nicene Creed, specifically in the section on the Holy Spirit. Whereas the original Creed affirmed that the Holy Spirit proceeds "from the Father" without reference to the Son, the revision declared that the Spirit "proceeds from the Father *and from the Son*" (Latin, *Filioque*).

Since this interpolation first appeared in conjunction with the Council of Toledo (589), a regional synod, the insertion probably first occurred in Spain. From Spain the Creed with the *Filioque* would have passed through France to Germany. Here Charlemagne not only embraced this expanded version of the Creed but used it to accuse the Byzantine church of heresy for *not* reciting this longer version. Increased use of the *Filioque* in the west created consternation in the east. The Nicene Creed had been formulated by ecumenical council, and tampering with the wording seemingly violated the repeated conciliar prohibitions.

Theologically, some have claimed that the *Filioque* was added to guard against Arianism since the Arians had subordinated the Son to the Father. Certainly the absence or the insertion of the *Filioque* had implications for defining the intra-Trinitarian relationship of the Father, the Son, and the Holy Spirit. Presumably, both the original single procession of the Holy Spirit from the Father and the added double procession from the Father *and the Son* required not only theological reasoning but the citation and counter-citation of biblical texts.

As we have seen, from Christianity's beginnings there were profound cultural differences between the western church and the eastern church. There emerged clear differences in the understandings of institutional authority, although both models were hierarchical, with the office of bishop at the top of the pyramid, and with episcopal succession unbroken from the original apostles appointed by Jesus Christ. But in the west, the view prevailed that the bishop of Rome had God-granted primacy over the church universal. In the east, the view remained that God-given leadership came through bishops acting collectively.

The *Filioque*, possibly more than any other single factor, called attention to the divergent understandings of ecclesiastical authority that resulted in the so-called Great Schism of 1054. In other words, the *Filioque* placed Jesus as the Son at the very center of the controversy that divided the one catholic and orthodox church into the western Catholic Church and the Eastern Orthodox Church. Like empire, like church!

Two occasions, briefly identified, situate this separation in the particularity of time and place – both involve bitter confrontations between the papacy and the patriarchate of Constantinople. First, in the 860s, Pope Nicholas I objected to the appointment of Photius as patriarch. Photius wrote a letter to his fellow patriarchs denouncing the use of the *Filioque* and pronounced those who used the *Filioque* to be heretics. He later called a council that declared that the pope had been excommunicated as a heretic. After Photius himself was deposed by the Byzantine emperor, the eighth ecumenical council convened in Constantinople in 869–70, by which Photius was roundly condemned for various crimes and misdemeanors – although the eastern church never recognized this council.[5] Photius later had his condemnations struck from the record by a subsequent council, and he was reinstated as the patriarch of Constantinople. Secondly, in 1054, Pope Leo IX dispatched legates to Patriarch Cerularius, seeking a settlement of several contentious issues. But instead of settlement, the events led the leader of the papal delegation to place a bull of excommunication against Cerularius on the altar of the church of Hagia Sophia. Among the accusations was the claim that the Greeks had omitted the *Filioque* from the creed. This intrafaith fighting between the Latin church and the Greek church was about to be transformed into interfaith fighting. Christianity and Islam were on the brink of war.

Jesus as the Christ of Eastern Orthodoxy: Creed, Liturgy, and Spirituality

The Jesus of the Eastern Orthodox tradition is the Christ of scripture as interpreted by the first seven ecumenical councils. As the Son of God, Jesus Christ is one person of the Holy Trinity who for our salvation became incarnate through Mary his virgin mother, the *Theotokos*. The Nicene Creed (381) and the definition of Chalcedon I (451) represent historic statements of Christian belief shared by the Eastern Orthodox Church and the Roman Catholic Church, with one exception. As we have seen, the Orthodox version of the Creed does not include, in the article about the procession of the Holy Spirit, the phrase *Filioque* ("and the Son"). This affirmation of Jesus as the Christ continues to be communicated and experienced in the corporate worship, the sacred rituals, and the devotional practices of the Orthodox faithful.

The Eastern Orthodox Church identifies its principal order of corporate worship as the Divine Liturgy, which is centered on the Eucharist. Although several forms of the Byzantine eucharistic liturgy took shape in the early centuries, three remain in common use today, including the form bearing the name of John Chrysostom (359–407). This one-time patriarch of Constantinople's stirring preaching earned him the nickname by which he has been remembered, "Golden Mouth."

The "Divine Liturgy of St. John Chrysostom," through the opening words of the priest, immediately places the worshipers in the presence of the Triune God: "Blessed is the kingdom of the Father and the Son and the Holy Spirit, now and forever and to the ages of ages." Throughout the liturgy occur repeated references to "the Holy Trinity" and "the Father and the Son and the Holy Spirit."

Near the beginning of the liturgy, the hymn "Only-begotten Son" (*Monogenes*) celebrates the Son's becoming flesh as the Word through his virgin mother Mary, the *Theotokos* – a hymn attributed to the sixth-century Byzantine Emperor Justinian. The liturgy itself falls into two main parts, each of which reflects a period in Jesus' public life as the incarnate Son.

The first part of the service, for catechumens learning about the faith, recalls Jesus' ministry of teaching. This part begins with a procession of clergy through the church bearing the Gospel Book – the Lesser Entrance. Subsequently, the epistle and the gospel readings of the day are read and, traditionally, the homily is spoken.

The second part of the service, for the faithful, recalls events of Jesus' last days leading to his death on the cross. The transition to this part of the service involves the "Cherubic Hymn" extolling the Trinity and another procession of clergy, but this time they bear the bread and the wine – the Great Entrance. Having affirmed their faith through the Nicene Creed, the worshipers have reached the highest moments of the liturgy. The priest recites Jesus' words of institution at the Last Supper over the bread and the wine. He then invokes the Holy Spirit to make the bread the body of Christ and the wine the blood of Christ. After other words, prayers, and the Lord's Prayer, the priest receives communion and invites others to come forward and to do likewise. After communion, the liturgy continues with a prayer of thanksgiving and finally words of dismissal. The priest's final blessing sounds the Trinitarian note with which he began: "May the Holy Trinity protect all of you."

These two parts of the eucharistic liturgy presuppose at least two "mysteries" (from the Greek) or "sacraments" (from the Latin) – symbolic rituals that confer God's grace upon the recipients. These two mysteries are baptism and the Eucharist, both explicitly instituted by Jesus Christ. Not until the seventeenth century, perhaps under the influence of Catholicism, did the Eastern Orthodox Church, through local councils, identify the number of mysteries or sacraments as seven, although not limited to seven. Besides baptism and the Eucharist, the seven sacraments include chrismation, or anointing of the Holy Spirit by means of holy oil, immediately following baptism; repentance or confession; anointing of the sick, by means of holy oil; holy matrimony; and holy orders.[6]

Icons play an important and distinctive role in Orthodox worship and personal devotion, in accordance with the guidelines of the seventh ecumenical council (Nicaea II). The subjects of icons include Jesus the Christ, Mary the *Theotokos*, the four Evangelists, and other saints. In churches, an iconostasis ("icon stand"), which bears icons in a specified order, separates the sanctuary from the nave. Icons also may be found on the walls of churches and homes. Orthodox Christians show respect toward icons by kissing them or by using incense and candles. Icons mediate between the heavenly and the earthly realms and usher worshipers into the presence of the divine.

The "Jesus prayer" has also occupied an important place in the spiritual tradition of eastern Orthodoxy. Originating with the Desert Fathers, the prayer had special significance in the Hesychastic (Greek, meaning "stillness") tradition represented by Symeon the New Theologian (949–1033) and Gregory Palamas (1296–1359) – the former a monk in Constantinople, the latter a monk on Mount Athos who subsequently became the archbishop of Thessalonica. The Jesus prayer itself was a brief formulaic prayer focused on the divine name that could be uttered repeatedly, such as, "Lord Jesus Christ, Son of God, have mercy on me, a sinner." The goal of this spiritual practice was to still the mind and to induce an experience of the divine, be it a warm feeling or a perception of light. The gospel-based model for this desired heartfelt experience was the experience of Peter, James, and John at the transfiguration of Jesus.[7]

The Crusades: Warriors for Christ

In our history of how Jesus has been received, a persistent theme has been the *imitatio Christi*, the imitation of Christ. This theme expresses itself in the gospel narratives where Jesus often beckons, "Follow me." More specifically, he also declares: "If any want to become my followers, let them deny themselves and take up their cross and follow me" (Mark 8:34).

In the early centuries of Christianity, followers of Jesus imitated him by accepting persecution and execution at the hands of the authorities. After Christianity became a legal religion in the empire, followers of Jesus began forsaking family and fortune and withdrawing into desert places to live, alone or together, away from the allures of this world. Thus martyrs imitated Jesus by their faithfulness unto death, and monastics imitated him by their disciplined lives in the world.

However, on November 27, 1095, the notion of imitating Jesus by taking up the cross took a bizarre turn. On that day Pope Urban II, at a synod in Clermont in eastern France, issued a public call for Christians "to take up the cross" by undertaking a military campaign to reclaim the Holy Land, with its sacred sites, from Islamic control. Urban was responding to a request for assistance from Byzantine Emperor Alexius I (1081–1118), who felt threatened by actions of the Muslim Turks along his borders. Much debate continues about Urban's motives and his exact words, but their effects are certain. Between 1095 and 1291, the western church launched at least nine expeditions, or crusades, toward the Holy Land.

The first crusade, 1096–9, was the most successful territorially. The crusaders found their way through Constantinople to the Holy Land and established there the Latin Kingdom of Jerusalem, which lasted until its recapture in 1187 by the great Muslim leader Saladin. The second crusade, 1147–8, was the most intriguing. The Cistercian monk Bernard of Clairvaux, at the height of his celebrity, became the crusade's principal recruiter and organizer, perhaps consistent with his knightly ancestry, but seemingly contrary to his advocacy of devotion to the Virgin Mary. The fourth crusade, 1200–4, was the most tragic. The crusaders involved themselves with Venetian sailors, barbarically sacked the still Christian city of Constantinople, and established Latin rule over the Byzantine empire for seventy years, thus ending the possibility of any immediate reunion between the Roman Catholic Church and the Eastern

Orthodox Church. The fall of the Syrian city of Acre to the Muslims in 1291 erased the last vestige of territory under Christian rule.

"To take the cross" became the standard way of expressing commitment to the crusades. The crusader vow was accompanied by sewing a cross-shaped cloth onto one's clothing. In fact, the words "crusade" and "crusader" are themselves derived from the Latin *cruciare*, "to mark with a cross." Thus this period in the reception of Jesus, and other moments like it, represent a parody of his saying in Mark 8:34. Now the words of Jesus as the one crucified provided the sanction for his followers to wage a holy war by killing others in the name of Christ – whether Muslim, Jew, or fellow Christian.

Popes such as Urban II (1088–99), Eugene III (1145–53), and Innocent III (1198–1216) not only called for Holy War but also granted various heavenly blessings and earthy benefits to supporters and participants through a series of pronouncements, decrees, and bulls. However, there seem to have been some uncertainties among those in the field as to exactly what the benefits were. The promise of the remission of all confessed sins was a given. But did dying in battle against Muslim infidels in that day ensure crusaders immediate access to paradise? In other words, were some papal declarations in that day understood by Christian crusaders as some Muslims today interpret the blessed consequences of dying in a war against western infidels?

Within the social setting of medieval Europe, the crusades seem to have been the perfect venue for kings and knights to give expression to their testosterone – and their piety. Perhaps the third crusade (1189–92) started out with the strongest leadership, with three great armies respectively under the Holy Roman Emperor Frederick Barbarossa (1152–90), King Richard I (the Lionheart) of England (1168–99), and King Philip Augustus of France (1179–1223). Frederick died by drowning, not enemy fire; but Richard and Philip survived to return to their home countries.

The crusaders' initial success in reclaiming the Holy Land even led to the formation of military religious orders. These religious orders united the crusader zeal for fighting with monastic spiritual disciplines. Their original aims were to defend the Latin kingdom and to protect pilgrims.

The most famous of these orders was founded in Jerusalem, in 1118, around a French knight, Hugues de Payens. Because their initial headquarters were adjacent to the Temple Mount, they named themselves the Poor Knights of Christ and the Temple of Solomon, or simply, the Knights Templar. Later, when Bernard of Clairvaux became a patron of the order, they adopted the white Cistercian habit or cloak and added a red cross.

The Knights of St. John, or the Hospitallers, and the Teutonic Knights, modeled themselves as military religious orders after the Knights Templar. However, the Hospitallers had a prior history of caring for the sick among pilgrims dating back to the earliest centuries of Christian pilgrimage to Jerusalem. The Teutonic Knights, a German-based order, also protected pilgrims and cared for the ill among them. The Knights of St. John displayed a white cross on their black cloaks; the Teutonic Knights, a black cross on white. Each of these military religious orders has its own interesting story that extends beyond the crusades to the present day. The Knights Templar, for example, were at the center of recent scholarly, ecclesiastical, and popular debate in response to Dan Brown's novel *The DaVinci Code* (2003) and its subsequent movie adaptation that involved Leonardo's masterwork, *The Last Supper*, and the claim that Mary Magdalene was herself the so-called "holy grail," who had carried and preserved Jesus' bloodline.

Beyond Monasticism: Monks, Mendicants, and Mystics

Throughout the Middle Ages in western Europe, the papacy competed for turf with non-ecclesiastical authority, from the Holy Roman Emperor, through kings, to more local rulers. During this period, the papacy represented by the bishops of the church also had to contend with networks of monasteries under abbots and with monks, some priestly, others non-priestly. There were also communities of religious women and convents of nuns.

The Rule of Benedict, dating from the sixth century, became the common order to be followed. The most important reform movement within Benedictine monasticism, which called for a more rigorous following of founding principles, emanated from the monastery founded in 1098 at Citeaux, near Dijon in France. Thus the Cistercian movement came into being, and within a century there were affiliated monasteries across the European landscape.

Among the Cistercian leaders was Bernard of Clairvaux (1090–1153), whom I have already mentioned for his role in the crusades. He was a vigorous preacher and often celebrated the very name of Jesus in his sermons. He also advocated a Christ-centered mysticism in a series of sermons based on the biblical book of the Song of Songs. Therein, he interpreted these erotic poems allegorically, but in language no less erotic than the poems themselves: the beloved is the soul, who longs for the lover; the lover is Jesus the bridegroom, who kisses and unites with his beloved in the bridal chamber.

A contemporary and admirer of Bernard was Hildegard of Bingen (1098–1179), for whom the Song of Songs was also a favorite book. Her parents had turned Hildegard over to the care of a nun at an early age, and she later established two women's religious communities. She was a visionary of great learning and great talent, writing on a variety of topics and even composing music. Like Bernard of Clairvaux, she became a public figure as a traveling preacher through the Rhineland, and her views were sought by kings and popes.

During the Middle Ages the papacy reached the zenith of its power under the reign of Pope Innocent III. He dominated his royal contemporaries, conducted crusades abroad and at home, and charted the future of the Roman Catholic Church by convening the Fourth Lateran Council (1215).

Whereas the crusades to the Holy Land had seen the creation of military religious orders, so the papacy of Innocent III witnessed the emergence of another kind of religious order: the mendicants. Mendicant orders received this designation because their founders aspired to support their public preaching by begging (from the Latin *mendicare*, to beg). Here the theme of the *imitatio Christi*, again based on the gospel narratives, reconfigures itself through the initiatives of Francis of Assisi (1182–1226) and Dominic Guzman (1170–1221), the founders respectively of the Franciscan and the Dominican orders.

Francis continues to be identified by the town where he was born – Assisi, in the hill country of central Italy. His father was a cloth merchant of comfortable means. As a young man, Francis was carefree and enjoyed a good time. But all that began to change. Francis later recalled an encounter he had with lepers, in which his immediate revulsion was transformed into compassion. He also told about an experience before a crucifix in the ruined church of St. Damian outside Assisi, where he was commanded to rebuild the church. He finally discovered his true calling upon hearing the gospel being read at the church of Portiuncula, also near Assisi, on February 24, 1208. The text came from the missionary discourse in Matthew where Jesus commands his disciples: "As you go, proclaim the good news … Cure the sick … Take no gold, or silver, or copper in your belts" (Matt. 10:7–42).

Imitating Jesus as the Christ, Francis joyously embraced both preaching and poverty, both of which ran against the grain of the ecclesiastical behavior of the church in the thirteenth century. Although the priesthood, including monks, affirmed the vow of poverty along with chastity and obedience, the wealth and power of the church had became increasingly obvious.

Francis – already known locally – preached repentance, wore the plainest of garb, and relied on the generosity of others. He attracted like-minded companions, who accompanied him around Assisi and across the Umbrian countryside. They communicated and embodied a message of peace and brotherly love. For his earliest associates he developed a simple Rule, no longer extant, that probably consisted of a few gospel passages emphasizing Jesus' injunctions on poverty. Along the way, Francis finally received approval for his activities and plans from Pope Innocent III.

Among those attracted to the Franciscan life of humility and poverty, as exhibited among the male brothers, was a young woman of Assisi named Clare (1194–1253), who in 1212 began what became the second order of Franciscans, the Poor Clares. Still later there was formed the third order, or tertiaries, a secular order for men and women who could not desert their families and work to enter one of the other orders. Perhaps the story that best depicts Francis at the height of his audaciousness is that of his venture to the Middle East during the fifth crusade, where he witnessed the carnage at first hand. In Egypt, sometime around 1219, he sought a meeting with Sultan Malik-al Kamil, the nephew of Saladin, on which occasion he urged the sultan to accept Jesus as the Christ – and lived to tell about it.

By the time of Francis' death, in 1226, the band from Assisi had continued to grow in numbers and had been shaped into a religious order. With Cardinal Ugolino – later Pope Gregory IX – as his patron, Francis developed two subsequent Rules to govern the Order of Friars Minor (OFM) – one in 1221, the other in 1223. Just prior to his death, Francis dictated his *Testament*, in which he bequeathed in writing to the Brothers a reminder of what it meant to be a Franciscan.

However idiosyncratic Francis' ways, and however wonderful his "Canticle to Brother Sun and Sister Moon," being Franciscan to him meant being faithful to the doctrines and the order of the church as the overarching framework for his devotion to Jesus as the poor, crucified Christ. This verbal image, which underscores poverty and crucifixion, serves as a reminder of two distinctive contributions made by Francis to Jesus' continued reception. First, Francis contributed to the world the *crèche*, or the manger scene, commonplace during the Christmas season – the time for celebrating the incarnation of God's Son as Jesus through the Blessed Virgin Mary. Secondly, during his final two years Francis received in his own body the five stigmata, or wounds, of the crucified Christ – one in each hand, one in his side, and one in each foot.

Although a contemporary of Francis, Dominic Guzman presented a contrasting figure. Dominic was a Spaniard from Castille. He distinguished himself as an excellent student during his years of study at the University of Palencia. He entered the priesthood and became associated with the cathedral in Osma.

In 1203 Dominic accompanied Bishop Diego on a trip that took him to Toulouse, where he encountered adherents of deviant beliefs and practices, who were a powerful force in the region. The Albigensians (named for the town of Albi) or Cathars (cognate meaning "pure" or "perfected") were a dualistic sect that sharply contrasted spirit with matter, as had the Paulicians and Bogomiles in the early Byzantine empire, the Manichees of Augustine's day, and the Gnostic sects even earlier. Certainly the views of the Albigensians were an assault on the orthodox understanding of God as creator and Jesus as God's Incarnate Son.

As a result of his experiences, Dominic came to consider the need for a religious order dedicated to combating deformed ideas with preaching based on well-formed ideas. He became convinced that persuasion, not compulsion, was the way to win heretics to the orthodox faith. Like Francis of Assisi, Dominic had been attracted to the gospel-based model of Jesus' itinerant preaching with his disciples and their sharing lives of poverty. But unlike Francis, Dominic desired followers who were well educated and priests.

Dominic's visit to Pope Innocent III in 1206 led to his being sent back to the area around Toulouse to combat the Albigensians. He succeeded in establishing a convent to protect women from the influence of the heretics. But two years later in 1208, the circumstances of Dominic's mission changed. The pope's legate to the region was assassinated. Suddenly, the crusades had come to France, spearheaded by Simon de Montfort. Over the next decade or so, the Albigensian heresy was eliminated by the brutal extermination of the heretics themselves.

Dominic continued his own mission and gathered around himself a small group of fellow-preachers. In 1215 they were given a house in Toulouse. Dominic's dream of a world-wide order of preachers was about to be fulfilled. That very same year, Pope Innocent III convened the Fourth Lateran Council in Rome, whose actions charted the path for the order popularly known as the Dominicans.[8]

The council condemned heretics by declaring: "Catholics who have girded themselves with the cross for the extermination of heretics shall enjoy the indulgences and privileges granted to those who go in defense of the Holy Land." Although the word "extermination" may have been contrary to Dominic's preferred strategy of persuasion, it accurately described what was then occurring against the Albigensians. The council also placed restrictions on new religious orders by declaring, "whoever wishes to found a new religious house should take the rule and institutes from already approved religious orders." Shortly thereafter, Dominic's band adopted the time-honored Rule of Augustine. Before the end of 1216, the order of preachers (OP) had been approved by the recently elected Pope Honorius III (1216–27).

Dominic's order moved quickly. Preachers established themselves in the cities, often those with a university. Dominicans took up residence in Paris, Rheims, and Toulouse; in Barcelona, Verona, and Bologna. In Bologna, the first meeting of the general chapter was held in 1219. Also in Bologna, Dominic died in 1221. As with the Franciscans, the Dominicans came to consist of three orders: the order of preachers, the order of the Dominican sisters, and the third order, or tertiaries.

Dominic was obviously a faithful son of the church. The church's doctrine and discipline provided the context for his devotion to Jesus as the Christ. He has even been associated with the origin of the Catholic devotional practice known as the rosary – the use of beads in conjunction with the repetition of the "Hail Mary" and the "Our Father" to meditate on the life of Jesus Christ. But Dominic's preoccupation with heresy, however well intended for the salvation of heretics, tends to evoke a verbal image of Jesus as an inquisitorial Christ. Even the tradition about the rosary's origin with Dominic brings with it the claim that he developed the rosary as a means by which to transform practicing heretics into recovering heretics. Today the rosary bead chain bears a crucifix – a figure of Jesus being crucified, not crucifying others.

Whereas Pope Innocent III had dealt with heresy by delegating responsibility to bishops, special legates, and local courts, the papacy in 1233 established a permanent Holy Office or Inquisition with the task of ferreting out heretics by whatever means necessary and turning them over to secular courts for appropriate punishment – such as being burned at the stake. The Dominican order became a principal source of inquisitors. But the Dominicans produced not only Torquemada (1420–98), the Grand Inquisitor of Spain, who became a terror to both Jews and Muslims, but also Thomas Aquinas (1225–74), possibly the greatest of all Christian theologians.

Scholastic Theology: The Trinity, the Incarnation, and the At-one-ment

The earliest Christian writings confessed Jesus to be the Christ and associated with him a variety of other honorific names such as the Son of God, the Good Shepherd, the Word, the Bread of Life, the Prophet, and the Son of Man. These writings use a variety of categories to affirm that God through Jesus as the Christ has effected what has come to be called the at-one-ment, or atonement, between God and humankind: salvation, redemption, reconciliation, adoption, among others. These writings also understand the death of Jesus, evidenced by his blood and symbolized by his cross, to be necessary for atonement.

The four ecumenical councils of the fourth and fifth centuries developed doctrines of the Triune God and the Incarnation by which to gauge orthodox views of God as Trinity and Jesus as the Incarnate Son. But none of these councils nor their immediate successors explicitly addressed the question of exactly "how" God through Jesus effected the atonement between God and humankind. Although the Nicene Creed speaks about "salvation" as the reason "why" the Lord Jesus Christ as the only-begotten Son of God became incarnate even unto death by crucifixion, it does *not* explain "how."

In the early eastern church, atonement seemed more related to the movement of God's incarnation in the Son than specifically to his death by crucifixion, as suggested by the use of the concept of *theosis* (Greek, "divinization"). Athanasius, the defender of Nicene orthodoxy, stated in his treatise *On the Incarnation*: "For [God] became human as we are so that we [humans] might become what He is [God-like]."[9]

But in the western church an early theological explanation of the "how," which became common, expressed what has been called the "ransom" view (with support from Mark 10:45). Among many others, Irenaeus, the second-century bishop of Lyon, was a proponent of this position. According to this view, humans had been kidnapped and held hostage by the devil; and the life and death of Jesus as God's Son became the ransom for which the hostages were set free.

Not until the eleventh century, with the rise of scholastic theology, did there appear other reasoned alternatives for a doctrine of the atonement. Scholasticism is the name given to the theology of the Middle Ages that wrestled with the relationship between faith and reason, analyzed the traditional teachings of the church, and attempted to provide a comprehensive summary of those teachings. In what follows, I will first examine how Jesus was received by scholastic theologians by considering the views on the atonement set forth by Anselm and Abelard.[10] Then I will consider the view of Thomas Aquinas within the context of his systematic exposition of Christian theology.[11]

Anselm (ca. 1033–1109), perhaps the most important thinker since Augustine, articulated what has been described as the "satisfaction" view of the atonement. He was born in the town of Aosta, in northern Italy. He became a monk, later the prior, and still later the abbot, at the Benedictine abbey of Bec in Normandy. Here he taught and wrote for more than thirty years. His treatises included *Proslogium*, on the existence of God, *Monolgium*, on the being of God, and *Cur Deus Homo*, on the incarnation of God. During Anselm's long tenure at Bec, the Normans under William conquered England in 1066. Subsequently, in 1093, Anselm himself was elected archbishop of Canterbury; and, after prolonged dispute over matters of protocol, he eventually assumed the office.

Anselm's explanation of the atonement occurred in response to the question implied in the title of his treatise *Cur Deus Homo*, or *Why God Became Human*. His treatment of the subject reflects both the categories of feudal society as well as the penitential system of the medieval Roman Catholic Church.

God as the creator expected to receive honor from God's human creatures. But when humans dishonored God by rebelling against God, they needed to satisfy their incurred debt in accordance with God's justice. But humans could not satisfy their indebtedness. Only God could. So God sent Jesus, who was both divine and human, who lived in perfect obedience to God, and thus was not required to die as the penalty for sin. Nonetheless, Jesus, as the God–Man, accepted the penalty of death not for his sins, but for the sins of others. Jesus' death, which was not required of him, became a work of supererogation, or a meritorious act, that did satisfy the human stain of having dishonored God. So God's sending of the Son not only expressed God's love for humankind but also upheld God's principle of justice.

Abelard (1079–1142), a brilliant and tragic figure, was born in a village ten miles east of Nantes in Brittany. He proposed a "moral influence" view of the atonement as an intentional alternative to the view of Anselm. Abelard decided on an academic career early in life, traveled about France learning from various masters, and finally settled in Paris as a combative teacher of philosophy and theology – until something happened around the year 1118. Abelard became a private tutor to and fell in love with Heloise, the learned niece of a canon at the cathedral. She bore Abelard's child. His *Story of My Calamities* narrates, with frankness, how he was vengefully emasculated and how circumstances led him to enter a monastery and her to become a nun. But he continued his reading and writing. Twice he was censured for his writings. In 1121, a regional synod at Soissons condemned as heretical his interpretation of the Trinity. In 1141, with Bernard of Clairvaux as his chief adversary, Abelard was condemned for ideas by a synod at Sens, an action upheld by Pope Innocent II (1130–43).

Among Abelard's ideas so condemned was his understanding of the atonement that he expressed in his *Commentary on the Epistle to the Romans.* In this work, Abelard rejected the notion that atonement required the death of Jesus Christ as God's Son – either as a ransom paid to the Devil or as the satisfaction of an indebtedness owed to God. Instead, Abelard viewed the life and the death of Jesus as a demonstration of such divine love that humans would thereby be transformed and would respond with just such love toward God and each other.

Consequently, both the "ransom" and the "satisfaction" views of atonement can be described as objective because they involve transactions respectively with the Devil and with God. By contrast, the "moral influence" view appears subjective since it requires a change within persons themselves. With regard to the doctrine of the atonement, the medieval church would finally discard the "ransom" idea and reject "the moral influence" notion and follow a path similar to the "satisfaction" view of Anselm.

By the thirteenth century, the monastic and cathedral schools were being complemented by universities as centers of learning. Many of the works of Aristotle had been transmitted to the west by the Jews of Spain, who had received them from the Muslims. The mendicant orders, especially the Dominicans, had early on committed themselves to formal study and learning.

Thomas Aquinas and his writings represent the noblest expression of scholastic theology; and he has repeatedly been recognized by the Roman Catholic Church as the church's theologian *par excellence*.[12] Born in southern Italy, near Aquino, he entered the Dominican order around 1244 and later was ordained into the priesthood. He studied under his much-respected fellow Dominican Albertus Magnus, both in Cologne and in Paris, at the university – from which he received his bachelor's, master's, and doctor's degrees. Thomas devoted his life to preaching, teaching, and writing not only in Cologne and Paris, but also in Rome and various other towns around Italy. He rejected offers to become the archbishop of Naples and the abbot of Monte Cassino. At his death, his magisterial *Summa Theologiae* remained unfinished.

With an indebtedness to Aristotle, on the one hand, and church tradition and scripture on the other, Thomas created a systematic synthesis between philosophy and theology, between reason and faith, between natural revelation and special revelation. Natural revelation discloses the existence and the oneness of God; but special revelation makes God known to Christians as triune, the Father, the Son, and the Holy Spirit. Natural law consists of the four cardinal virtues, which are expected of all persons (prudence, justice, fortitude, temperance); but special revelation discloses the three theological virtues, which are expected of Christians (faith, hope, love).

As the chief and definitive representative of medieval Roman Catholic orthodoxy, it is understandable that Thomas' own reflections on the basic doctrines related to Jesus as the Christ would move within the framework of inherited teachings about the Triune God, about the Incarnation, and about the Atonement.[13] But he does make his own contributions by refining traditional statements. He clarifies the meaning of God's personhood. He suggests that God would not have become human if the first human had not sinned. He synthesizes the objective and subjective views about the atonement by reaffirming that Jesus' work was a satisfaction for human sin, which also earned merit, and that Jesus' work also empowers humans to love.

Thomas was probably the only theologian to have had his own theological magnum opus, his *Summa Theologiae*, complemented by a comparable literary magnum opus, *The Divine Comedy* by Dante Alighieri (1265–1321). These works stand like twin peaks in the cultural landscape of medieval Europe. Dante's epic poem also belongs to a reception history of Jesus – although Jesus as a character nowhere appears in the poem.

In this epic poem, Dante the pilgrim wends his way out of hell, through purgatory, and into paradise. Here Dante passes his theological exams on faith, hope, and love (*Paradiso*, cantos 24–6). But whereas Virgil and Beatrice have served as his guides thus far, it is Bernard of Clairvaux who intercedes with the Virgin Mary on the pilgrim's behalf by praying that Dante be allowed to behold in a beatific vision the Love that moves the universe (*Paradiso*, cantos 31–3) – the Triune God.[14]

Jesus as the Christ of Roman Catholicism: Creed, Liturgy, and Spirituality

The Jesus of the Roman Catholic Church is the Christ of scripture as interpreted by the early ecumenical councils. As the Son of God, Jesus Christ is one person of the Holy Trinity who for our salvation became incarnate through Mary his virgin mother.

The Nicene Creed (381) and the definition of Chalcedon (451) represent historic statements of Christian belief shared by the Eastern Orthodox and the Roman Catholic churches. However, as we have seen, the Roman Catholic version of the Creed includes, in the article about the Holy Spirit, the phrase *Filioque* ("and the Son"). This affirmation of Jesus as the Christ continues to be communicated and experienced in the corporate worship, the sacred rituals, and the devotional practices of the Roman Catholic faithful.

Like the Eastern Orthodox Church, the Roman Catholic Church also centered its principal order of corporate worship in the

Eucharist, but came to identify the entire ceremony as the Mass. The term "Mass" (from Latin, "dismissal") originated from the formula with which the ceremony was concluded: "Go, it is the dismissal" (*ite est missa*).

The Mass as it has developed within Roman Catholicism has had a more complicated history than the Divine Liturgy of Eastern Orthodoxy. In the western church, many variations appeared in the service early on. The initial attempt to create some uniformity of the Latin rite resulted from Charlemagne's request of Pope Adrian I for a copy of the eucharistic service believed to have been composed by Pope Gregory I (590–604). The king of the Franks wanted his people to share a common liturgy. So the combination of the liturgy observed in Rome – including the Gregorian chant – with the Frankish liturgy created the Roman rite that became the principal form of eucharistic liturgy for the Roman Catholic Church. Of particular interest for the reception of Jesus was the introduction of the Nicene Creed into the Roman Mass during the pontificate of Benedict VIII (1012–24) prior to the 1054 schism between Eastern Orthodoxy and Roman Catholicism.

Two major events have occurred in the subsequent history of the Mass. One was the Council of Trent (1545–63), which met to reform the Catholic Church in response to the Protestant Reformation.[15] The council took actions that resulted in the formulation of the Tridentine Mass in Latin, which – in 1570 – was promulgated by Pope Pius V (1566–72) and made mandatory for the western church. The second event was the more recent Second Vatican Council (1962–5), which was called by Pope John XXIII (1958–63).[16] The liturgical changes emphasized the use of vernacular languages and allowed for more options in the observance of the Mass.

By its focus on the eucharistic sacrifice, the Mass – from whatever historical period – centers on the Incarnation. Therefore, the continued inclusion of the Nicene Creed in the Mass, as decreed in the revision by Vatican II and published in 1970 under the name of Pope Paul VI (1963–78), still places the Incarnation within an explicitly Trinitarian framework. Even if the more succinct Apostles' Creed is used in celebrations of the Mass with children, as is allowed, the Trinitarian framework remains.[17]

Furthermore, the opening greeting and the final blessing of the Mass are pronounced in the name of the Father, and the Son, and the Holy Spirit.

Thus, for the Catholic faithful, liturgical life revolves around the Eucharist and the other six sacraments: baptism; confirmation; penance or reconciliation; holy matrimony; holy orders, and anointing of the sick and dying. The Fourth Lateran Council, the twelfth ecumenical council by Catholic reckoning, formally established the number of sacraments at seven. Later in the thirteenth century, Thomas Aquinas in his *Summa Theologiae* provided commentary on the seven sacraments along with their scriptural basis. His exposition included the use of the Aristotelian categories of "form" and "substance" to explain how in the Eucharist the form of the bread and the wine is transubstantiated into the actual body and blood of Jesus. Eastern Orthodoxy makes a similar claim, but simply acknowledges the transformation as a divine mystery without providing a philosophical explanation.

In the Middle Ages, the Easter liturgy itself became the setting for the beginnings of religious drama. In the liturgy were four lines that began with the question asked by angels of the women visiting the tomb of Jesus, "Whom do you seek?" (in Latin, *Quem quaeritis?*) This dramatic exchange eventuated into Easter plays within the church and later developed into passion plays, enacted more publicly, about the last week of Jesus' life. Individual actors now played the gospel-based roles, including the role of Jesus. The best known of these plays is that performed regularly since 1634 in the Bavarian village of Oberammergau. Until recent decades, the script and the performance reinforced the themes long characteristic of Christian anti-Judaism and anti-Semitism.

Virtually from Christianity's beginnings, pilgrimages have been undertaken as devotional acts to holy sites related to holy people, or saints, whether to Canterbury or to Rome or to Jerusalem. In the Middle Ages there emerged a devotional act more suitable for individuals who could not travel such great distances – the Stations of the Cross. These so-called stations represent and depict in some manner the stages along Jesus' way to the cross. The numbered stations may be erected out of doors, but they have also become commonplace in Catholic churches. Central to this devotion is meditation upon the passion, or suffering, of Jesus, as participants move sequentially from one station to the next. Although the number of stations has varied, the prescribed number is now fourteen, beginning with Jesus' condemnation by Pontius Pilate and ending with the placing of Jesus' body in the tomb.

Our recognition of the way Jesus was received by the church in the Middle Ages deserves a cautionary observation. Historically, Christian theological writings, Christian scripture, Christian liturgy, and Christian devotional acts have both contributed to and reflected an anti-Judaism epitomized by the accusation that Jews were "Christ-killers." On October 28, 1965, Vatican Council II issued the declaration *Nostra Aetate* ("Our Times") that condemned anti-Semitism and displays of anti-Semitism. As other branches of Christianity developed after the Middle Ages, they too would harbor an anti-Semitism for which their twentieth-century ecclesiastical bodies would also issue apologies

Rome and the Papacy: Exile, Schism, and Dissent

By the fifth century, the papacy was increasingly claiming primacy for itself and responsibility for the one, catholic, or universal, church – both in the west and in the east. In 1054 the Great Schism had occurred between the Latin church and the Greek church of the Byzantine empire. Thereafter, the papacy was no longer competing with other patriarchal churches for primacy but wrangling with emperors and kings over such issues as lay investiture. That is, only clerics were allowed to give the symbols of ecclesiastical office, such as staffs or rings, to appropriate recipients. The struggle now was whether ecclesiastical authority or royal authority would be supreme in Christendom.

Innocent III, the quintessential embodiment of papal power – as previously noted – certainly believed that ecclesiastical authority should be supreme; and during his eighteen-year tenure, it was. A later papal successor, Boniface VIII (1294–1305), shared Innocent III's convictions about church–state relations. In fact, his *Unam Sanctam* (1302) declared that the church had two swords, the one spiritual and the other temporal. The spiritual sword was exercised by the church through the papacy and the temporal sword was exercised by secular authorities for the church. However, Boniface VIII possessed neither the wisdom nor the skills of Innocent III to translate his views into socio-political reality.

Furthermore, times were changing. In the fourteenth and fifteenth centuries, the medieval papacy soon found itself no longer at the height of its power, but sinking toward its lowest point, however measured. From 1309 until 1377, the papacy had relocated from Rome to Avignon in southeastern France. During this period, the papacy became a ward of the French, and all six popes elected during the period were French. When the papal exile ended and the papacy returned to Rome, there commenced a period of schism during which two, and sometimes three, popes ruled. Finally, all three popes were deposed, and Pope Martin V (1417–31) was elected by the Council of Constance (1414–18).[18]

Personal responses to these papal troubles came from four women with mystical inclinations. Two of the four were from different ends of Europe, Bridget of Sweden (1303–73) and Catherine of Siena (ca. 1340–80), but they shared a devotion to Jesus and a concern for the return of the papacy to the city of Rome.

Bridget came from a prominent and pious family. Early in life she experienced visions of the life of Christ. She married and bore eight children. After her husband's death, she established a community of nuns in Sweden, but later traveled to Rome and to Avignon where, in 1370, she received approval for her religious community from Pope Urban V (1362–70). Bridget urged Urban V to return home to Rome. Catherine of Siena, the youngest child in a large Italian family, was also a visionary, and had a vision in which Jesus appeared and entered into a "spiritual marriage" with her. She became a Dominican tertiary, preached on repentance, and cared for the poor and the sick. She reached out to the world through letters, many of which survive, including several written to Pope Gregory XI (1370–8). Catherine asked him to reform the clergy and to reestablish Rome as the seat of the Church.

Two other women from these troubled times, both English, who did not confront popes but who were confronted mystically by Jesus, were Julian of Norwich (ca. 1342–1417) and Margery

Kempe (1373–1440). Julian was an anchorite, a religious recluse, living in a cell attached to a church. She experienced a series of sixteen visions, about which she wrote in her *Revelations of Divine Love*. Although theologically Trinitarian, she spoke about the divine in feminine terms, using phrases such as "the Motherhood of God" and "Christ our true Mother." By contrast, Margery had been married, and had fourteen children. Increasingly over-whelmed with a sense of the love of Christ, she sought spiritual direction from Julian. When her husband agreed to a mutual oath of celibacy, she entered into a "spiritual marriage" with Jesus, even wearing a ring with his named inscribed thereon. She later undertook pilgrimages, including a visit in 1414–15 to Constance while the council was still meeting.[19]

The Council of Constance, which finally ended more than a hundred years of papal exile and schism, also signaled the possible fate of those who threatened the law and order of the church. John Wyclif (1328–84) was an Oxford-educated priest and reformer who was responsible for the first translation of the Latin Vulgate Bible into the English language of his day. The council condemned him and ordered that his long-dead body be exhumed from the consecrated sod of his former parish at Lutterworth, that his remains be burned, and his ashes be scattered in the river Swift.

Jan Hus (1373–1415) was a Prague-educated priest and an advocate of reforming views similar to those of Wyclif. Although Hus had been promised safe passage to the Council of Constance, he was imprisoned, condemned, and – less fortunate than Wyclif – burned alive. Thus ecclesiastical reform was brewing well before the Reformation.

Material Culture: Architecture and the Visual Arts

Constantine adapted the Greco-Roman basilica, with its rectangular footprint, and used it as the architectural model of his church-building programs, in Rome and then in Constantinople. Just as the empire in the fourth century and the church in the eleventh century divided, so the building patterns for western Christianity and eastern Christianity also followed separate

Figure 3 Mosaic of Christ Pantocrator (thirteenth century) from the magnificent imperial church of Hagia Sophia in Constantinople, which had been rebuilt by the Emperor Justinian (482–565), and later became a mosque under the Ottoman Turks in the renamed city of Istanbul (fifteenth century). *Reproduced by courtesy of Murat Sen/istockphoto. com*

trajectories. The worship of Jesus as the Christ, the Son of God, within Roman Catholicism and Eastern Orthodoxy came to be expressed in physical settings of differing designs.

In the Rome-centered western church, the basilica remained the preferred form for church buildings through the Middle Ages and beyond, as reflected in the continued importance of the rectangular floor plan, whether the architectural style was Romanesque, Gothic, or Renaissance. With the addition of a transept at right-angles to the long nave in the basilica design, the church buildings in the west often assumed the shape of the Latin cross.

However, in the sixth century the Byzantine Emperor Justinian undertook a building program of his own that carried eastern Christianity in a different architectural direction. Justinian's builders created churches based on a central plan with a central dome covering the interior space where the floor plan reflected the shape of a Greek cross, with the four arms having the same length. In Constantinople, Constantine's original Hagia Sophia had burned to the ground in 532, and Justinian was determined to rebuild it in a new style, with even greater ostentation – although it required two attempts. The first great dome built in 558 collapsed, necessitating a modified replacement in 563.

Orthodox churches with a dome, and even multiple domes, were later constructed elsewhere, through the Balkans and into Russia, none fancier than those in Moscow. Ivan III (1462–1505), *not* the Terrible, founded the Russian state and rebuilt the Kremlin walls that still contain three gleaming cathedrals: the Assumption, the Annunciation, and the Archangel. The cathedral of the Annunciation displays icons of Jesus by Andrei Rublev (ca. 1360–1430), arguably the finest of all icon painters. Outside the Kremlin walls stands the candy-swirl-domed cathedral of St. Basil. In some Orthodox circles, especially after the fall of Constantinople to the Ottoman Turks in 1453, and the conversion of Justinian's great church of Hagia Sophia into a mosque, Moscow came to be viewed as the "third Rome."

In western Europe, around the turn to the second millennium, there emerged that monumental style of architecture known as Romanesque, which in the twelfth century soon evolved into the Gothic style. Medieval cathedrals, abbeys, and churches in both styles continue to dot the European countryside and cityscape. These churches generally have elaborations externally at the west end, a point of entry, and internally at the east end, the altar end.

Predominantly Romanesque churches have a massive, fortress-like appearance, with small windows and block towers. Durham cathedral in England represents a wonderful example of Romanesque or Norman architecture – as the style is called there, in homage to the Norman conquest of England in 1066. By contrast, Gothic ecclesiastical structures are characterized by verticality, with pointed arches, towers, or spires, flying buttresses used to support the walls, and much glass. Among thirteenth-century Gothic foundations are Salisbury cathedral in England, León cathedral in Spain, and Cologne cathedral in Germany.

Christian art has come a long way from the catacombs of Rome. Medieval cathedrals, in particular, provided the space and the surface for the visual arts in a variety of media including sculpture and stained glass. The cathedral became the "Bible" for those unable to read. Although the cross of Jesus and the crucifix had been slow in emerging as central symbols for Christianity, now the full story of Jesus as the Christ could be displayed in stone and glass. The images of the Christ lent support for the liturgy, the sermons, and even the public religious plays that became common in many locales.

However, Jesus the Christ himself received continuing support from his mother and "Madonna," the Blessed Virgin Mary. Theologically, the three persons of the Trinity were eternally co-equal, and the Son became incarnate to mediate salvation to humans; but devotionally it was Jesus' mother who obediently enabled the divine to become human. In a feudal, hierarchical, society, seekers of salvation approached the Savior through the one most approachable to them – the Son of God's mother. Understandably perhaps, many if not most medieval cathedrals were dedicated to Mary. Even the divinity school of the Church of Scotland where I began my theological education, at the University of St. Andrews, still bears her name: St. Mary's.

The cathedral of Chartres, in north-central France, was rededicated in 1260 to Mary as a successor to the structure virtually destroyed by fire in 1194. Its prized relic was the veil believed to have been worn by Mary at the birth of Jesus. The cathedral has appropriately received acclaim for its comprehensive, well-designed, and beautifully executed decorative program. With nine portals, or doorways, to enhance with stonework and nearly two hundred windows on three levels for stained glass, the artists had much opportunity to practice their crafts. Representations of Mary and her son Jesus, in stone and glass, are placed within the broader history of salvation and even local history. But only brief observations related to the Jesus story are possible here.[20]

Outside, above the central portal at the west end, Christ appears in majesty. On the statue-column dividing the central portal of the south transept, which overlooks the town, Jesus stands as a teacher inviting the people to enter. Once inside, the people can view a triptych of windows at the west end, featuring the genealogy of Christ, the life of Christ, and the passion and resurrection of Christ. People can also see windows depicting the parables of the Good Samaritan and of the Prodigal Son. At the east end, centrally placed in stained glass, appears Mary as the Virgin in majesty – with her infant Son.

By the beginning of the fourteenth century, cultural shifts were already signaling the dawn of another age: the Renaissance. The grandest ecclesiastical structure of the Renaissance period, of course, would be St. Peter's basilica in Rome, built in 1506–1626, as a successor to "Old" St. Peter's that had been first constructed under Constantine. However, as we anticipate the transition from the Middle Ages to the Renaissance, I want us to think small – about as small as the Scrovegni chapel (also known as the Arena chapel), in Padua, Italy.[21]

This family chapel, dedicated to the Virgin Mary in 1305, was built at the expense of Enrico Scrovegni, whose father Reginaldo, a wealthy merchant, is consigned to literary hell for greed or usury by Dante in *The Divine Comedy*. The small nave without side windows provided an unbroken surface for story-telling. The early Renaissance master Giotto (1267–1337), using the painting technique of fresco, created a strikingly beautiful visual narrative of the lives of Mary and Jesus – thereby telling the story of the Incarnation, up close and personal. The Mary cycle includes scenes from the non-canonical Infancy Gospel of James. The Jesus cycle represents a harmonizing of the four canonical gospels.

Giotto executed his plan by arranging the frescoes on each wall sequentially in three tiers. Scenes from the life of Mary appear on the upper tier and scenes from the life of Jesus on the middle and lower tiers. The frescoes in the chancel area at the east end have the Annunciation of Gabriel to Mary as their principal subject and provide the transition from the Mary story to the Jesus story. Over the door at the entrance, or exit, appears a large representation of the Last Judgment, which, like most medieval visualizations of the theme, was intended to frighten the hell out of those who gazed upon it. But Enrico Scrovegni created a moment of hope for himself by having the artist show him beneath the empty cross presenting a model of the chapel to the Virgin. Such was life and death in the Middle Ages.

Notes

1   "Second Council of Constantinople – 553 AD," <http://www.piar. hu/councils/ecum05.htm>, *Decrees of the Ecumenical Councils*, trans. Norman P. Tanner.
2   "Third Council of Constantinople – 680–1 AD," <http://www.piar/ hu.councils/ecum06.htm>, *Decrees of the Ecumenical Councils*, trans. Norman P. Tanner.
3   "Second Council of Nicaea – 787 AD," <http://www.piar.hu/coun cils/ecum07.htm>, *Decrees of the Ecumenical Councils*, trans. Norman P. Tanner.
4   Timothy Ware, *The Orthodox Church*, new edn. (London: Penguin, 1997), 30–42.
5   "Fourth Council of Constantinople – 869–70 AD," <http://www. piar.hu/councils/ecum08.htm>, *Decrees of the Ecumenical Councils*, trans. Norman P. Tanner.
    For an overview of worship in the Orthodox tradition, including the "Divine Liturgy of St. John Chrysostom," see Ware, *The Orthodox Church*, 264–88. A variety of liturgical texts are readily accessible on the website of the Greek Orthodox Archdiocese of America, <http:// www.goarch.org>.
7   Ware, *The Orthodox Church*, 64–70, and John A. McGuckin, "Christian Spirituality in Byzantium and the East (600–1700)," in Arthur Holder, ed., *The Blackwell Companion to Christian Spirituality* (Oxford: Blackwell Publishing, 2005), 100–2.
8   "Fourth Lateran Council – 1215 AD," <http://www.piar.hu/coun-cils/ecum12.htm>, *Decrees of the Ecumenical Councils*, trans. Norman P. Tanner.
9   Athanasius, *On the Incarnation of the Divine Word*, in *Nicene and Post-Nicene Fathers*, vol. 4, 2nd series (Grand Rapids, MI: William B. Eerdmans, repr. 1991), 65.
10 Gustaf Aulén, *Christus Victor: An Historical Study of the Three Main Types of Atonement*, trans. S. G. Hebert (New York: Macmillan, 1961).

11 LaDue, *The Trinity Guide to the Trinity* (Harrisburg, PA: Trinity Press International, 2003), 71–4.

12 St. Thomas Aquinas, *Summa Theologiae: Latin Text and English Translation, Introductions, Notes, Appendices, and Glossaries*, ed. Michael Cardinal Browne, OP, and Father Aniceto Fernandez, OP, 60 vols. (New York: McGraw-Hill, 1964–).

13 These topics are discussed by Thomas in the 60-volume "Dominican" edition of his *Summa Theologiae*, ed. Browne and Fernandez: the Trinity, vols. 6 and 7; the Incarnation, vol. 48; the Atonement, vols. 49 and 50.

14 Dante Alighieri, *The Divine Comedy*, trans. John Ciardi (New York: W. W. Norton, 1977).

15 "The Council of Trent [1545–63]," <http://history.hanover.edu/early/trent/htm>, *The Canons and Decrees of the Sacred Ecumenical Council of Trent*, ed. and trans. J. Waterworth (London: Dolman, 1848).

16 Holy See Archive – Documents of the II Vatican Council, <http://vatican.va/archive/hist_councils/ii_council/index.htm>, "Constitution on the Sacred Liturgy" (Dec. 4, 1963).

17 Basic Texts for the Roman Catholic Eucharist – The Order of Mass, <http://catholic-resources.org/ChurchDocs/Mass.htm>.

18 "Council of Constance 1414–18," <http://www.piar.hu/councils/ecum16.htm>, *Decrees of the Ecumenical Councils*, trans. Norman P. Tanner.

19 Gordon Mursell, gen. ed., *The Story of Christian Spirituality: Two Thousand Years from East to West* (Minneapolis: Fortress Press, 2001), 115–18.

20 Jean Favier, *The World of Chartres* (New York: Harry N. Abrams, 1988).

21 Frescoes in the Cappella Scrovegni (Arena Chapel), Padua, <http://wga.hu/html/g/giotto/padova/index/html>.

Chapter 4

Jesus and Challenges
to Christian Orthodoxy
(Since the Fifteenth Century)

The Jesus who ruled the Middle Ages, and in whose name medieval culture was shaped, was the Christ of scripture as interpreted primarily by the emerging Roman Catholic and Orthodox churches. As the Son of God, Jesus was one co-eternal and co-equal person of the Holy Trinity – Father, Son, and Holy Spirit. For the salvation of humankind, the Son of God became incarnate through Mary, his virgin mother.

Therefore, the worldview of Christianity – based on Christian scripture – had been defined during the earliest centuries of the Christian movement as a triune monotheism. This worldview differed from the monotheistic confessions characteristic of ancient Judaism and Islam. For Jews, the *Shema*: "Hear O Israel, the LORD our God, the LORD is one." For Muslims, the *Shahada*: "There no god but Allah and Muhammad is the messenger of Allah."

Between the Middle Ages and modernity, three successive and overlapping cultural waves pounded against the bulwark of the orthodox understanding of Jesus as the Christ. These waves have been identified by later historians as the Renaissance, the Reformation, and the Enlightenment. Each wave, in its turn, threatened and further undermined the traditional verities, or truths, of Christian belief and practice. Whereas the culture of the Middle Ages had an intrinsic predisposition toward God, toward the transcendent, and toward all things religious, by the nineteenth century the culture of modernity was well on its way to developing a predisposition against God, against the transcendent, and against the religious dimension of life. The era of Christendom was being eclipsed. The triune theistic worldview of what became known as western culture was being superseded by a worldview, or worldviews, that included openly Unitarian, agnostic, and even atheistic options.

The Renaissance: Back to the Classics

The Renaissance (from the French, "rebirth" or "new birth") is the name given retrospectively to that first cultural wave that crashed against the bulwark of the orthodox understanding of Jesus as the Christ. As a historical period, the Renaissance began in the late Middle Ages, in fourteenth-century Italy, and subsequently spread throughout Europe and extended itself chronologically into the seventeenth century.

As a broad cultural movement, the Renaissance generally carried forward the traditional Trinitarian understanding of Jesus as the Christ, the Son of God, who came into the world to save humankind. The Renaissance also elaborated on the traditional but varied theme of the *imitatio Christi*.

In fact, this period saw the appearance of a devotional manual that soon became and remains an influential spiritual classic, bearing the straightforward title, *The Imitation of Christ*.[1] The book opens with the words of Jesus from John 8:12, "Whoever follows me will never walk in darkness." There follows an exhortation to the reader to study the life of Jesus Christ with the chiding observation that scholarly discourse about the Holy Trinity counts for nothing if the reader lacks the humility of Jesus Christ. First published anonymously in Latin around 1418, the book has been attributed to Thomas à Kempis (1380–1471), a Catholic priest and Augustinian monk. Thomas had been educated in a school run by the Brethren of the Common Life – a religious community, primarily of laypersons, dedicated to the dissemination of learning through a network of schools, especially in the Low Countries and Germany. As reflected in the opening words of *The Imitation of Christ*, the Brethren followed the spiritual path of the *Devotio Moderna* ("modern devotion"), which accepted church

Figure 4 Fresco of "Handing over the Keys" on the wall in the Sistine Chapel in Rome, depicting Peter receiving the keys of the kingdom from Jesus; painted by Pietro Perugino (1445–1523). *Reproduced by courtesy of Vatican Museums and Galleries, Vatican City/Bridgeman Art Library*

teaching about Jesus as the Christ, but emphasized Jesus Christ as the example for daily living.

Although there was continuity of religious belief and practice between the Middle Ages and the Renaissance, the name given to the latter period served notice that "newness" was occurring in many areas of life. Cities grew in size. Universities multiplied. Commerce and trade became increasingly global in the wake of far-ranging explorations over land and by sea. However, the dimension of life that most readily comes to mind at the mention of "the Renaissance" is that of the arts – architecture, sculpture, and especially painting, both in diversity of technique and breadth of subject matter.

We have already mentioned the frescoes of Giotto in the Scrovegni chapel in Padua and the construction of St. Peter's basilica in Rome. But between Padua and Rome lay the city of Florence, which under the family of the Medici became the center of the artistic explosion. The Roman Catholic Church, popes, and other church and civic leaders, priestly and non-priestly, were among the greatest patrons of the arts. Notable popes in this regard included Nicholas V (1447–55), who founded the Vatican Library, and Julius II (1504–13), who initiated the construction and beautification of the new St. Peter's. Among the artists who served the church were those whose genius and breadth of interests and skills became proverbial models for the person who can do everything. Leonardo da Vinci (1452–1518) and Michelangelo (1475–1564) were certainly the foremost among such "Renaissance men" – although Hildegard of Bingen had been a "Renaissance woman" three hundred years before her time. With the Renaissance, "beauty" had seemingly taken its place as the aesthetic virtue among the four cardinal and the three theological virtues as espoused by the Thomistic scholasticism of the Middle Ages.

However, the most distinctive dimension of the Renaissance, presupposed by the visual splendor, was its humanism – an intellectual movement based on a love for the languages and literature of the ancient Greeks and Romans. Humanism developed an approach to learning based more on historical reasoning, in contrast to scholastic reasoning intended to resolve logical contradictions and to create a comprehensive system of established viewpoints.

Francesco Petrarch (1304–74), a Latin scholar, a collector of manuscripts, and a celebrated poet, continues to receive recognition as the "father" of the humanist movement. Although born in Italy, he spent much of his early life in Avignon, where the papacy under Clement V (1305–14) had begun its long exile from Rome. A letter written by Petrarch to a friend, during his middle years, contained a biting critique of the papacy that referred to Avignon as "the Babylon of the West." Therein, he also condemned church leaders for their deceitful entrapment of Christians for their own benefit by unfavorably comparing these leaders to Jesus, who had cast nets to obtain sustenance for others (based on Luke 5:1–11).[2]

Thus Renaissance humanists were not necessarily anti-God, anti-Christ, or anti-Bible, but there was an increasingly astringent criticism of the papacy and the church. Counted among the humanists were the Italians Giovanni Boccaccio (1313–75), Giovanni Pico della Mirandola (1463–94), and Niccolò Machiavelli (1469–1527); the Frenchman Jacques Lefèvre (1455–1536), the German Johann Reuchlin (1455–1522); and the Englishman Thomas More (1478–1535).

Humanists were not, of course, the first Christians to read the classics insofar as Latin had become the language of the church and then the university. Furthermore, before and after the fall of the Byzantine empire in 1453, Greek scholars had come to the west bringing with them classical Greek literature as well as Greek manuscripts of the Bible. The humanists' study of the classical authors in their original languages fostered a shift of focus away from the other world to this world, from the eternal to the temporal, and from the future to the past. Ancient figures and the world they inhabited became the objects and the subjects of study and discourse. These classical authors included Plato, the dramatists, and the representatives of Stoicism and Epicureanism from among the Greeks, and Cicero, Virgil, and Livy from among the Romans. The turn of humanism to the past led to the emergence of what in the future would become two important academic disciplines: one, historical criticism, the other, textual criticism.

Historical criticism examines evidence from the past, documentary or otherwise, and uses that evidence to evaluate tradition, to reconstruct anew, and to interpret past events. The development of historical criticism is associated with the Italian humanist Lorenzo Valla (1407–57). Born in Rome, Valla acquired expertise in Latin and Greek. He pursued a university career before becoming secretary to King Alfonso of Naples. He finally returned to Rome where he served positions under Pope Nicholas V and his successor Pope Callistus III (1455–8).

Valla was committed to the humanistic approach to learning based on a careful analysis of language and literature. He also had a propensity for scrutinizing "authoritative" texts.[3] He developed arguments against tradition based on the language of the documents and an understanding of the history of their transmission. The best-known case in this regard was his demonstration that the "Donation of Constantine" was a forgery. This document claimed to be a deed by which Emperor Constantine, when he moved his capital from Rome to Constantinople, around 330 CE, donated to Pope Sylvester both the city of Rome and much of the land that had constituted the western Roman empire. The deed had been used to legitimate the temporal authority of the pope and his rule over the Papal States – a geopolitical entity that endured until 1870. A second case involved Valla's argument that the familiar Apostles' Creed, still in liturgical use today in the Roman Catholic Church and in many Protestant denominations, could not have originated with the twelve apostles on the day of Pentecost as traditionally claimed. Still another case involved Valla's critique of the Latin Vulgate, the church's Bible, and his identification of awkward style and incorrect translation. Although Valla did not challenge belief in the doctrine of the Trinity, he used the doctrine to criticize Thomas Aquinas' scholastic use of Aristotelian categories, and advocated a return to the common-sense language of the Church Fathers.[4]

Around the year that Lorenzo Valla died in Rome, in 1457, there occurred one of those rare events that would eventually alter the lives of people everywhere: the use of movable type to produce a printed book. The place was the German town of Mainz. That book was the Latin Vulgate version of the Bible, which is usually remembered simply as the Gutenberg Bible in honor of the printer Johannes Gutenberg (1400–68). The transmission and the reception of Jesus and his story had suddenly taken on a new form.

It was this transition from handwritten manuscript to the printed book that necessitated the emergence of the second academic discipline that sprang from the humanist movement. The development of textual criticism, at least as it relates to the New Testament, is associated with the Dutch humanist from Rotterdam, Desiderius Erasmus (1466–1536).[5]

Erasmus received his early education in schools sponsored by the Brethren of the Common Life where he – like Thomas à Kempis – learned the path of the *Devotio Moderna*. He was ordained to the priesthood and entered an Augustinian monastery. With ecclesiastical permission, Erasmus was allowed to spend his life as a peripatetic student and an independent scholar, whose early competence in Latin was later complemented by his learning Greek. He established himself in academic circles not only in the Low Countries, but also in England, France, Italy, and Germany, both through his presence and his publications.

Erasmus' *Handbook of the Christian Soldier* (1504) used martial imagery to describe the Christian life, but the crusade to be waged was not against external enemies but represented the internal struggle within every person who strives to follow Christ in accordance with the ideals of the *Devotio Moderna*. Erasmus' *Praise of Folly* (1511), in which Folly foolishly praises herself, represents a biting satire on the church and humankind.[6] But to discover how traditional and orthodox were Erasmus' own views of Jesus as the Christ one need only read his exposition about the boy Jesus, which he composed for the students at the St. Paul's school for boys in London. He concluded his plain-spoken exposition with an exhortation for the students to sit at the feet of Jesus their teacher.[7]

However, Erasmus' greatest gift relative to the reception of Jesus by others lay in his having been responsible for the printing and publication of the first New Testament in the original language – Greek.[8] He was inspired by his discovery of Lorenzo Valla's annotations on the Latin Vulgate version, and the printing was enabled by the printer Johann Froben of Basle, in Switzerland. The date was 1516.

Erasmus had only a handful of medieval Greek manuscripts to use in his reconstruction of the Greek New Testament text. None of his Greek manuscripts contained the familiar final words of Jesus from the Lord's Prayer: "For the kingdom, and the power, and the glory, are yours forever. Amen" (Matt 6:13). Therefore, Erasmus did not include the words in his Greek text, although the words had been in the Latin Vulgate. He was playing the textual critic. Textual criticism is that discipline that examines all the manuscript evidence available and decides which reading was probably in the original manuscript.

Erasmus remained a Catholic in spite of the urgings by others, including Martin Luther, for him to join those who had separated themselves from the Roman Catholic Church. But when Luther published his New Testament in German in 1522 he based his translations on Erasmus' printed Greek text.

The Reformation: Back to the Bible

The Reformation constitutes the second cultural wave that pounded against the bulwark of the orthodox understanding of

Jesus as the Christ. This Reformation identifies that period in the sixteenth century when longstanding efforts to reform the Roman Catholic Church had failed and actions undertaken by such leaders as Martin Luther (1483–1546) eventually resulted in the separation of western Christianity into Roman Catholicism and Protestantism.[9] Consequently, world Christianity – such as it was in the sixteenth century – was reconfigured into the three main branches that continue today: Eastern Orthodoxy, Roman Catholicism, and Protestantism. If Christianity had been a complex and varied phenomenon before the sixteenth century, it had become even more so with the events of that century and thereafter. The Roman Catholic Church countered with a reformation of its own centered in the Council of Trent.

Protestantism encompassed a variety of movements that differentiated themselves from the Catholic Church and papal authority. Most of these emerging churches shared a cluster of beliefs and emphases that created commonality among them. This commonality, representing something of a Protestant "orthodoxy," included these affirmations: that God's authority resides in the Bible, not in the pope and later church tradition; that God justifies individuals by grace through faith in Jesus Christ, not through belief and meritorious deeds; that all believers constitute a priesthood who receive forgiveness from God, independent of the pronouncement of God's forgiveness by a priest. Protestant movements tended to continue the observance of only two, not seven, sacraments: baptism and the Eucharist (known as the Lord's Supper or Communion).

Thus among the cries heard from Protestant reformers were *Sola scriptura!* (By scripture alone!), *Sola gratia!* (By grace alone!), and *Sola fide!* (By faith alone!). However, according to Luther and other reformers, the phrase *sola scriptura* meant scripture as interpreted by the first four ecumenical councils of Nicaea, Constantinople, Ephesus, and Chalcedon. The pronouncements of these early councils were considered to be consistent with scripture. Therefore, in spite of the earlier differences between Eastern Orthodoxy and Roman Catholicism and the sharp differences between Roman Catholicism and Protestantism, all three branches carried forward the belief in the Triune God as the

Father, the Son, and the Holy Spirit, and the affirmation that Jesus as the Christ, the Son of God, came into the world to save humankind.[10]

Out of the Protestant Reformation came three principal ecclesiastical traditions, the Evangelical (Lutheran), the Reformed (Calvinistic), and the Anglican (Church of England), plus other traditions such as the Anabaptists, who rejected the practice of infant baptism in favor of adult baptism. Therefore, although the three main branches of Christianity retained the "Christ" in "Christianity," Jesus as the Christ was not only becoming "Protestantized" but "denominationalized." How was Jesus received within these principal Protestant traditions?

On the eve of All Saints' Day, October 31, 1517, Martin Luther, an Augustinian monk, a parish priest, and a lecturer at the University of Wittenberg in the German territory of Saxony, posted his now fabled Ninety-Five Theses on the door of the local castle church. Written in Latin, these propositions were intended for discussion and debate. The first thesis invoked the name of Jesus Christ and provided an introduction to the entire list: "When our Lord and Master Jesus Christ said, 'Repent' (Matt. 4:17), he willed the entire life of believers to be one of repentance." Whereas the church had interpreted these words as a command to observe the sacrament of penance, Luther suggested that repentance was a way of life for the believer. Luther's subsequent theses concerned questionable practices related to the sacrament of penance – specifically, the sale of indulgences – and the related belief in purgatory.[11]

Through the sacrament of penance, the believer could experience sorrow for sin (contrition), verbalize sorrow to a priest (confession), and receive God's forgiveness for the acknowledged sin (absolution); but God's justice also required some imposed temporal punishment to compensate for the sin forgiven (satisfaction). A work of satisfaction might consist of special alms-giving, special prayers, special fasting, or even a pilgrimage to sacred sites. An indulgence constituted a certified remission of temporal punishment and thereby afforded forgiven sinners an opportunity to satisfy whatever temporal penalty had been imposed by the priest. Otherwise, the penalty would be satisfied after death in purgatory.

Figure 5 Triptych created by Lucas Cranach the elder (1472–1553) for the city church in Wittenberg (installed 1547), which features scenes that include the Reformers Martin Luther and Philip Melanchthon. *Reproduced by courtesy of Church of St. Marien, Wittenberg, Germany/The Bridgeman Art Library*

The immediate occasion for Luther's action was the sale of indulgences to support the (re)building of St. Peter's in Rome, as preached by Johann Tetzel (1470–1519), commissioned through Albert of Brandenburg, the archbishop of Mainz (1490–1545), and authorized by Pope Leo X (1513–21). Luther's theses allude to a saying attributed to indulgence salesmen, such as Tetzel, that goes something like this, "When the coin in the coffer rings, the soul from purgatory springs."

Therefore, the theological issue that ignited what became the Protestant Reformation was soteriology – the doctrine of salvation, specifically God's forgiveness of sins as mediated through Jesus Christ. Luther's posting his theses presupposed years of personal struggles over his own salvation and his search for understanding the basis of salvation for all humans.

In 1505, shortly after receiving a degree from the University of Erfurt, Luther entered the Augustinian order in response to a promise made in a prayer for deliverance during a violent thunderstorm. Two years later he was ordained as a priest. But neither the grace offered through the Eucharist nor the absolution provided through penance brought him a sense of God's forgiveness. He was a tormented, soul-sick man. The leader of Luther's order, Johann von Staupitz, provided him kindly counsel about the love of God and selected him for further education and a possible teaching career. Having earned degrees in theology in 1509 and 1512, Luther began teaching the Bible at the University of Wittenberg. He first lectured on the Psalms and then on Romans.

It was Luther's regular study of the Bible that gradually gave him new views of God, of God's relationship to humankind, and of the mediating role of God's son, Jesus Christ. As it had been for Augustine centuries earlier, so it was for Luther. Paul's letter to the Romans provided the catalyst for Luther's personal transformation and, at last, peace with God.

For Luther, Romans 1:16–17 represented the core teaching of the Bible that expressed itself in the phrase: "Justification by God's grace through faith." "Justification" (or "righteousness") meant for humans to be put right with God, who loves them and intends to be reconciled with them, not for humans simply to be judged by the God whose holiness demands perfection. "Grace" meant that being put right with God was truly God's free gift, without humans having to earn merit through their own works. "Faith" was trust in Jesus Christ, the incarnate Word, the crucified Savior, not simply rational assent to a creed. According to Luther, through Jesus Christ humans remained sinners but became forgiven sinners.

When in 1517 Luther affixed his Ninety-Five Theses to the door of the castle church, he did so as a reformer, not as a revolutionary. But events moved swiftly against him, although he had already attracted supporters. In 1519, at a disputation in Leipzig, he was driven to deny the final authority of the pope and to affirm the fallibility of church councils. In 1520 he wrote his best-known treatises, *To the Christian Nobility of the German Nation*, the *Babylonian Captivity of the Church*, and *On Christian Liberty*.[12]

By January 1521 Luther had already been excommunicated by the pope. Later that year, at the Diet of Worms, called by Charles V, the Holy Roman Emperor, Luther was asked to recant the ideas in his writings; but he refused, and uttered his memorable words: "Here I stand, I can do no other. God help me. Amen." The subsequent Edict of Worms declared him to be an outlaw to be seized and turned over to the authorities. Only Luther's sequestered protection at Wartburg castle by the sympathetic Elector of Saxony, Frederick the Wise (1486–1525), enabled Luther to write for another day. It was during his months at Wartburg that Luther became an even more significant transmitter of Jesus and his story by translating the New Testament from Greek into the vernacular German (1522). The protest that began as a gesture for reformation had indeed become a revolution. The authority of the pope had been overthrown and replaced by the authority of the Bible.

Perhaps understandably, Luther claimed that theologically the Gospel of John and the letters of Paul ranked far above the other three gospels. Therein he had discovered and finally experienced the way to salvation. But it should also be recognized that Luther's sermons, delivered over the course of his lifetime, often drew on stories and sayings from the gospels of Matthew, Mark, and Luke.

In 1530 Emperor Charles V convened the Diet of Augsburg to resolve the persistent religious question that had divided Germany between Catholics and Protestants. Although Luther was still considered an outlaw and could not attend, his compatriot since Wittenberg days, Philip Melanchthon (1497–1560), drew up a lengthy statement of faith known as the Augsburg Confession (1530) to represent the Lutheran position. Articles I and III reiterate the Lutheran belief in the Triune God and in Jesus as the Incarnate Son of God through the Virgin Mary. Article IV sets forth the Lutheran emphasis on justification by faith in Jesus Christ, by whose death satisfaction was made for human sins. Although intended to be conciliatory, this confession was not accepted by the Catholics, nor even by all the Protestants, present. Nonetheless, the statement represents a foundational document for Lutheran churches to the present day.

In 1555, after twenty-five years of sometimes armed conflict, the Catholics and the Protestants agreed to the so-called Peace of Augsburg. Germany became divided along Catholic and Evangelical (or Lutheran) lines even before Germany was unified as a nation. The religion of the ruler of each territory would be the religion for that territory. But those folk who lived in each area had only an either/or choice. Thus, within a decade of Luther's death in 1546, the town of his birth and the territory in which he spent most of his life – Eisleben, in Saxony – had officially become Lutheran country. By the close of the sixteenth century, Lutheranism had also established itself in Scandinavia, Denmark, Norway, and Sweden.

Alongside and interactive with Evangelical or Lutheran Protestantism, there developed the Reformed tradition, originally centered in Switzerland, whose major founders were Ulrich Zwingli (1484–1531) and John Calvin (1509–64). German-speaking Zurich became the locale of Zwingli's reforming activities, whereas French-speaking Geneva served as the main focus of the French-born Calvin's work.

Zwingli's reforming ideas did not grow out of a personal spiritual crisis, and they initially took shape independently of Martin Luther. Zwingli's humanistic studies at the University of Basle, where he received degrees in 1504 and 1506, provided the impetus toward what became his commitment to the reforming principles of *sola scriptura, sola gratia, sola fide,* and his antipathy not only to indulgences but also to images considered idolatrous – even images of Jesus.

After serving as a parish priest for more than a decade, Zwingli was chosen, in 1519, to become priest and preacher at the largest church in Zurich. By 1525, with the support of the civil authorities, reform had come to Zurich. But the struggle between Catholics and Protestants continued, so a meeting was arranged between Lutherans and Zwinglians to resolve theological differences between the parties as the basis for possible political co-operation. Attended by Luther and by Zwingli, this so-called Marburg Colloquy considered fifteen propositions developed by Luther (a strength of his). The parties agreed on fourteen. The point of disagreement involved how Jesus was received in the

Eucharist. Luther had rejected the scholastic understanding that the bread and the wine were transformed into the body and blood of Christ; but he still insisted on a "real presence." He claimed that Jesus' "is" meant "is": "This *is* my body. ... This *is* my blood ..." (Matt. 26:26, 28). By contrast, Zwingli had come to view the sacrament as simply symbolic, with Jesus' words meaning, perhaps, "This *signifies* my body ... This *signifies* my blood ..."

On October 11, 1531, Ulrich Zwingli's own blood was spilled in battle, fighting on the side of Zurich against an allied army representing five of the Swiss Catholic cantons or territories. Thus, like Germany, Switzerland became divided along religious lines. The focus of the Reformation in Switzerland soon shifted from Zurich to Geneva, from Zwingli to Calvin.

John Calvin, a native of Noyon in northern France, took a degree at the University of Paris in 1528 before studying law in Orléans and Bourges. His humanistic interests led to a study of the ancient languages, Latin, Greek, and Hebrew. In the early 1530s, Calvin moved about Paris in humanistic circles, became familiar with the questions raised by the Protestants, and experienced a "sudden conversion" that won him over to the Protestant cause. He was soon working on what became his magisterial systematic exposition of Reformed theology, *The Institutes of the Christian Religion* (first published in 1536). The preface to this edition, addressed to Francis I, the king of France, contained a defense of those Protestants who were being persecuted for their beliefs.

These were perilous times, so Calvin sought refuge in Switzerland. He ended up in Geneva in 1536, where he joined William Farel in the latter's attempt to win over the city for Protestantism. Although the two were banished in 1538, Calvin was invited back in 1555. Under his leadership, working through the civil authorities, Geneva became a model religious community and attracted Protestant refugees from throughout Europe, including John Knox, who later spearheaded the Reformation in Scotland.

As interpreted by Calvin in the final edition of his *Institutes* (1559), Jesus as the Christ conformed to the Protestant mold – although Calvin certainly emphasized the majesty and sovereignty of God as creator. Perhaps it was this theocentric emphasis that led to his being accused of Arianism during his initial sojourn in Geneva. But in his *Institutes*, he explicitly defended the doctrine of the Triune God and the validity of using categories such as "Trinity" and "person" in speaking of God. Calvin also explained how the two natures of Jesus as the incarnate Word (John 1:14), divinity and humanity, made one person. The divinity of Christ was demonstrated by his miracles, which were performed by his own power as the Son of God.[13]

The importance of the Trinity and the Incarnation for Calvin was made evident by his retrospectively unfortunate involvement in the well-known burning, in 1555, of Michael Servetus as a heretic because of his repudiation of these teachings. In fact, according to Calvin, Servetus' pejorative name for Trinitarians was "atheists."

Calvin, as did other reformers, articulated a view of the atonement similar to the "satisfaction" theory of Anselm.[14] But whereas Anselm thought that Jesus' death was a payback to God on behalf of sinners who had infringed on God's honor, Calvin considered that Jesus' death was his taking the punishment for sin – namely death – on behalf of sinners. This characteristically Protestant interpretation has been designated the penal-substitution view. Calvin positioned himself between Luther and Zwingli as to the presence of Christ in the sacrament of the Lord's Supper. Christ was present, but only spiritually. Thus to Calvin the sacrament was more than a bare memorial.

However, what really set Calvin's view of Jesus Christ apart from the views of other reformers came from the theological framework within which he viewed Jesus' person and work: his doctrine of "double" predestination, or "the eternal decree" by which God has elected some people for eternal damnation and others for eternal salvation. According to Calvin, the efficacy of Jesus' atonement was limited to those elected for salvation.[15]

By the time of Calvin's death in Geneva in 1564, the Reformed tradition, or Calvinist teaching, had become influential in the Netherlands and in Scotland. Some years after his death, the synod of Dordrecht or Dort (1618–19) articulated for the Dutch Reformed Church what became known as the "five points of

Calvinism." These points have been epitomized by the acronym TULIP: Total depravity; Unconditional election; Limited atonement; Irresistible grace; and Perseverance of the saints. The Calvinist teaching of the Church of Scotland later influenced those who gathered in London and formulated the Westminster Confession of Faith (1646). This influence appears most obviously in chapter 3, "Of God's Eternal Decree."

England produced the third major ecclesiastical tradition to originate out of the Protestant Reformation – the Anglican tradition of the Church of England. The Lutheran and the Calvinistic traditions and churches had been shaped by driven individuals who received political support from territorial and civic political leaders. By contrast, the Anglican tradition grew out of the machinations, travails, and statecraft of the English Tudor dynasty, from Henry VIII (1509–47), through his son Edward VI (1547–53) and his daughter Mary (1553–8), to his daughter Elizabeth I (1558–1603).

Henry VIII, a confirmed Catholic and married to Catherine of Aragon, forbade the dissemination of Luther's writings, wrote against them, and in the early 1520s earned from Pope Leo X the title "Defender of the Faith." But his failed attempts to have his marriage to Catherine dissolved through church channels and his continued bickering with the papacy led to the Supremacy Act of 1534 by which Parliament declared Henry and his successors to be the "only supreme head" of the Church of England. In effect, the king of England had displaced the pope. However, his headship did not involve ecclesiastical privileges such as ordination and administration of the sacraments. Thomas Cranmer (1489–1556) had become archbishop of Canterbury and provided leadership in such matters. It was he who finally declared an end to Henry's marriage with Catherine.

In spite of Henry's dissolution of the monasteries and the execution of those who stood in his path, such as his second wife Anne Boleyn, he remained Catholic in his sentiments throughout his life. The Church of England also remained Catholic in its beliefs and liturgy. The Jesus Christ of the Church of England remained Catholic as the incarnate Son of God, whose body and blood were received by communicants through the transubstantiation of the elements in the Eucharist.

In 1547 Edward VI, the 9-year old son of Henry's third wife Jane Seymour, succeeded his father. England had its own reforming tradition dating back to John Wyclif and was not immune to Protestant influences from the continent. Edward was surrounded by advisors with Protestant sentiments. In 1549, Parliament enacted an Act of Uniformity that required the universal use for worship of a prayer book in the English language. By 1552, Cranmer was also engaged in the formulation of a creedal statement consisting of Forty-Two Articles, to which John Knox, the Scottish reformer, had contributed. However, the shift toward Protestantism in England was abruptly reversed when the sickly Edward died.

In 1553 Mary, the daughter of Henry's scorned first wife Catherine, ascended the throne. The ecclesiastical legislation passed under Edward VI was repealed. Worship was restored to the forms practiced under Henry VIII. The authority of the pope was reaffirmed and heresy laws re-enacted. In the subsequent persecution, which earned for Mary her "Bloody" nickname, hundreds were burned, including the excommunicated former archbishop, Thomas Cranmer. But Mary too was short-lived, although she died of natural causes.

So, in 1558, Elizabeth, the indomitable daughter of Henry's second wife Anne Boleyn, became queen of England. With the determination and savvy of her father, she charted a forward-looking course for the nation and the national church. In 1559, Parliament passed both another Act of Supremacy with the ruling sovereign as the "Supreme Governor" of the church and another Act of Uniformity that required the universal use of a newly revised prayer book for worship. In 1563 the Forty-Two Articles of 1553 were reduced to the Thirty-Nine Articles of Religion that became, and remain, the creedal statement of the Church of England. This confessional statement disclosed that the Church of England had been reformed, but was grounded in the historic Catholic tradition.

Although the sixteenth-century English Reformation interpreted Jesus as the Christ through the Thirty-Nine Articles, this Jesus had become the speaker of the English language in those four gospels included in English Bibles. John Wyclif, along with others, had translated the Latin Vulgate into the English language of the fourteenth century; but his Bibles were handwritten. However, in the New Testament of William Tyndale printed in 1526, Jesus spoke in a modern English idiom as translated from Greek – from the 1516 Greek New Testament of Erasmus. Tyndale had been forced to print his New Testament in Protestant territory on the continent. Over there he was eventually arrested and executed by Catholic authorities. This English-speaking Jesus was later featured in a succession of sixteenth-century English Bibles. These included the Coverdale Bible (1535), "Matthew's" Bible (1537), the Great Bible (1539), the Geneva Bible (1560), and the Bishops' Bible (1568). This tradition of English versions culminated in the King James Version (1611). This latter Bible, commissioned by Queen Elizabeth's successor, James I (1603–25), became the most influential English translation among English Protestants for more than three hundred years –. although the earliest English colonists to America used the Geneva Bible, which had been translated by English-speaking refugees in Calvin's Geneva. The Douay–Rheims Bible (1582–1609/10), the translation work of English exiles on the continent, became the Roman Catholic counterpart to the King James Version.

Not all ecclesiastical reform movements of the sixteenth century represented the Evangelical (Lutheran), Reformed (Calvinistic), or Anglican (Church of England) traditions. The overlapping categories of Anabaptists and Radical Reformers have been used to designate groups and individuals whose beliefs and practices deviated in various ways from the main tenets of these aforementioned movements. Both Thomas Müntzer (1489/90–1525) and Menno Simons (1496–1561) were Catholic priests. Both have been described as Anabaptists insofar as they came to advocate adult or believers' baptism and to reject the baptism of infants. But they were "radical" in very different ways and had oppositional views of Jesus.

In July of 1524 Müntzer – from Saxony, as was Luther – delivered a sermon to the nobility of Saxony based on the book of Daniel with an appeal to the book of Revelation. With apocalyptic fervor, Müntzer called upon the princes to kill godless rulers, and cited Jesus' words in Matthew 10:34 about not bringing peace, but a sword. Müntzer became a leader in the peasants' revolt, was captured, tortured, and beheaded. By contrast, Simons – from the Netherlands – gave his name to the Mennonites, "peace" churches whose members sought to live in accordance with Jesus' non-violent admonitions in the Sermon on the Mount (Matt. 5–7). The Mennonites formulated the Dordrecht Confession (1632), whose sixteen articles reaffirmed traditional belief in the Trinity and the Incarnation, but also acknowledged characteristically Mennonite practices such as non-resistance to evil (Matt. 5:38–42).

There were also those "radicals" who, like Servetus, expressed strong anti-Trinitarian views. Among them were the Italians with the Latinized names of Laelius Socinus (1525–62) and his nephew Faustus Socinus (1539–1604). They identified themselves as Unitarians, and rejected the belief that Jesus had existed before his birth. Their movement, which flourished for a while in Poland, has been remembered as Socinianism. In England, the Quakers, founded by George Fox (1624–91), also looked askance at traditional doctrinal statements, emphasized the "inner light" available to every person, and like the Mennonites stressed following Jesus' pacific teachings against violence (Matt. 5:38–42).

The word "reformation" does not apply exclusively to the emerging Protestant churches. Roman Catholicism itself experienced reformation – sometimes referred to as the Counter-Reformation. Even prior to the furor around Martin Luther, Roman Catholics had initiated the publication of the Bible into the original languages of Hebrew and Greek. The humanistic scholar Erasmus had published the first edition of the Greek New Testament in 1516. But at the University of Alcalá in Spain, Cardinal Francisco Ximenes de Cisneros (1437–1517) was already overseeing the production of a polyglot Bible, meaning a Bible in many languages. This so-called Complutensian Polyglot, in six volumes, included appropriate texts in Hebrew, Aramaic, Greek, and Latin. The completed work was circulated with papal permission around 1522.

One of the new religious orders, often identified with the Catholic Counter-Reformation, took its name not from the founder or the order but from the founder of the religion. This order was the Society of Jesus – the Jesuits, established by Ignatius of Loyola (1491–1556).[16] Born in northern Spain, in Basque country, Ignatius was wounded as a young man while defending the town of Pamplona against the French. During his convalescence, he was inspired by reading about the life of Jesus and the saints. Later in life, he wrote his classic, *Spiritual Exercises*, to be practiced under the guidance of a spiritual director, and based the four-week regimen of introspection on the gospel narrative of the life of Jesus. Ignatius' own spiritual experiences pointed him toward education and the priesthood – from Alcalá to Salamanca, from Paris to Rome. Although Ignatius had not set out to found an order, Pope Paul III (1534–49) eventually approved the establishment of the Society of Jesus in 1540. In addition to the traditional vows of poverty, chastity, and obedience, Ignatius and his companions pledged themselves to serve the pope, the "Vicar of Christ," wherever and however he directed them. The Jesuits have done this and have continued to do so – especially through their work in education and missions.

Pope Paul III was also the pontiff who finally called a general council to definitively articulate Roman Catholic teaching over against Protestant heresies and to correct the abuses that had marred the church's inner life. The Council of Trent, which we have already cited for its revision of the Mass, met in northern Italy for three sessions between 1545 and 1563.

The council's agendas, discussions, and decisions were far-ranging. It recognized the Bible to be the source of divine revelation, and church tradition, together with the Bible, also to be a source. The scope of the biblical canon was defined; and the Latin Vulgate was held up as the authoritative text for sermons and disputations. The council also dealt with the doctrine of justification, and identified the many related heresies promulgated by Protestants. The sacraments again were numbered as seven with the doctrine of transubstantiation reaffirmed. Once again, Jesus had become Catholic. The Tridentine Creed was formulated to provide a confessional overview of the decisions made and positions taken by the council.

The medieval Roman Catholic Church had increasingly defined boundaries between orthodox and heretical beliefs or behaviors. The reformation of the medieval church in the sixteenth century had not only fractured both the church and western Christendom but created parallel Catholic and Protestant orthodoxies. Furthermore, the principal Protestant movements and bodies came to define themselves by adopting their own confessions of faith and creedal statements, thereby creating their own normative standards for faith and practice.

Among the Protestant statements that continue to be important for churches in their respective traditions are the Lutheran Augsburg Confession (1530); the Reformed, or Presbyterian, Westminster Confession (1646), the Anglican Thirty-Nine Articles (1563); and the Mennonite Dordrecht Confession (1632). Most Protestant churches, therefore, have developed standards for their own denominational orthodoxies.[17] Thus Protestant confessions usually reflect three layers: Catholic orthodoxy (agreements with the church of Rome), Protestant orthodoxy (agreements with other Protestant churches), and denominational orthodoxy (distinctive beliefs or practices).

The Peace of Westphalia, which ended the Thirty Years War (1618–48), sometimes declared the last of the religious wars in Europe, has been used as a chronological marker for the end of the Reformation period. Obviously, the Peace of Augsburg (1555) had failed. Catholics and Protestants had been at it again, using military means to advance their respective causes, particularly in that checkerboard collectively called Germany. But Germany also figured prominently in the next stage of Jesus' journey from the first to the twenty-first centuries.

The Enlightenment: Not Revelation, but Reason

The Enlightenment constituted the third cultural wave that eroded the orthodox understanding of Jesus as the Christ. The term Enlightenment (German, *Aufklärung*) has been used narrowly to describe an eighteenth-century intellectual movement centered in Germany. In 1784 the German philosopher Immanuel Kant (1724–1804), well into his academic career, published an essay in a periodical intended for the general public, with the byline of his hometown of Königsberg, in eastern Prussia. Therein Kant answered the question, "What is Enlightenment?"[18] Kant described enlightenment as a process of maturation as individuals developed the capacity of thinking for themselves in all areas of life. In religious matters, therefore, enlightened thinking involved the primacy and autonomy of reason and the freedom from the traditional appeal to divine revelation based upon the Bible as dictated by ecclesiastical authority.

What cultural developments during the intervening two centuries could have effected such a shift away from the Bible-based fervor of Martin Luther and the Protestant reformers to a world that seemed destined to replace revelation with rationalism?

The Reformation period had already witnessed the beginnings of the modern sciences. Through the observations and computations of the Polish and Italian astronomers Nicolaus Copernicus (1473–1543) and Galileo Galilei (1564–1642) and the English mathematician Isaac Newton (1642–1727), the ancient Ptolemaic view of the universe with the earth at the center was overturned by a model having the sun at the center of what became the solar system and an immense universe. This Newtonian system operated mechanistically, governed by natural laws such as gravity and motion. Ahead lay the turn from the macrocosm of the physical universe to the microcosm of human origins and the inner life through Charles Darwin (1809–82) and Sigmund Freud (1856–1939).

Out of the Reformation period also came a growing separation between philosophy and theology. The Protestant reformers themselves often drew upon the theological reflections of Augustine and other early theologians, who had utilized Greek philosophy. But they rejected the medieval scholastic synthesis between Aristotelian philosophy and theology as articulated by Thomas Aquinas.

After fifteen centuries, philosophy would again find its own way. Theistic assumptions, whether derived from the Bible or the church, were no longer a necessary starting point for seeking to understand the world. The English Francis Bacon (1561–1626) advocated an empirical method based on observation and experimentation to establish laws governing nature. Although a faithful Catholic, the French mathematician René Descartes (1596–1650), often called the father of modern philosophy, introduced systematic doubt into his epistemological reflections with his famous dictum about individual existence as the foundational certainty,

Cogito, ergo sum – "I think, therefore I am." But what began as skepticism led to "clear and distinct ideas." Bacon and Descartes had contributed to the emergence of two philosophical approaches to understanding "reality": empiricism and rationalism.

During the Reformation had appeared anti-Trinitarians, or Unitarians, who in various ways continued to affirm a belief in God while repudiating the traditional teachings about the Trinity, the Incarnation, and the Atonement. With the new view of the universe, which operated in accordance with certain natural laws, and the growing divide between philosophy and theology, there emerged – in seventeenth-century England – a rationalistic philosophy known as Deism (from the Latin, *Deus*, meaning "God").[19] Although Deism itself was a phenomenon with a variety of viewpoints, Deists sometimes viewed God as the creator who set the natural universe in motion; the universe then ticked away on its own without divine intervention. One early Deist, Lord Herbert of Cherbury (1583–1648), advocated five basic beliefs and practices: the existence of God; the worship of God; the worship of God through piety and virtue; the repentance of sins with God's promised pardon; and God's rewards for the good and punishment for the bad, in this life and the next. Notice the absence of any reference to Jesus. Later Deists such as Thomas Woolston (1669–1733), Peter Annett (1693–1769), and Thomas Chubb (1679–1746) dismissed Jesus' virgin birth, and the miracles and the resurrection of Jesus, as contrary to natural law, and advocated a natural religion based on reason, not revelation. Writings of many English Deists found their way into Germany.

In England, however, the period of Deistic rationalism was followed by a century of the "Methodist" revival initiated by John Wesley (1703–91) and Charles Wesley (1707–88). Both brothers were Oxford graduates and Anglican priests, and they remained Anglicans until their deaths. Now reason gave way to the heart, with outdoor preaching and hymn-singing. John Wesley's testimony to his own moment of genuine faith – which occurred in London, on May 24, 1738, at an evening prayer meeting – disclosed an interesting line of transmission in his immediate experience of Jesus Christ. On that occasion in the gathering on Aldersgate Street, as Luther's preface to Paul's letter to the Romans was being read, John felt his heart "strangely warmed," and he became convinced that Christ had indeed died for him. The subsequent Methodist revival spread Jesus Christ across England and into Wales, Scotland, Ireland, and even across the ocean to Britain's American colonies.

Among John Wesley's acts, late in his life, was his editing and reducing in number the Thirty-Nine Articles of the Church of England to twenty-four for use by American Methodists. After the treaty ending the American Revolutionary War with Great Britain was signed in 1783, American Methodists organized themselves into an autonomous church independent of Anglicanism and even independent of British Methodism. They adopted John Wesley's edited version of the Anglican articles – to which they added a twenty-fifth for inclusion among their Articles of Religion (1784).

Meanwhile, in 1580, the Lutherans in Germany had published *The Book of Concord*. This volume contained those authoritative documents considered to be in harmony with the scriptures – such documents as the early ecumenical confessions and the Augsburg Confession. Thus, within a century, the church founded by Martin Luther was devolving into an ecclesiastical institution that prided itself on dogmatic correctness, and in which faith in Jesus Christ once again had become creedal assent and worship dull formalism. However, Philipp Jakob Spener (1634–1705), educated at Strasbourg and later the pastor in Frankfurt before moving to positions in Leipzig and Dresden, gave impetus to new life in the church. Spener called for a deeper experience of Christ-like living through Bible study and prayer in small group settings and for reaching out to those in need. Here too reason gave way to heart. Spener wrote about his program for renewal in his influential *Pious Desires* (1675). Those committed to this agenda became known as Pietists. In 1692, the University of Halle was founded and became a center for Pietism. Spener became the godfather of Nikolaus von Zinzendorf (1700–60), who would become the patron of the Moravian or United Brethren (*Unitas Fratrum*) – a pre-Reformation Protestant community and the spiritual descendants of Jan Hus, who had been martyred in 1415. Zinzendorf allowed the refugees to build the settlement of Hernnhut on his estate. Later he became a Moravian bishop himself. It was through Zinzendorf that Spener's influence was mediated to John Wesley – particularly Wesley's gathering of believers into small bands. Therefore, in the Protestant circles of Methodism, Moravianism, and Pietism, the Jesus as the Christ of creed was also the Christ of personal regeneration.

Although the Enlightenment of Kant's day was centered in Germany – not yet a unified nation – the burst of brilliance emanated from many lands. Among its luminaries were John Locke (1632–1704), from England, David Hume (1711–76), from Scotland, and Thomas Jefferson (1743–1826), from the United States.

Immanuel Kant had not only been born in Königsberg but also came of age, attended university, joined the university faculty, and became a well-known thinker and writer there, and he died in the city of his birth. Through his family and his early schooling, Kant was nurtured in the devotional discipline of Pietism. But his advanced education led him away from the study of theology to his eventual career in philosophy.

As a philosopher, Kant was initially indebted to the thought of his fellow Germans, Gottfried Leibniz (1646–1716) and Christian Wolff (1670–1757), until the writings of David Hume, the Scottish empiricist and critic of miracles, aroused Kant "from his dogmatic slumbers." Whereas Leibniz and Wolff were rationalists, Hume the empiricist had convinced Kant that all knowledge began with discrete sense data. Thereafter, Kant devoted himself to the philosophical problem of epistemology, that is, of knowledge. Sometime thereafter, he published his three "criticisms": *The Critique of Pure Reason* (1781, 1787), on knowledge of the physical world; *The Critique of Practical Reason* (1788), on moral knowledge; and *The Critique of Judgment* (1790), on aesthetic knowledge.

What about Kant's view of Jesus? Having pruned the supernatural away from the natural in the gospel narratives, Enlightenment thinkers generally were left with a Jesus recognized for his moral teaching. So Kant, not a theologian but a philosopher, interpreted Christianity, the gospels, and Jesus from the vantage point of what he called *Religion within the Limits of Reason Alone* (1793).[20] Just as Kant interpreted Christianity as morality, so herein he wrote about the moral example, the moral ideal, and the moral archetype as though the referent were Jesus. However, Kant never identified the referent by the personal name "Jesus," thereby suggesting that the example, the ideal, or the archetype could be realized by every person. However, the biblical story – including the Jesus story – was the subtext of this treatise. And when Kant epitomized Christianity as a natural religion or as morality he cited more than forty verses of Jesus' teachings, all from the Gospel of Matthew, most from the Sermon on the Mount (Matt. 5–7).

Therefore Kant's Jesus, the Enlightenment's Jesus, was pre-eminently a moral teacher. But it would be another Enlightenment figure who would not only quote Jesus' words but offer a non-traditional historical reconstruction of Jesus' public activity that concluded with his death on the cross. But first we must briefly note the influence of Jesus Christ on the material culture from these centuries of transition from the Middle Ages to modernity.

Material Culture: Architecture, Visual Arts, and Printed Books

The separation of western Christianity into Protestantism and Catholicism presupposed and resulted in profoundly different views on ecclesiastical authority and how Jesus as the Christ, the Son of God, mediates salvation. The Protestant advocacy of alternative beliefs and liturgical practices in the name of Jesus Christ made an impact on material culture in architecture, the visual arts, and the printed book.

The first churches used by Protestants for worship had been Catholic churches that were variously adapted for Reformed use. But by the end of the Thirty Years War, in those territories and cities that had become Protestant – especially in Germany, Switzerland, and the Low Countries – reconstruction or new construction had begun, as needed.

Whether Protestant churches had been converted from prior Catholic use or were new constructions, and in spite of the diversity within Protestantism, there had already appeared those interior markers that would distinguish Protestant churches. The worship space became a single room, or a sanctuary, where the gathered congregation could see and hear, pray and sing. Luther himself – and later Charles Wesley – were composers of hymns. Since the Bible, as the written Word of God, had become the foundational authority, the pulpit was often moved front and center on a dais. Reading the Bible and the sermon as the spoken Word of God, delivered by the preacher, became central acts of worship. The altar, so definitive for the Catholic Mass, became a table placed in front of the pulpit for the Lord's Supper where communion with Jesus as the Christ was celebrated.

The interiors of churches, particularly in the Reformed Protestant tradition, were generally devoid of statues and images – whether murals or stained glass. Whereas the crucifix had become commonplace in Catholic worship and devotional practice, Protestants preferred the empty cross, not only to symbolize Jesus' death and resurrection, but also to avoid idolatry. Ulrich Zwingli, John Calvin, and John Knox opposed images, appealing to the prohibition against images in the Ten Commandments (Exod. 20:4 and Deut. 5:8), although Martin Luther had been more accepting of pictorial representations for educational purposes.

There was therefore a strong iconoclastic tendency among Protestants. Significant outbreaks of iconoclasm occurred in such locales as Zurich in 1523, Geneva in 1535, and St. Andrews in 1559. The stone ruins of the cathedral in St. Andrews, the largest church structure in Scotland, still stand as a stark reminder of what happened when iconoclasts went wild.

Nonetheless, the Roman Catholic Church had been a rich source of art in the name of Jesus Christ. This tradition, which began in the catacombs of Rome, eventually became ubiquitous in the medieval church and included both portraits of Jesus and cycles of the Jesus story, in varied media, such as those we have already considered in Ravenna, in Padua, and in Chartres. Although images of Jesus did not disappear with the Reformation – even in Protestant lands – changes in their creation and use can be observed by considering selectively visual representations of Jesus from Rome, from Isenheim, from Wittenberg, and from The Netherlands.

The Sistine chapel, where papal conclaves convene to elect new popes, is located in Rome – now more properly in Vatican City.[21] The chapel bears the name of the pontiff who commissioned its construction, Pope Sixtus IV (1471–84). It was the same pope who initiated the artistic program for the interior. This visual program included a cycle of paintings based on the Moses narrative down the south wall and a cycle based on the Jesus narrative down the north wall. Both cycles were executed by leading artists of the time. The Jesus cycle highlights seven moments in his life: his baptism, his temptation, his call of the disciples, the Sermon on the Mount, his handing the keys of the Kingdom to Peter, the Last Supper with his disciples, and his resurrection. Pietro Perugino painted the fresco of the fair-haired Jesus transferring keys to a kneeling Peter, which depicts, in the background, the triumphal arch of Constantine and the temple of Solomon. This scene conveys the central message of the lavishly decorated chapel: that the popes as the successors to Peter have received through Jesus Christ the authority to head the church that has superseded historic Israel and the Roman empire. Years later, Michelangelo's renowned paintings of God's creation and humanity's fall, on the ceiling (1508–12), and of Christ's presiding at the Last Judgment, on the altar wall (1535–41), placed the claim of papal authority in an even more universal setting.

The Isenheim altarpiece, now preserved in a museum in Colmar in the Alsace region of northern France, was painted around 1515 by the German artist Matthias Grünewald for use in a chapel associated with a monastery and a hospital.[22] The monks belonged to the order of St. Anthony, whose mission involved care for victims of diseases that manifested themselves visibly on the body. This large altarpiece is a polyptych, meaning that it has two wings that can be adjusted to provide worshipers with three different views.

The first view, with wings closed, involves a grotesquely graphic crucifixion of Jesus, with John the beloved disciple and the two Marys, on the left, and a pointing John the Baptist with a white lamb holding a cross, on the right. To the left of the crucifixion scene appears a painting of St. Sebastian, a patron of plague-sufferers, and to the right a painting of St. Anthony, the reputed founder of monasticism and patron of those with the ailment then known as "St. Anthony's fire." The predella, or painted panel beneath the crucifixion scene, likewise displays the whelp-ridden dead body of Jesus.

The second view, with the wings opened, shows three scenes of hopeful celebration: the annunciation to Mary, a choir of angels heralding Mary and her newborn child, and the resurrected Christ standing triumphantly on the fallen cross with stunned soldiers lying at his feet.

The third view, again with open wings, depicts on the left St. Anthony's meeting in the desert with St. Paul, his fellow hermit, and, on the right, a terrifyingly ghoulish encounter between St. Anthony and the desert demons. Surprisingly, viewers also see between these two painted scenes carvings of St. Anthony flanked by St. Augustine and St. Jerome. Thus this altarpiece, with the suffering but gloried Christ, who was surrounded by a multitude of saints, provided prayerful therapy for the monks of Isenheim and for those entrusted to their care.

The visual programs of the Sistine chapel and the monastic chapel at Isenheim exhibited a correspondence between the Jesus portrayed and his social or liturgical setting. This correspondence also appears in the altarpieces created for Lutheran churches in the latter half of the sixteenth century. These altarpieces served the important pedagogical function of holding before the congregation the basic tenets of Lutheranism. This was often accomplished by incorporating into their scenes the familiar likenesses of the reformers themselves.

The Wittenberg altarpiece, painted by the German artist Lucas Cranach the Elder (1472–1553), was installed in the city church of Wittenberg in 1547 – the church where Luther had often preached, the town where it all began thirty years earlier.[23] Luther had died the preceding year.

This altarpiece is a triptych, displaying scenes on the three panels and a scene on the predella below. The predella shows Luther to the right, preaching from the pulpit, and the congregation across the room to the left, apparently listening to a sermon on Luther's theology of the cross, because the space between congregation and pulpit is occupied by the solitary figure of Jesus on the cross. Appropriately, the central painting above is a scene of the Last Supper. Jesus and his disciples are seated around a circular table.

Jesus is placing the bread on Judas' lips while Luther himself, seated across the way, prepares to drink from the cup. Lutherans received communion in both kinds – bread and wine. On the left panel, Melanchthon, as a John the Baptist figure, is sprinkling water on a baby crawling on the edge of the font. On the right panel, Pastor Johannes Bugenhagen of the Wittenberg church, as a Peter figure holding the keys, is hearing a parishioner's confession. Lutherans practiced infant baptism and emphasized the importance of confession and absolution for all believers.

One day in my New Testament class, I asked the students to examine the twenty-two images of Jesus scattered about in our secondary textbook and to select the one image with the greatest appeal. These images represented a variety of visual media, different historical periods, a multiplicity cultures, and a range of specific poses or subject matter. More than half of the thirty students selected the same work of art: an etching, *Christ with the Sick around Him Receiving Little Children* (ca. 1649), by the Dutch artist Rembrandt van Rijn (1609–69). Rembrandt created this recognized masterwork out of moments in the ministry of Jesus narrated in Matthew 19. The students in my class who selected this representation of Jesus expressed a connection with this Jesus who was concerned for those who are socially vulnerable, the sick and the young.

As with Rembrandt, so with most artists who take on Jesus as a subject, the road leads back to those ancient texts that preserve the Jesus story. With the invention of mechanical type in the fifteenth century, printed books soon superseded handwritten manuscripts as the principal means of transmitting literature, including the Bible, and therein the Jesus story. The Latin Vulgate, the Bible of the western church translated by Jerome in the fifth century, became the first book to be printed in the mid-1450s. Before the end of the fifteenth century, at least some portion of the Bible had found its way into print in many of the European vernacular languages. Jews in Italy had also printed their scriptures in Hebrew. Not long thereafter, Cardinal Ximenes and Desiderius Erasmus printed the New Testament in Greek.

If the Renaissance had encouraged a return to the classics, so the Reformation called for a return to the Bible and further encouraged the translation and publication of the Bible in the vernacular languages. The sixteenth century witnessed the printing of Bibles, or portions thereof, in German by Luther, in English by William Tyndale, and in French by Jacques Lefèvre. As might be expected, it was Luther's Bible that came to be adorned with woodcut images illustrating and dramatizing the Jesus story.

Notes

1 Thomas à Kempis, *The Imitation of Christ*, trans. Ronald Knox and Michael Oakley (New York: Sheed & Ward, 1960).
2 "Petrarch, Letter to a friend, 1340–53," <http://www.fordham.edu/halsall/source/14cpetrarch-pope.html>; from J.H. Robinson, *Readings in European History* (Boston, 1904), 52.
3 R. V. Laurence, "Influence of Lorenzo Valla on the Reformers," in A. W. Ward, et al., eds., *The Cambridge Modern History* (New York: Macmillan, 1907), 2:694.
4 Charles Trinkaus, "Lorenzo Valla on the Problem of Speaking about the Trinity," *Journal of the History of Ideas*, 57/1 (Jan. 1996), 27–53.
5 Roland H. Bainton, *Erasmus of Christendom* (New York: Scribner's, 1969).
6 Both the *Handbook of the Christian Soldier* and the *Praise of Folly* are available in *The Erasmus Reader*, ed. Erika Rummell (Toronto: University of Toronto Press, 1990), 138, 154.
7 Bainton, *Erasmus*, 102.
8 Bruce M. Metzger and Bart D. Ehrman, *The Text of the New Testament: Its Transmission, Corruption, and Restoration*, 4th edn. (New York: Oxford university Press, 2005), 142–50.
9 Roland H. Bainton, *Here I Stand: A Life of Martin Luther* (Nashville, TN: Abingdon Press, 1950).
10 William J. LaDue, *The Trinity Guide to the Trinity* (Harrisburg, PA: Trinity Press International, 2003), 75–7.
11 CRTA website: " 'The Ninety-Five Theses' by Martin Luther," <http//www.reformed.org/documents/95_theses.html>.
12 Martin Luther, *The Three Treatises* (Philadelphia: Muhlenberg Press, 1943).
13 *Institutes of the Christian Religion*, ed. John T. McNeill and Ford Lewis Battle, Library of Christian Classics (Philadelphia: Westminster Press, 1960), vol. 1, bk. 1, ch. 13, pp. 120–59.

14 *Institutes*, vol. 1, bk. 2, chs. 12–17, pp. 464–534.

15 *Institutes*, vol. 2, bk. 3, chs. 21–4, pp. 920–87.

16 *St. Ignatius of Loyola: The Spiritual Exercises and Selected Works*, ed. George E. Ganss, Classics of Western Spirituality (Mahwah, NJ: Paulist Press, 1991).

17 John Leith, *Creeds of the Churches*, 3rd edn. (Atlanta, GA: John Knox Press, 1982).

18 Immanuel Kant, "An Answer to the Question: 'What is Enlightenment?', Königsberg in Prussia, 30th September, 1784," <http://philosophy.eserver.org/kant/what-is-enlightenment.txt>.

19 *Catholic Encyclopedia* website: "Deism," <http//www.newadvent.org/cathen/04679b.htm>.

20 Immanuel Kant, *Religion Within the Limits of Reason Alone*, trans. Theodore M. Greene and Hoyt H. Hudson, The Cloister Library (New York: Harper & Row, 1960).

21 Fabrizio Macinelli, *Die Sixtinische Kapelle* [*The Sistine Chapel*] (Vatican City: Ufficio Publicazioni e Reproduzioni dei Musei Vaticani, 2000).

22 Web Gallery of Art, image collection, virtual museum, <http://www.wga.hu/frames-e.html?//html/g/grunewal/2Isenhei/index.html>.

23 Sacred Destinations – Wittenberg, Germany, <http://www.sacreddestinations.com/germany/wittenberg-pictures/slides/stadtkirche cranach-altar-hc.htm>.

Chapter 5

Jesus and the Historical Quest
(Since the Eighteenth Century)

The challenges to Christian orthodoxy posed by the Renaissance, the Reformation, and the Enlightenment were many. But the greatest challenge came from the Enlightenment. Claims were made on behalf of human reason at the expense of divine revelation. Traditional authority was challenged in all areas of life – including religion, whether that authority be the hierarchy and tradition of Roman Catholicism, or the scriptures as elevated by Protestantism.

The Trinitarian view of God as Father, Son, and Holy Spirit and the doctrine of the Incarnation, that the Son became flesh through Mary, had been interpreted to mean that Jesus was true God and true Man, divine but also human. Therefore, Christian orthodoxy had always affirmed that Jesus was a historical figure who lived and died in the first century. But it was Enlightenment thinking expressed through historical reason that analyzed the gospels as literary documents and used the results to reconstruct what Jesus' life was really like.

In the nineteenth and twentieth centuries, this move to accentuate Jesus as a historical figure resulted in a distinction between what became known as "the Christ of faith" and "the Jesus of history." The Christ of faith referred to Jesus as confessed and proclaimed to be the Christ by and within Christian communities, including Jesus as presented in the New Testament writings, Jesus as adored in the liturgy, Jesus as affirmed in creedal statements, and Jesus as the subject of theological reflection. By contrast, the

Jesus of history referred to Jesus as he walked, talked, and died in first-century Palestine. Or, more precisely, the phrase referred to what could be established about Jesus, his aims, his public activity, and his death, using appropriate historical evidence guided by principles of historical interpretation. The biography, or "life," of Jesus became the characteristic literary representation of the historical Jesus.

In recent decades, scholars have rightly noted the limitations of the phrases "Christ of faith" and "Jesus of history." They have proposed various alternatives. Marcus J. Borg introduced the categories of "the post-Easter Jesus" and "the pre-Easter Jesus" to clarify how Jesus was viewed, experienced, and talked about before and after the Easter event.[1] John P. Meier has distinguished between the "real Jesus" and the "historical Jesus" as a way of acknowledging that there was more to Jesus than can be established by the historian as historian.[2] C. Stephen Evans rejected the validity of the distinction by reversing the modifiers and speaking about the historical Christ and the Jesus of faith. Herein we recognize the limitations of this bifocal distinction while continuing to use the phrases Christ of faith and the Jesus of history as helpful ways to highlight the issues involved in the modern quest.[3]

Therefore, for more than two centuries, Jesus has posed a problem that expresses itself as a question: What is the relationship between the Christ of faith and the Jesus of history? Contributors to and opponents of this historical quest for Jesus have wrestled with two related questions: Is it methodologically possible to undertake this quest? Is it theologically legitimate?

This chapter provides an overview of how Jesus has been received by theologians and historical scholars, and, through them, a broader public, by sketching the principal periods that prepared for and now constitute this modern quest. Each period reflects a dominant assumption about the relationship between the Christ (of faith) and the Jesus (of history) and offers distinctive answers to the questions of methodological possibility and theological legitimacy. However, there is interplay among the periods, and each period includes viewpoints that remain options today for understanding Jesus as a historical figure.[4]

Pre-Quest Period: Christ = Jesus (before 1778)

From their origins as expressions of faith in Jesus as the Christ, the four gospels themselves were used within Christian communities for guidance in matters of belief and practice. But no distinction was made between the Christ of faith and the Jesus of history. Strictly speaking, there was no problem and no quest. However, church leaders as well as their opponents were well aware of the obvious differences among the four gospels. Over the centuries, attempts have been made to harmonize and to defend the apparent discrepancies in the gospel accounts.

In the fifth century, Augustine produced a meticulous work on *The Harmony of the Gospels* in which he explained how the four gospels agreed with each other in spite of their apparent differences.[5] He explained the glaring differences between Matthew, Mark, and Luke, on the one hand, and John, on the other, by using Christological categories. On this view, the first three gospels focused on "those things which Christ did through the vehicle of the flesh of man," and the Gospel of John expressed the "true divinity" and "divine nature" of Jesus Christ. Augustine also wrote about the origins of the individual gospels and the chronological order in which they were written. He articulated the view that prevailed for centuries, namely, that the gospels were written by their namesakes in the order in which they now appear in the canon: Matthew, Mark, Luke, and John.

Already two centuries before Augustine, not long after the four canonical gospels had been gathered together, a believer from Mesopotamia named Tatian had settled in Rome and skillfully woven the four gospels into a continuous narrative called the *Diatessaron* (paraphrased, "four-in-one"), as we have already noted.[6] Whatever Tatian's intention and whether he wrote initially in Greek or Syriac, it was the Syriac version that gained considerable popularity. His harmony was widely used within the Syriac-speaking church until the fourth and fifth centuries and exerted its influence well beyond its original time and place through its translation and adaptation into such languages as Armenian, Arabic, and Latin.

The Protestant Reformation witnessed the formulation and circulation of more gospel harmonies. The renewed emphasis upon scripture and the new availability of printing made this both desirable and feasible. Sometimes the gospels were woven together into a continuous account of the Jesus story. At other times the gospels were printed separately but in parallel columns. John Calvin, the great reformer of Geneva, followed something of the latter approach in his biblical commentary, *A Harmony of the Gospels of Matthew, Mark, and Luke* (1555).[7] He placed similar passages from these gospels next to one another and followed them with verse-by-verse comment.

The Enlightenment brought a sharp distinction between the natural and the supernatural, and a growing scientific, philosophical, and even theological assault on the supernatural. Now both the gospels and Jesus were often considered without regard for the traditional ways they had been viewed by the church or – by now – the churches. In 1774–5, the German textual scholar J. J. Griesbach published what he called a "synopsis" of the three gospels of Matthew, Mark, and Luke whereby these three gospels were arranged in Greek in parallel columns.[8] Thus began the practice of identifying Matthew, Mark, and Luke collectively as the Synoptic Gospels because they together ("syn-") view ("optic") the Jesus story. Although Griesbach himself reaffirmed the written priority of Matthew, he claimed that Luke was literarily dependent upon Matthew and that Mark was dependent upon both. His arrangement of these three gospels in parallel columns would become important in future scholarly discussions over the literary relationship among the three, and thus the identification of which sources might be the earliest and thus of greatest historical value.

Old Quest Period: Christ // Jesus (1778–1906)

The name most often associated with the beginning of the historical quest has been Hermann Samuel Reimarus (1694–1768).[9] Reimarus was a respected professor of Oriental languages in the German city of Hamburg, where he was born and where he died.

He maintained a public silence throughout his life about his negative views of Christianity, which had been honed under the influence of the English Deists, because there were limits to free speech even in a so-called enlightened age. A transgression of those limits could lead to loss of employment, social ostracism, and even arrest, so that the negative views of Reimarus became known only after his death. Between 1774 and 1778, that man of letters G. E. Lessing published anonymously several fragments of a sizable manuscript written by Reimarus. The year 1778 was the date of the publication of the seventh fragment, entitled "On the Intentions of Jesus and his Disciples."[10] The importance of this document for the quest lies in its sharp delineation between the Christ of faith and the Jesus of history.

Whereas traditional Christianity and the gospels understood Jesus to have been a spiritual messiah who died for the sins of humankind, who was resurrected from the dead, and who would return in glory, Reimarus claimed that Jesus' intention historically had actually been to establish an earthly kingdom in the immediate future with himself as the kingly messiah. Reimarus found support for this political interpretation in the gospels themselves, especially in Matthew, which he considered the oldest of the four gospels.

According to Reimarus, Jesus epitomized his message with the political phrase, "the kingdom of heaven" (or the "kingdom of God"). When Jesus entered Jerusalem riding on an ass with a colt in fulfillment of the royal passage in Zechariah 9:9, the crowds acclaimed him as king. The sign over the cross publicized the charge on which he was executed, "King of the Jews." The words spoken by Jesus from the cross expressed his attitude toward his own death, "My God, my God, why have you forsaken me?" (Matt. 27:46). Reimarus accepted these words as historical and concluded that Jesus' intention had been to deliver his people from Roman oppression and to establish a worldly kingdom. However, Jesus died in despair because he had not achieved his goal.

Subsequently, after Jesus' unexpected execution, his disciples stole his body and fabricated what became the traditional Christian view that Jesus was a spiritual messiah. As Reimarus declared: "the new system of a suffering spiritual savior, which no one had ever known or thought before, was invented only because the first hopes had failed."[11] Reimarus thus perceived a historical truth underlying the stolen body story in Matthew 28:11–15 to support his claim that Jesus' followers had indeed stolen Jesus' body. The reason the disciples undertook their deception was their desire to avoid returning to their more mundane ways of making a living in Galilee.

The historical reconstruction of Reimarus may be objectionable in retrospect, not only on theological but also on literary and historical grounds. But he had made the crucial distinction. Jesus the spiritual messiah of church teaching and the canonical gospels was quite clearly not identical with the historical, political messiah presupposed by the gospel narratives.

Reimarus' specific understanding of the historical Jesus as a messianic figure with political aims did not prevail. But his recognition of discontinuity between the Christ of faith and the Jesus of history became a prominent assumption in the nineteenth century. This fundamental assumption of discontinuity also involved related assumptions. It was widely held that it was methodologically possible and theologically important to seek and to recover the shape and substance of Jesus' historical ministry.

Those persons who engaged in the quest for Jesus assumed that it was possible to recover what he was like as a historical figure. If they rightly used the gospels, they believed that they could reconstruct his life and ministry. Individual interpreters, of course, often defined what was a right use of the gospels as historical sources. Sometimes they seemed to pick and choose arbitrarily those details in the gospel accounts that supported what they claimed to be establishing historically. At other times they allowed a rigid understanding of natural law to lead them to approach the miracle stories in the gospels with great skepticism. They explained away the miracles as natural occurrences, dismissed them as products of primitive superstition, or just ignored them. Reimarus himself often appeared arbitrary in his use of the gospel accounts and approached the miracle stories with skepticism.

One of the first critical treatments of Jesus in the United States was undertaken by Thomas Jefferson (1743–1826), the remarkable third president of the new republic, who had served as the principal author of the nation's Declaration of Independence, which had been declared publicly to the world on July 4, 1776. Jefferson himself had also been nurtured on the thought of English Deism and corresponded with, among others, the transplanted English scientist and dissenting clergyman Joseph Priestley (1733–1804). Jefferson finally created – perhaps in 1820 – what he called *The Life and Morals of Jesus of Nazareth*.[12] He had acquired gospel texts in four languages: Greek, Latin, French, and English. He then went through the four gospels and literally "cut out" all references to supernatural events such as virginal conception, miracles, and resurrection. Among Jesus' sayings, he also separated "the gold from the dross," attributing the former to Jesus and the latter to Jesus' followers. The surviving bits of gospel text were then joined together into a truncated but linear narrative and displayed in parallel columns in the four languages. Consequently, Jefferson's Jesus emerged pre-eminently as a teacher, a great moralist. For him the greatness of Jesus was to be found in his most benevolent teachings and parables, such as the sayings in the Sermon on the Mount (Matt. 5–7) and the commandments on love (Matt. 22:40; Mark 12:28–31, 32, 33). Here was an American scissors-and-paste version of Immanuel Kant's religion within the limits of reason alone.

During the nineteenth century, however, the debate over the literary relationship among the four gospels was perceived to have important consequences for the historical quest. Although J. J. Griesbach had earlier reaffirmed the priority of Matthew, his printed Greek synopsis of Matthew, Mark, and Luke proved to be a valuable tool for those scholars who later sorted through the many possibilities of how these three gospels were literarily related.

One such scholar was H. J. Holtzmann (1832–1910), who in 1863 set forth a "two-document hypothesis" to explain the similarities and differences among the gospels of Matthew, Mark, and Luke.[13] The earliest document was understood to be the Gospel of Mark, that was later used independently by the authors of Matthew and Luke. The second source was a hypothetical document identified by the German word *Quelle* (meaning "source") and thereafter called by its first letter "Q." The evidence for such a "missing" document lay in those gospel passages now found in the gospels of Matthew and Luke, but not in Mark. Thus, what was the source for the Lord's Prayer, as reported in Matthew 6:9–13 and Luke 11:2–4? The authors of Matthew and Luke did not borrow it from Mark insofar as it does not appear therein. Where did they get it? From a hypothetical source called "Q."

The Gospel of John, traditionally recognized as the last of the four to be written, was increasingly regarded as irrelevant to the search for the historical Jesus because of both its lateness and its radically different characterization of Jesus. Both the priority of Mark and the peculiarity of John had enormous consequences for the nineteenth-century quest. Mark was often viewed as presenting the most trustworthy narrative account of Jesus' public ministry. The source called Q – whether written or oral tradition – as an early collection of Jesus' teachings, came to be regarded as crucial for access to what Jesus had taught during his ministry. John was shunted to the side as a theology in narrative form and thus not a source for recovering what Jesus was like historically.

Furthermore, there emerged in the nineteenth century the indisputable recognition that the historian should interpret Jesus against the background of his own distinctive environment – first-century Palestinian Judaism. Reimarus had already shown considerable historical sensitivity in this regard. For him, Jesus was a Jew whose cultural and religious "home" was not the Christian church but ancient Judaism. He examined gospel passages about Jesus in relation to Jewish thought and custom as he knew them. Consequently, he understood Jesus' kingdom message and ministry as reflections of the traditional Jewish hope for a worldly deliverer.

Methodologically, therefore, it was considered possible to reconstruct the life and ministry of Jesus. What Jesus was really like could be known. What Jesus was really like ought to be known. Theologically, it was assumed to be necessary to reconstruct the life and ministry of Jesus.

Reimarus had secretly sought the historical Jesus in order to discredit traditional Christianity. Thomas Jefferson was also writing over against the church's dogmatic interpretation of Jesus as the Savior, the Son of God. But many after them sought Jesus in order to support Christian belief. The nineteenth century saw the rise of that theological movement known as Protestant "liberalism," a term suggesting a movement seeking liberty or freedom. Liberal theologians sought freedom from the traditional Christ of church doctrine and sought to establish a firm foundation for Christian belief and practice. They sought that foundation neither in the traditional creeds nor in the New Testament writings generally. Instead, they sought that foundation in the personality and religion of Jesus. Liberal theology emphasized Jesus not so much as savior but as teacher and example. It stressed not so much faith *in* Jesus but the faith *of* Jesus as he taught the Fatherhood of God and the brotherhood of man (to use nineteenth-century phrasing). Liberal theology also understood the kingdom of God as that realm to be realized on earth as Jesus' followers, ancient and modern, obeyed his command to love God and neighbor. Liberal theologians characteristically contrasted the dogmatic Christ of Paul with the historical figure of Jesus discovered through the gospels.

The German scholar H. J. Holtzmann serves as an appropriate symbol for the relationship in the nineteenth century among liberal theology, the quest of the historical Jesus, and gospel criticism. I have already mentioned Holtzmann as having set forth the two-document hypothesis, which claimed Mark to be the first gospel written. He concluded his 1863 study of the Synoptic Gospels with a short description of the life of Jesus. Following the basic outline of Mark's Gospel, he arranged Jesus' ministry into specific stages of activity and suggested how Jesus' awareness of his messiahship developed over the course of his ministry. Holtzmann's source analysis of the four gospels and his presentation of the historical Jesus became quite influential in liberal theological circles.

The nineteenth-century quest – or the old quest as it came to be called – was characterized by great variety. There was variety of motive and variety of result. There was variety of philosophical and theological perspective. Dozens of biographies, or "lives," of Jesus were written. Both professional historians and amateurs retold the story of Jesus by arranging his life into distinct periods and by probing his understanding of himself. Like most biographies, therefore, these biographies of Jesus often displayed extensive sequencing of his life and intensive probing of his consciousness.

Among the most famous, or infamous, writings from this era were the *Life of Jesus Critically Examined* by David Friedrich Strauss (1835–6; first translated into English in 1846)[14] and the *Life of Jesus* by Ernest Renan (1863).[15] In upbringing and family background, Strauss was a German Protestant and Renan a French Catholic. But both suffered for their writings about Jesus. The former forfeited his hopes for an academic career. The latter lost his academic position. The biography of Jesus was the principal literary expression of the old quest; but any book that presents itself as a "life'" of Jesus with detailed chronologizing and psychologizing, whatever its date, represents in some sense a throwback to the old quest.

For a comprehensive account of the nineteenth-century quest as pursued in continental Europe one should consult the classic survey written in 1906 by Albert Schweitzer, translated from German into English with the title *The Quest of the Historical Jesus* (1910).[16] Schweitzer's reflections as a commentator and a contributor established him as a transitional figure in the history of Jesus research. The date of his publication serves as a convenient date for marking the shift from the "old quest" period to a period of no quest.

No Quest Period: Christ // Jesus (1906–1953)

Albert Schweitzer became known to the world as the humanitarian missionary doctor of West Africa. He spent the last fifty years of his life battling tropical diseases, until his death in 1965. But before he studied medicine he had already distinguished himself as a biblical scholar at the University of Strasbourg. His writings about Jesus in many respects both ended the old quest period and anticipated a period of no quest.

On the one hand, Schweitzer ended the old quest period by demonstrating how his nineteenth-century predecessors, such as H. J. Holtzmann, had failed to recover Jesus as he really was during his historical ministry. Schweitzer claimed that liberal interpreters had modernized Jesus and made him over in the likeness of their own philosophical and theological ideas. He concluded his exhaustive review with biting words rejecting the nineteenth-century liberal understanding of Jesus: "The Jesus of Nazareth who came forward publicly as the Messiah, who preached the ethic of the Kingdom of God, who founded the Kingdom of heaven upon earth, and died to give his work its final consecration, never had any existence. He is a figure designed by rationalism, endowed with life by liberalism, and clothed by modern theology in an historical garb."[17]

On the other hand, Schweitzer anticipated the no quest period by saying that the historical Jesus he had discovered was for the most part insignificant for twentieth-century faith and practice: "But the truth is, it is not Jesus as historically known, but as spiritually risen within men, who is significant for our time and can help it. Not the historical Jesus, but the spirit which goes forth from Him and in the spirit of men strives for new influence and rule, is that which overcomes the world."[18]

The historical Jesus discovered by Schweitzer, therefore, both differed from the figure of his liberal predecessors and rendered Jesus as a historical figure insignificant for later generations. Jesus during his lifetime, according to Schweitzer, had proclaimed that God in the near future would establish his supernatural kingdom through the supernatural messiah known as the "Son of Man'" (cf. Dan. 7:13). Jesus believed that God had designated him to be revealed at the kingdom's arrival as that supernatural messiah; and he acted to hasten that climactic moment. Schweitzer described his viewpoint as one of thoroughgoing or consistent eschatology. Jesus both proclaimed and acted out his apocalyptic beliefs.

Albert Schweitzer found support for his interpretation of Jesus in the gospels themselves. For him, Matthew 10:23 was a crucial text. Here Jesus, before sending out his disciples two by two, said to them: "When they persecute you in one town, flee to the next; for truly I tell you, you will not have gone through all the towns of Israel, before the Son of Man comes." Accordingly, at this point in his ministry, Jesus had thought that the persecution of his disciples would constitute those sufferings before the end-time that were expected within traditional Jewish apocalyptic speculation. Jesus had thought that he, therefore, would be revealed as the messianic "Son of Man" before they completed their rounds. But the disciples returned to Jesus. They had not suffered. The kingdom of God had not arrived. He had not been glorified as the "Son of Man."

So Jesus had to rethink the course of his ministry. He subsequently decided that he had to take on himself the sufferings before the end. He shared this decision with his disciples. As Schweitzer explained: "In the secret of his passion which Jesus reveals to the disciples at Caesarea Philippi the pre-Messianic tribulation is for others set aside, abolished, concentrated on Himself alone, and that in the form that they are fulfilled in His own passion and death at Jerusalem."[19] But Jesus' own death still did not usher in God's supernatural kingdom and his glorification as the "Son of Man." The historical, apocalyptic Jesus had miscalculated – not once, but twice.

Hermann Samuel Reimarus had initiated the nineteenth-century quest by considering Jesus against the background of Jewish expectation for a political messiah and an earthly kingdom. Albert Schweitzer surveyed that quest by considering Jesus against the background of Jewish eschatological expectation for a transcendent messiah and a supernatural kingdom. Both Reimarus and Schweitzer agreed that Jesus during his ministry had failed to achieve his intended goal. They also agreed that there was a difference between the gospel portrayals of Jesus and Jesus the historical figure.

This assumption about discontinuity between the Christ of faith and the Jesus of history was carried forward from the old quest period into the subsequent period of no quest. Some scholars early in the twentieth century called for the suspension of efforts to seek the Jesus of history. This no quest attitude stemmed from a growing realization that it might be methodologically impossible to write a life of Jesus and theologically illegitimate to base Christian faith on the uncertainties of historical research. These scholars and theologians began to emphasize the importance of the Christ of faith.

The seekers after the historical Jesus in the nineteenth century had proceeded with the methodological confidence that they could use the gospels to rediscover what Jesus had been like. But gradually this confidence was eroded. Historical skepticism asserted itself. There were even those who denied that a historical figure named Jesus from Nazareth ever lived. Others did not deny the existence of Jesus but did say that it was impossible to write a detailed biography about him. A number of developments led to these expressions of historical skepticism.[20] But it was the development of form criticism that brought this skepticism to full flower. Form criticism emphasized the transformative influence of the early church on the oral tradition of the Jesus story before that story became written gospels. Some form critics called into question the historical reliability of the outline of Jesus' ministry in Mark. Others emphasized how the early church may have created many of the stories and sayings of Jesus now preserved in the gospels. Therefore, the nature of the gospels themselves made a quest of the historical Jesus seem difficult, if not impossible.

A principal representative of the no quest attitude toward the historical Jesus was Rudolf Bultmann, a longtime member of the faculty at the University of Marburg. Throughout his lengthy career as biblical scholar, theologian, and preacher, he clung steadfastly to the view that the quest of the historical Jesus was methodologically impossible and theologically suspect. His historical skepticism, of course, was related to his pioneering work in form criticism. Bultmann could make positive comments about Jesus the historical figure, and published a small book on Jesus' teaching called *Jesus and the Word* (1926; translated into English in 1934).[21] But he denied that any interpreter could write a full biography of Jesus. Bultmann's theological reluctance to undertake biographical writing about Jesus, even if possible, was related to his existentialist theology. The term "existentialism" generally refers to a theology or a philosophy that emphasizes the human individual as a decision-making agent. Bultmann himself emphasized that Christian faith was the individual's affirmative response to the church's *kerygma* (from the Greek, meaning "proclamation") of Jesus as the Christ. He even said that faith requiring the external props of historical research into the life of Jesus was simply not faith. To Bultmann, therefore, both the nature of the gospels and the nature of faith made the writing of a life of Jesus impossible and illegitimate.

Rudolf Bultmann has often been recognized as the outstanding biblical scholar of the twentieth century in terms of technical scholarship and for his theological reflection. However, it should be noted that the period of no quest was centered especially among scholars on the European continent.

In the United States, scholars representing American liberalism such as those of the "Chicago school," centered at the University of Chicago, continued to pursue the historical Jesus. In 1927, during the heyday of the social gospel, Shirley Jackson Case wrote *Jesus a New Biography* in which Jesus – in characteristically American fashion – emerged as a social prophet who challenged institutionalized authority and achieved martyrdom as a "potential insurrectionist."[22]

In Great Britain after World War II, a diverse quartet of scholars, A. M. Hunter, T. W. Manson, Vincent Taylor, and C. H. Dodd, reconstructed their own historical "lives" of Jesus.[23] Although not without differences over particulars, all four confidently acknowledged that Jesus knew himself to be the messiah but did not publicly use the title for himself. Instead, he chose as his own self-designation the ambiguous phrase the "Son of Man"; and he interpreted his own mission in the light of the "Suffering Servant" passages of Isaiah – especially Isaiah 53. Thus all four of these scholars presented Jesus as a messianic suffering servant.

However, at mid-century in Germany, in spite of Bultmann's methodological and theological reservations about the quest for the historical Jesus, a lecture by one of his own former students called for a renewed interest in such a figure. So the period of no quest was superseded by the period of a new quest.

New Quest Period: Christ › Jesus (1953–1985)

The search was initiated by a lecture delivered by Ernst Käsemann in 1953. The occasion for the lecture was a reunion of Rudolf Bultmann's former students, many of whom had assumed important teaching positions in European universities. The lecture was published and translated with the title "The Problem of the Historical Jesus."[24]

In his concluding remarks, Käsemann distinguished between his interest in the Jesus of history and the attitudes of earlier representatives of the old quest and the no quest. Käsemann firmly rejected the possibility of writing a biography of Jesus in the manner of the old quest. The gospels, he said, did not allow for the extensive chronologizing and the intensive psychologizing reflected in the older "lives" of Jesus. Käsemann also rejected the kind of historical skepticism that was partly responsible for the no quest disinterest in the earthly career of Jesus. The gospels, he said, may not allow for a full biographical treatment of the Jesus story, but they do refer to a real person of flesh and blood. Ernst Käsemann therefore summarized his view of the issue in these terms: "The question of the historical Jesus is, in its legitimate form, the question of the continuity of the gospel within the discontinuity of the times and within the variation of the kerygma."[25]

The scholarly movement in the 1950s initiated by Käsemann's call became known as the new quest of the historical Jesus. He and his successors maintained the distinction between the Christ of faith – the kerygmatic Christ – and the Jesus of history. But they neither sought the Jesus of history at the expense of the Christ of faith nor elevated the Christ of faith to the exclusion of the Jesus of history. Instead, they desired to establish continuity between the Christ of faith and the Jesus of history. They believed that within limits it was methodologically possible to reach relatively certain historical conclusions about Jesus, especially about his message. They also believed that it was theologically necessary to seek these historical conclusions as a reminder to Christian faith that Jesus the Christ was indeed a human being.

Within four years of Käsemann's challenge there appeared a full-scale treatment of Jesus from among those who had studied with Rudolf Bultmann. The author was Günther Bornkamm; the book, *Jesus of Nazareth* (1956; translated into English in 1960).[26] The work of Bornkamm stayed within the guidelines set forth by Käsemann. The very title of the book had significance in this regard. The book was not called a "life," or biography, of Jesus. Throughout the volume, there was only the slightest interest in

Figure 6 Etching by Rembrandt (1606–69), *Christ with the Sick around Him, Receiving Little Children* (based on Matthew 19). *Photo: AKG Images*

the sequence of events in the ministry of Jesus, and virtually no interest in Jesus' self-understanding. However, Jesus proclaimed the dawning "kingdom of God" and confronted his hearers in a radical way with the "will of God." The authority of God expressed through Jesus' words and deeds established continuity with the messiahship conferred on him by the later church. Bornkamm wrote this volume for a general audience as well as scholars, and it became one of the most widely read historical treatments of Jesus over the quarter-century after its initial publication.

The renewed interest in Jesus, initiated by Käsemann and popularized by Bornkamm in the 1950s and 1960s, attracted followers throughout the scholarly world. The very name given to this approach to the Jesus problem was bestowed by American scholar James M. Robinson in his sympathetic review of its beginnings, *A New Quest of the Historical Jesus* (1959).[27] Because of its origin and development within Bultmannian scholarly and theological circles, the new quest approach to Jesus possessed a kind of homogeneity lacking in that diverse movement known as the old quest. Three unifying characteristics should be briefly mentioned.

First, new quest scholars recognized the faith-based, or kerygmatic, nature of the gospels. The gospels were not modern biographies but faith documents with every story and saying reflective of that faith. Simultaneous with the renewed interest in the historical Jesus was the development of redaction criticism. Günther Bornkamm was a pioneer of this school of criticism, which analyzed how each gospel writer had redacted, or edited, his sources to create his gospel so that each gospel reflected the theological interests of its author and his intended audience. Thus Bornkamm was well aware of the possible gap between the Christ of the gospels and the Jesus of history when he affirmed the possibility and necessity of bridging that gap by historical investigation into Jesus' earthly career.

Second, new quest scholars understood the academic discipline of history and history-writing more in terms of "event" than "sequence of facts." The gospels do not allow interpreters to write a modern biography, a "life," about Jesus. But the gospels do allow them to write about the life of Jesus. Every story and every saying as an interpreted event may have originated with Jesus in his earthly ministry.

Third, new quest scholars accepted the view that the burden of proof rested upon those who claimed that material in the gospels was "authentic" – that is, originated with Jesus in his earthly ministry. These scholars, therefore, inherited and further developed certain principles or criteria that would enable them to establish the authenticity of the gospel material, and they passed on these criteria to the next generation of Jesus scholars. Later in this chapter I will list and discuss several criteria that continue to be used, in various ways, to establish the historical probability of Jesus' words and deeds.

Third Quest Period: [Christ] Jesus (since 1985)

During the 1960s and 1970s interest in the historical Jesus began to extend well beyond new quest scholars and their sympathizers.

That Jesus research had entered another stage, or period, in recent decades has received general recognition among scholars working in the field. To distinguish this preoccupation with the historical Jesus from the nineteenth-century "old" or "first quest" and the mid-twentieth-century "new" or "second quest," scholars have used different phrases to describe the widespread interest in the historical Jesus that erupted both in scholarly and popular circles toward the end of the twentieth century.

Herein I have adopted the phrase "third quest" to designate this most recent period of the quest.[28] The year 1985 serves as a convenient date to mark the transition to the current phase of the quest. In that year, two events occurred that clearly signaled the emergence of still another phase in the history of Jesus research.

First, there appeared E. P. Sanders' volume, *Jesus and Judaism*.[29] Sanders' academic career had carried him from McMaster University in Canada to the University of Oxford in England and, eventually, back to Duke University in his native America. Having published significant volumes on Paul's relation to Judaism, Sanders turned his attention to Jesus. In the introduction to this Jesus book, Sanders listed a number of works on the historical Jesus that had appeared in the years immediately prior to his own. He suggested that these scholarly works shared a feature with his own presentation: a disinterest in "the debate about the significance of the historical Jesus for theology." Sanders recognized that the renewed interest in the historical Jesus, unlike the old quest, the no quest, and the new quest, was neither driven nor dominated by the traditional question of the relationship between the Christ of faith and the Jesus of history. Just as philosophy had earlier declared its independence from theology as a result of the Enlightenment, so Sanders suggested that historical inquiry into the life of Jesus was now being pursued independent of Christology. The question of the historical Jesus was considered interesting in itself without any necessary linkage to the church's traditional confession of Jesus as the Christ. The focus now rested on Jesus as a historical figure.

Second, in March of 1985, the same year that Sanders published his Jesus book, there convened in Berkeley, California, the first meeting of the Jesus Seminar – initially a group of thirty or so scholars who had gathered at the invitation of Robert W. Funk.[30] After many years as a scholar and teacher at such institutions as Vanderbilt University and the University of Montana, Funk began to think that it was time for him to set forth his own historical reconstruction of the ministry of Jesus. In order to facilitate his task, he sought two scholarly aids. He tried to locate a "raw list" of all the sayings by, and stories about, Jesus as reported in ancient literature – within and without the New Testament. He also looked for a "critical list" of words and deeds generally considered by scholars, after two hundred years of critical sifting, to have been actually said and done by Jesus. He failed to find an exhaustive list of either kind. Therefore, Funk invited a group of scholarly colleagues to participate in an ongoing seminar that eventually met twice annually in four-day sessions. He later described the purpose of this Jesus Seminar as twofold. The first task was to compile a list of all words attributed to Jesus in the first three centuries (roughly to the establishment of Christianity as a legal religion under Constantine). The second task was for participants to work systematically through this raw list and to determine by their collective judgment which sayings preserved the very voice (*ipsissima vox*) of Jesus and which sayings represented later stages of the Jesus tradition.

John Dominic Crossan, who served as co-chair of the Jesus Seminar, designed and edited the raw list of Jesus' words: *Sayings Parallels* (1986).[31] Robert Funk assumed principal responsibility for the volumes that eventually represented the critical list of Jesus' words and the lists of propositions distilled from Jesus' deeds: *The Five Gospels* (1993) and *The Acts of Jesus* (1998).[32] The Jesus Seminar became known in academic and popular circles for such procedures as face-to-face discussion of position papers, voting by dropping colored beads in a box on the authenticity of individual sayings and specific deeds, and color-coding the voting results, with only around 20 percent of Jesus' reported words and deeds being judged historically probable (red: highly probable; pink: probable; gray: possible, black: improbable).

Sharp differences have distinguished the work of E. P. Sanders from that of the Jesus Seminar both in approach and result. Nonetheless, in 1985, both Sanders and the Jesus Seminar, without conscious reference to each other, had seemingly agreed that their interest in Jesus was historical, not theological – although the Westar Institute, which sponsored the Seminar, came to address theological issues of contemporary import with the public at large.

In the years following 1985, biblical scholars continued to note how the current phase of Jesus research exhibited a general disinterest in theological matters. Walter P. Weaver, for example, observed: "what seems characteristic of this new movement is a lack of interest in the theological significance of its subject."[33] M. Eugene Boring also observed that "the 'Third Quest' proclaims its separation from the theological enterprise – although it does this in strikingly different ways."[34] Dennis C. Duling described this period of Jesus research as "theologically neutral."[35]

Thus an assumption for many practitioners in this phase of the historical quest can be described as methodological possibility but theological neutrality or disinterest. However, the use of words like "neutrality" and "disinterest" is intended to identify a distinctive dimension of what has been going on in recent Jesus studies and not to suggest that all participants are disinterested in what has traditionally been described as the relationship between the Christ of faith and the Jesus of history.

John P. Meier, a Roman Catholic priest and biblical scholar, has provided further confirmation of the concern of many contemporary Jesus scholars to bracket out their own faith commitments as they pursue their work as historians. On the opening pages of what has already become more than a thousand pages of his own judicious rethinking of the historical Jesus, *A Marginal Jew* (three volumes have been published to date, 1991, 1994, 2001). Meier acknowledges that he writes out of "a Catholic context." However, as a way of not allowing his theological commitments to get in the way of his historical investigations, he playfully imagined what he called an "unpapal enclave."[36] This gathering would involve a Catholic, a Protestant, a Jew, and an agnostic – all competent historians of religious movements in the Greco-Roman–Palestinian world. They would be locked up in the Harvard Divinity School Library, allowed only a meager diet, and allowed to exit only after producing a consensus document on who Jesus was within the setting of his time and place. This document would be based exclusively on historical arguments and appropriate evidence.

Perhaps this general lack of overt interest in the theological implications of Jesus research relates to another distinctive dimension of recent Jesus scholarship – a strong emphasis upon Jesus as a Jew who was continuous with the Judaism of his own time, however that continuity be understood. In a post-Holocaust world, biblically related scholarship has had to come to terms with Christianity's role in the origins and perpetuation of anti-Judaism and anti-Semitism.

In the closing years of the twentieth century, major works attested to Jesus' Jewishness. Note the titles of the previously mentioned works by E. P. Sanders, *Jesus and Judaism*, and John P. Meier, *A Marginal Jew*. Among other major works were James H. Charlesworth, *Jesus Within Judaism:* (1988); John Dominic Crossan, *The Historical Jesus* with the explanatory subtitle, *The Life of a Mediterranean Jewish Peasant* (1991), and Bruce Chilton, *Rabbi Jesus* (2000).[37] These writings were anticipated by the pioneering work of the Jewish scholar Geza Vermes, whose study on *Jesus the Jew* (1973) served as a harbinger of the current phase of Jesus research – the third quest. Since the publication of his pioneering work, Vermes has completed his projected trilogy that includes his *Jesus and the World of Judaism* (1983) and *The Religion of Jesus the Jew* (1993).[38] Among the volumes already mentioned in this chapter appear works that represent three principal historical models that have emerged in recent years for understanding Jesus as a first-century Jew.

First, E. P. Sanders, in his *Jesus and Judaism*, followed the path of Albert Schweitzer and portrayed Jesus as the eschatological prophet who proclaimed the imminence of God's kingdom, or rule, and expected the imminent restoration of Israel by God. Although not without differences among themselves, others have also bestowed upon Jesus the mantle of an eschatological prophet. These scholars have included Dale C. Allison, Bart D. Ehrman, and Paula Fredriksen.[39]

Secondly, the main alternative to the model of Jesus as eschatological prophet came from within the Jesus Seminar, whose collective judgment, as well as the writings of individual members such as Robert Funk and John Dominic Crossan, projected Jesus as a subversive sage whose parables and aphorisms challenged the conventional wisdom of his day and affirmed God's rule to be already present. Jesus was characterized as a Galilean peasant sage whose unconventional teaching and itinerant behavior even resembled that of the Cynic philosophers – although Jesus was indeed a Jew.

Thirdly, there were scholars whose understanding of Jesus the Jew could not be easily confined to seeing him in a singular role. Just as Geza Vermes had portrayed Jesus as a *Hasid*, or holy man, in the charismatic tradition of Galilee, so Marcus Borg has characterized Jesus as a Spirit-filled person who opposed "a politics of holiness" with "a politics of compassion." Jesus' teachings and actions marked him as a healer, a sage, a prophet, and a founder of a movement intending to revitalize Israel.[40]

John P. Meier has also emphasized how Jesus was "a complex figure, not easily subsumed under one theological rubric or sociological model."[41] Jesus proclaimed a paradoxical message of God's kingly rule as both future and already present. Among the roles reflected in his message and activity were those of an eschatological prophet, an exorcist and healer, a rabbinic teacher and interpreter of the law, and even a baptizer.

The most visible British scholar in the current period of the Jesus quest has been N. T. Wright, since 2003 the Anglican bishop of Durham. His major contribution to the historical quest, *Jesus and the Victory of God* (1996),[42] represents one volume of a larger project, "Christian Origins and the Question of God." Although Wright was the first to use the phrase "third quest," he used it not to identify a period in Jesus research but to place himself in the interpretive tradition of, among others, Albert Schweitzer and E. P. Sanders. Wright understands Jesus to have been an eschatological prophet, but for him Jesus was an "eschatological prophet/ Messiah." As such, Jesus consciously redefined the traditional markers of Jewish identity and acted out Israel's story of the return from exile, the defeat of evil, and the return of YHWH to Zion. Jesus' cross became the means and the symbol of "the victory of God," as declared by his resurrection from the dead by

God.[43] Therefore, unlike Schweitzer and Sanders, Wright considered the historical Jesus not to be irrelevant for contemporary faith; and Wright himself was neither disinterested in nor neutral about theological issues.

These contributors to the quest have in varying degrees employed in their historical reconstructions the insights of the social sciences such as cultural anthropology and archaeology. The differences among these and other historical portrayals of Jesus, past and present, have been based on several factors.

One factor involved the literature the historian admitted as evidence and how the interrelationship of this literature was understood. All four gospels? Only the Synoptic Gospels? Or, also – and even primarily – traditions represented by Q and the Gospel of Thomas? What about the Gospel of Peter? Certainly a reassessment of gospel literature has been a major factor in the recent renewal of interest in the historical Jesus.

Another factor involved the kind of Judaism – the specific Jewish context – within which to place Jesus. Did the eschatological traditions expressed by ancient Israel's prophets and their successors provide the context within which to understand Jesus? Whereas apocalyptic has been understood by some to be a kind of eschatology that projected a coming *end* of the world, other scholars view apocalyptic to be a dramatic way of talking about the end of the present evil age and the inauguration of a new age *within* history when God would somehow intervene and restore Israel. Or, did wisdom traditions compiled by Israel's sages in such books as Proverbs, with their focus on how to live now, provide the context within which to understand Jesus? In recent years, some scholars have rediscovered Jesus' parables and aphorisms as expressions of wisdom that does not reinforce but challenges traditional ways of viewing God and the world. Without denying Jesus' Jewishness, and observing how Galilee generally represented a much-Hellenized territory, others have established similarities between Jesus' teaching and the counter-cultural wisdom of those wandering philosophers known as Cynics. Or did the legal traditions grounded in the five books of Moses, and later codified by the rabbis in the Mishnah, provide the context within which to understand Jesus? Scholars generally have come to view Jesus' antagonism toward the Pharisees, as displayed in the gospels, to be more a reflection of conflict between the post-Jesus church and the synagogue than a recollection of conflict between Jesus historically and his Pharisaic contemporaries.

Still another factor that determined a historical reconstruction of Jesus' career involved the way the interpreter used specific principles, or criteria, for determining whether or not Jesus spoke this word or performed that act. Here are five criteria of the many that have been developed and invoked during the long search for the historical Jesus.[44]

First, the criterion of dissimilarity states that sayings or emphases of Jesus in the gospels may be considered authentic if they are dissimilar from sayings or emphases of the early church, on the one hand, and of ancient Judaism, on the other. This criterion assumes knowledge of both the early church and ancient Judaism with which comparison is made. Its limitation is that it confirms only of those aspects of Jesus' teaching that are peculiar to him and excludes those aspects that he may have shared with the early church or Judaism. Because this criterion tends to separate Jesus from Judaism, it no longer has the prominence it did among new quest scholars. Among the sayings and emphases often said to have been authenticated by this criterion are Jesus' proclamation of "the Kingdom of God" as not only future but also present; Jesus' interpretation of the Law without appeal to precedent; Jesus' address of God by the intimate name *Abba* ("Father"), and, generally, Jesus' distinctive parables and aphorisms.

Second, the criterion of multiple attestation states that sayings, themes, or kinds of behavior by Jesus may be considered authentic if they are attested in multiple gospel sources – traditionally Mark, Q, and John, plus M and L, as symbols for words and deeds of Jesus peculiar to Matthew and Luke. Most, if not all, of these sources depict Jesus as one who preached in parables, associated with social outcasts, debated with religious authorities, and performed healings and exorcisms. This principle obviously grew out of the source analysis of the gospels so characteristic of the old quest period. But the Gospel of Thomas and the Gospel of Peter have come to be viewed by some scholars in recent years as sources independent of the Synoptics and John. The Q document itself has been elevated, within some circles, to the status of Sayings Gospel Q that antedated the canonical narrative gospels.

Third, the criterion of embarrassment states that information about Jesus that would have been viewed by the early church as an embarrassment may be considered authentic since it is unlikely that the church would have made up such activities or sayings. Among details said to meet this criterion are Jesus' baptism by John, since it was a baptism of repentance for the forgiveness of sins; Jesus' conflict with his immediate family, since his mother Mary and his brother James later become prominent in the church; and Jesus' denial by Peter and his betrayal by Judas, since they were among his chosen disciples.

Fourth, the criterion of language and environment, more negative than positive, states that material about Jesus in the gospels may not be considered authentic unless it is compatible with the language and culture of Palestine and Palestinian Judaism. This principle also emerged out of the old quest. Participants in the nineteenth-century search took seriously the study of Jesus within the first-century setting in which he lived and died. No scholar in this century used this criterion with any more rigor than Joachim Jeremias.[45] Although a German contemporary of Rudolf Bultmann, he never accepted the no quest outlook and continued to work his way back through the gospel tradition to the historical Jesus. He even translated from Greek back into Aramaic such portions of the gospel tradition as Jesus' parables, the Lord's Prayer, and his words over the bread and wine at the last supper.

Fifth, the criterion of coherence states that sayings or emphases of Jesus in the gospels may be considered authentic if they cohere, or agree, with material established as authentic by other criteria. This criterion allows for the enlargement of the amount of authentic material. Debate about the different kinds of so-called "Son of Man" sayings preserved in the gospels has continued. But the futuristic apocalyptic "Son of Man" sayings could be accepted as authentic insofar as they cohere with the futuristic dimension of Jesus' kingdom proclamation.

Whatever else may be involved in the many and varied literary reconstructions of Jesus' aims, his words, his deeds, and his death as a historical figure, these "lives" in some sense bring the historical figure to life. Although visual representations of Jesus in varied media have been created since the second century, I turn now to consider briefly the representations of Jesus and his story in the performance media of stage and screen.

Dramatic Arts: From Passion Plays to Jesus Films

Over the centuries, Jesus and his story have been transmuted into a variety of visual forms, including passion plays. Toward the end of the nineteenth century, Jesus also became the subject of that visual and story-telling medium so characteristic of modern and postmodern culture – motion pictures, the movies, film.[46] Just as earlier representations of Jesus occasioned iconoclastic controversies and charges of anti-Semitism, so cinematic treatments of the Jesus story have sometimes elicited similar outrage, not through imperial decrees and sacked churches but through devastating film reviews, letter-writing campaigns, and picketed theaters.

During the first decade of commercial cinema in the 1890s, there appeared films advertising themselves as passion plays: the Horitz *Passion Play* (1897) and the *Passion Play of Oberammergau* (1898). Both were projected for paying audiences in Philadelphia and New York respectively. The former showed scenes of a traditional passion play performed for the camera in Horitz, Bohemia (today the village of Horice in the Czech Republic). The latter, contrary to its title, was filmed on the roof of a building in New York City using local actors. Of limited duration, these two silent moving pictures with scenes from the life of Jesus were accompanied by spoken commentary and live music.

Both of these early films were well received, and were even exhibited on the road. However, these experiences signaled that Jesus was no longer the property of the church. Now, through this new collaborative medium, Jesus had to find a public audience – or filmmakers had to find an audience for Jesus – out of diverse populations, although most viewers would have a prior knowledge of the Jesus story, a notion of how Jesus should look, and certainly some disposition toward the claims made for him as the Christ.

Figure 7 Portrait, *The Head of Christ*, by Warner Sallman (1892–1968); it has been reproduced tens of thousands of times since the 1940s. © *1941 Warner Press, Inc., Anderson, Indiana. Used with permission*

Nevertheless, in spite of the many challenges of bringing the Jesus story to life on the screen, an ever-lengthening tradition of Jesus films has emerged. My comments must of necessity be suggestive rather than comprehensive. But Jesus films must both connect with their audiences and also draw upon the familiar gospels of the Christian scriptures for their screenplays. The films in this cinematic tradition represent a spectrum of relationships to the four gospels.

The most common use of the gospels for creating a screenplay, anticipated by the staged and filmed passion plays, was to harmonize the gospels into a continuous storyline – no mean feat considering the diversity among the gospels, especially the differences between the Synoptics and John. Among the films taking this approach were Cecil B. DeMille's silent classic *The King of Kings* (1927) and the two sprawling epics of the 1960s, Samuel Bronston's *King of Kings* (1961) and George Stevens' *The Greatest Story Ever Told* (1965), both four hours in length with formal intermissions. Attracted by the possibility of more screen time, Franco Zeffirelli accepted the invitation to direct a six-hour, made-for-television, mini-series to be produced by RAI, Italian state television, and ATV, a British commercial company, to be called simply *Jesus of Nazareth* (1977).

These harmonizing films became increasingly inclusive in terms of material incorporated from the four gospels. Among these films, *Jesus of Nazareth* projected the most coherent characterization of Jesus by skillfully reporting the Synoptic scene of Peter's confession that Jesus was the Christ before integrating into the script Jesus' self-declarative "I am" sayings from John. Whereas Stevens' *The Greatest Story Ever Told* explicitly told the Jesus story as a Christian story by framing it with scenes in a church, Zeffirelli's *Jesus of Nazareth* emphasized the Jewishness of the Jesus story by depicting scenes that underscored the spiritual vitality of the Judaism in which Jesus came of age.

A common feature of most Jesus films shot in color stock from this period was the piercing blue eyes of the northern-European-looking Jesus character. In appearance, Robert Powell, who played Jesus, recalled Warner Sallman's *Head of Christ* (1940) that had become ubiquitous in Protestant church life in the America of the 1940s and 1950s.

Alongside the harmonizing approach, in recent decades Jesus films have appeared that base their stories on the narratives of individual gospels. Pier Paolo Pasolini premiered his stark, black and white, *The Gospel According to [St.] Matthew* (1964, Italian; 1966, English) during the Second Vatican Council (1962–5) and dedicated it to Pope John XXIII, who convened the council and who died before its close. The film *Jesus* (1979), produced at the initiative of Bill Bright and the evangelistic organization Campus Crusade for Christ, based its screenplay on the Gospel of Luke. The Jesus Film's regularly updated website has in recent years claimed that this movie has been made available in more than a thousand languages, received more than 6 billion viewings, and resulted in 200 million decisions for Christ.[47] More recently, Philip Savile's *The Gospel of John* (2005) followed the text and translation of the Good News Bible, word for word, in its three-hour narration of the Jesus story.

Still another cinematic approach has been the film adaptation of the Jesus story from other media, such as staged musicals. With Norman Jewison's *Jesus Christ Superstar* and David Greene's *Godspell* (both 1973), Jesus began singing his way across the screen in celebration of the hippie, or flower-power, generation. The rock opera *Jesus Christ Superstar*, filmed in the Israeli desert, had the structure of a passion play and focused on events from the last week of Jesus' life. *Godspell* used New York City as its urban set and drew on the Synoptic Gospels for its material as Jesus, in his Superman shirt, and his vaudevillian troupe acted out some of his best-known parables. The characterizations of Jesus in these films indicate the respective moods of these productions: a "woe-woe Jesus" in *Superstar*, and a "ho-ho Jesus" in *Godspell*.

In contrast to these musicals from the early 1970s, Jesus films have usually sought a certain verisimilitude by looking like ancient first-century Palestine. But only occasionally have Jesus films explicitly betrayed an awareness of the critical issues explored by the historical quest. However, Martin Scorsese's *The Last Temptation of Christ* (1988), adapted from the Nikos Kazantzakis novel, and Denys Arcand's *Jesus of Montreal* (1989, in French; 1990, English subtitles) confronted viewers with the problem of the historical Jesus.

In *The Last Temptation*, the historical problem was articulated in the long dream-fantasy of Jesus as he hangs dying on the cross. In an imagined verbal exchange between Jesus and Paul, Paul insinuates that he himself has deceptively created the belief that Jesus was the Christ, who has died and been resurrected, in order to meet the needs of the people. This affirmation of the fraudulent beginnings of Christianity recalls the similar claim by H. S. Reimarus, who inaugurated the historical quest in the eighteenth century.

In *Jesus of Montreal*, the premise of the film itself involves the claim that a traditional passion play performed at a shrine overlooking the city has been rendered out of date by newly discovered information about Jesus. An actor named Daniel Coulombe was commissioned by Father LeClerc to write and to stage a new passion play with Coulombe himself playing Jesus alongside his own company of actors. But later LeClerc strongly objected to the content of the play that he had commissioned. So, in a crucial face-off, the priest declared to the actor/playwright that people come to Mass to hear how Jesus loves them – not to learn about the most recent archaeological discoveries. This acknowledged preference by LeClerc for the Christ of faith over against historical investigation into the life of Jesus recalls the no quest attitudes of early twentieth-century theologians, such as Rudolf Bultmann.

With Mel Gibson's *The Passion of the Christ* (2004), the tradition of Jesus films returned to its origin in medieval passion plays with Gibson's own bloody depiction of the last twelve hours of Jesus' life – and his picking at the scabs of anti-Semitism, as many critics claimed. But this film became an unexpected box-office blockbuster with a worldwide gross of more than $600 million.[48]

With his Jesus film, Gibson joined other filmmakers of Catholic heritage who, in recent decades, have enlarged the tradition of Jesus films. Among them are Pier Paolo Pasolini, Franco Zeffirelli, Martin Scorsese, and Denys Arcand. Also, In spite of cinematic differences among Zeffirelli's *Jesus of Nazareth*, Scorsese's *The Last Temptation*, and Gibson's *The Passion*, all three films explicitly identify Jesus on the screen with the so-called "Suffering Servant" of Isaiah 53.

Notes

1   Marcus J. Borg, "Portraits of Jesus," in Hershel Shanks, ed., *The Search for Jesus: Modern Scholarship Looks at the Gospels* (Washington, DC: Biblical Archaeology Society, 1994), 86.
2   John P. Meier, *A Marginal Jew: Rethinking the Historical Jesus*, 3 vols. (New York: Doubleday, 1991, 1994, 2001), 1:21–40.

3 C. Stephen Evans, *The Historical Christ and the Jesus of Faith: The Incarnational Narrative as History* (Oxford: Clarendon Press, 1996).

4 See the diagram in W. Barnes Tatum, *In Quest of Jesus*, revised and enlarged edn. (Nashville: Abingdon Press, 1999), 109.

5 *Select Library of the Nicene and Post-Nicene Fathers of the Christian Church*, ed. Philip Schaff (1888; repr., Grand Rapids, MI: William B. Eerdmans, 1991), 678–80.

6 Bruce Metzger and Bart D. Ehrman, *The Text of the New Testament: Its Transmission, Corruption, and Restoration*, 4th edn. (New York: Oxford University Press), 131–4.

7 John Calvin, *A Harmony of the Gospels of Matthew, Mark, and Luke*, trans. A. W. Morrison, 3 vols. (Grand Rapids, MI: William B. Eerdmans, 1972).

8 William R. Farmer, *The Synoptic Problem: A Critical Analysis* (Dillsboro, NC: Western North Carolina Press, 1976), 1–3.

9 *Reimarus: Fragments*, ed., Charles H. Talbert, trans. Ralph S. Fraser, Lives of Jesus Series (Philadelphia: Fortress Press, 1970).

10 *Reimarus*, 21.

11 *Reimarus*, 151.

12 Thomas Jefferson, *The Jefferson Bible: The Life and Morals of Jesus of Nazareth* (Boston: Beacon Press, 1989).

13 H. J. Holtzmann, *Die synoptischen Evangelien: Ihr Ursprung und geschichtlicher Charakter* [*The Synoptic Gospels: Their Origin and Historical Character*] (Leipzig: Engelmann, 1863).

14 David Friedrich Strauss, *Life of Jesus Critically Examined*, ed. Peter C. Hodgeson, trans. George Eliot, Lives of Jesus Series (Philadelphia: Fortress Press, 1972).

15 Ernest Renan, *Life of Jesus*, Modern Library (New York: Random House, 1927; repr. 1955).

16 Albert Schweitzer, *The Quest of the Historical Jesus: A Critical Study of its Progress from Reimarus to Wrede* (Baltimore: Johns Hopkins University Press, 1998).

17 Schweitzer, *Quest*, 398.

18 Schweitzer, *Quest*, 401.

19 Schweitzer, *Quest*, 389.

20 This turn-of-the-century skepticism had become associated especially with William Wrede, according to Schweitzer, *Quest*, 330.

21 Rudolf Bultmann, *Jesus and the Word*, trans. Louise Pettibone Smith and Erminie Huntress Lantero (New York: Charles Scribner's Sons, 1934, 1958). A significant precursor of Bultmann and the "no quest" view was Martin Kähler, *The So-Called Historical Jesus and the Historic,*

Biblical Christ, trans. and ed. Carl E. Braaten (1st pub. in German, 1896; Philadelphia: Fortress, 1964).

22 Shirley Jackson Case, *Jesus: A New Biography* (Chicago: Chicago University Press, 1927).

23 A. M. Hunter, *The Work and Words of Jesus*, rev. edn. (Philadelphia: Westminster Press, 1973); T. W. Manson, *The Servant Messiah* (Grand Rapids, MI: Baker Book House, 1953); Vincent Taylor, *The Life and Ministry of Jesus* (Nashville, TN: Abingdon Press, 1955); C. H. Dodd, *The Founder of Christianity* (New York: Macmillan, 1970).

24 Ernst Käsemann, *Essays on New Testament Themes*, trans. W. J. Montague, Studies in Biblical Theology (London: SCM Press, 1964), 15–47.

25 Käsemann *Essays*, 46.

26 Günther Bornkamm, *Jesus of Nazareth*, trans. Irene McLuskey and Fraser McLuskey, with James M. Robinson (New York: Harper & Brothers, 1960).

27 James M. Robinson, *A New Quest of the Historical Jesus*. Studies in Biblical Theology (London: SCM Press, 1959).

28 The phrase "third quest" with reference to Jesus research originated with N. T. Wright. See Stephen C. Neill and N. Thomas Wright, *The Interpretation of the New Testament, 1861–1986* (Oxford: Oxford University Press, 1988).

29 E. P. Sanders, *Jesus and Judaism* (Philadelphia: Fortress Press, 1985), 2.

30 Robert W. Funk et al. *The Parables of Jesus: A Report of the Jesus Seminar* (Sonoma: CA: Polebridge, 1988), p. xii.

31 John Dominic Crossan, ed., *Sayings Parallels: A Workbook for the Jesus Tradition* (Philadelphia: Fortress Press, 1986).

32 Robert W. Funk, Roy Hoover, and the Jesus Seminar, *The Five Gospels: The Search for the Authentic Words of Jesus* (New York: Macmillan, 1993); Robert W. Funk and the Jesus Seminar, *The Acts of Jesus: The Search for the Authentic Deeds of Jesus* (San Francisco: Harper-SanFrancisco, 1998).

33 Walter P. Weaver, "Forward: Further Reflections on the Continuing Quest for Jesus," in James H. Charlesworth and Walter P. Weaver, eds., *Images of Jesus Today*, Faith and Scholarship Colloquies 3, Florida Southern College (Valley Force, PA: Trinity Press International, 1994), p. xiv.

34 M. Eugene Boring, "The 'Third Quest' and the Apostolic Faith," in Jack Dean Kingsbury, ed., *Gospel Interpretation: Narrative-Critical and Social Scientific Approaches* (Harrisburg, PA: Trinity Press International, 1997), 237–52.

35 Dennis C. Duling shared the phrase "theologically neutral" with me in a telephone conversation and later on a handout for his course at Canisius College, RST 305, Life and Teaching of Jesus (Spring 1998).

36 Meier, *A Marginal Jew*, 1:1–2.

37 James H. Charlesworth, *Jesus within Judaism*, Anchor Bible Reference Library (New York: Doubleday, 1988); John Dominic Crossan, *The Historical Jesus: The Life of a Mediterranean Jewish Peasant* (San Francisco: HarperSanFrancisco, 1991); Bruce Chilton, *Rabbi Jesus* (New York: Doubleday, 2000).

38 Geza Vermes, *Jesus the Jew: A Historian's Reading of the Gospels* (London: William Collins Sons, 1973); *Jesus and the World of Judaism* (Philadelphia: Fortress Press, 1983); and *The Religion of Jesus the Jew* (Minneapolis: Fortress Press, 1993).

39 Dale C. Allison, *Jesus of Nazareth: The Millenarian Prophet* (Minneapolis: Fortress Press, 1998); Bart D. Ehrman, *Jesus: Apocalyptic Prophet of the Millennium* (Oxford: Oxford University Press, 1999); Paul Fredriksen, *Jesus of Nazareth, King of the Jews* (New York: Alfred Knopf, 1999).

40 Marcus Borg, *Jesus: A New Vision* (San Francisco: Harper & Row, 1987).

41 Meier, *A Marginal Jew*, passim.

42 N. T. Wright, *Jesus and the Victory of God*. (Minneapolis: Fortress Press, 1996).

43 Wright, *Jesus and the Victory of God*, 62.

44 For a more detailed discussion, see Meier, *A Marginal Jew*, 1:167–95.

45 Joachim Jeremias, *The Parables of Jesus*, rev. edn., trans. S. H. Hooke (New York: Charles Scribner's Sons, 1963); *The Lord's Prayer*, trans. John Reuman, Facet Books (Philadelphia: Fortress Press, 1964); and *The Eucharistic Words of Jesus*, trans. Norman Perrin (New York: Charles Scribner's Sons, 1966).

46 W. Barnes Tatum, *Jesus at the Movies: A Guide to the First Hundred Years*, revised and expanded edn. (Santa Rosa, CA: Polebridge, 2004); Adele Reinhartz, *Jesus of Hollywood* (Oxford: Oxford University Press, 2007).

47 The Jesus Film Project website, <http://www.Jesusfilm.org>.

48 The Box Office Mojo website, <http://www.boxofficemojo.com>.

Chapter 6

Jesus and Christological Diversity
(Since the Eighteenth Century)

Since its beginnings in the eighteenth century, the modern quest for Jesus as a historical figure has presupposed the traditional confession of Jesus as the Christ of God. Participants in the search appealed to their varied reconstructions of what Jesus was like historically both to challenge and to support the orthodox teachings about Jesus Christ as expressed through the traditional creeds and such doctrines as the Trinity, the Incarnation, and the Atonement. Therefore, alongside – and intersecting with – the historical quest for Jesus have emerged increasingly diverse Christological perspectives on Jesus.

Since the historical appearance of Jesus in first-century Roman Palestine, his interpreters have inescapably fashioned their stories and teachings about him from their own vantage points, taking their own interests and the interests of their audiences as of paramount importance. Just as Albert Schweitzer accused his nineteenth-century predecessors of making Jesus over in their own image, so in the twentieth and twenty-first centuries the importance of the social location for all interpreters of Jesus has become increasingly recognized, whether they be historians or theologians. Christian theology has traditionally grappled with two basic questions about Jesus: Who was he? What did he do? That is, questions about his person and his work. But these questions are now supplemented by another: Whose is he? Here is the question about the context of the interpreter – their culture, place, time, ethnicity, gender, class, sexual identity, ideology, theology.

Like the preceding chapter on the historical quest, this chapter on Christological diversity proceeds chronologically, but more dialectically, and moves from approaches to Christology in western contexts toward alternative ways of understanding and affirming Jesus as the Christ in more global settings. We begin where the Protestant Reformation and the Enlightenment began – in Germany.

Modern Protestant Theology: Liberalism (Nineteenth Century)

Modern Protestant theology begins with Friedrich Schleiermacher (1768–1834).[1] His father was a Reformed, or Calvinist, pastor and military chaplain, but his own early education involved Moravian schooling. At the University of Halle, a Lutheran institution, he studied the philosophy of Kant, among others, and developed a skepticism about many tenets of orthodox Christianity – such as Jesus' death as a vicarious atonement.

While a young hospital chaplain in Berlin, Schleiermacher moved in Romantic intellectual and literary circles – Romanticism being the name given to a diverse, cosmopolitan movement across Europe, whose representatives both appreciated the Enlightenment critique of religion but also sought meaning beyond the sterile rationality of that critique. Out of his association with the Romantic movement, Schleiermacher published his own defense of religion: *On Religion: Speeches to its Cultured Despisers* (1799).[2]

After a brief teaching stint at the University of Halle, Schleiermacher became the first theologian appointed to the faculty of the newly founded University of Berlin, where he served from 1810 until his death in 1834. Not surprisingly, given his own diverse Protestant background, he supported the co-operation and eventually the union in Prussia between the Reformed and the Lutheran churches that became the Evangelical Church.

Schleiermacher articulated his mature Christology in what has been recognized as the most important systematic exposition of Christian doctrine between John Calvin's *Institutes of the Christian*

Religion, in the sixteenth century, and Karl Barth's *Church Dogmatics*, in the twentieth. Schleiermacher first published *The Christian Faith* in 1821–2 (it was revised in 1830–1).[3]

Central to Schleiermacher's presentation was how he identified the essence of religion, thereby overcoming the distortion of religion as set forth by Enlightenment thinking. For him the essence of religion was neither rationality nor morality, neither knowing nor doing. Rather, religion was essentially "feeling," which he associated with the phrase "immediate self-consciousness."[4] Perhaps something of his own experience of Moravian piety and Romantic aestheticism enabled him to find a middle way between knowing and doing. However, by "feeling" he did not mean some ephemeral psychological state, but the pervasive human sense of being relatively dependent upon and relatively independent from that beyond oneself. Foundational to this awareness of relative dependence and relative independence was an awareness of being absolutely dependent. The "Whence" of this feeling of absolute dependence was God.

With this understanding of religion, Schleiermacher proceeded to compare Christianity with other religions, including Judaism and Islam, and gave this memorable description: "Christianity is a monotheistic faith belonging to the teleological type of religion, and is distinguished from other such faiths by the fact that everything in it is related to the redemption accomplished by Jesus of Nazareth."[5] Within this broader framework, Schleiermacher laid out his Christology under the traditional headings of "the person of Christ" and "the work of Christ." He addressed these topics, as he did all topics in his systematic presentation, by appealing to the Christian consciousness within the framework of his own view of religion.

Who was Jesus? What set Jesus apart from other humans was "the constant potency of His God-consciousness."[6] Schleiermacher questioned the suitability of the traditional Christological categories of "one person" and "two natures" and considered these categories to be ill suited to express how "the God-consciousness in Him was absolutely clear and determined each moment, to the exclusion of all else." Schleiermacher also noted that the Protestant Reformers themselves uncritically carried forward the traditional creedal language about Christ; and he even expressed a preference for such simple New Testament affirmations as the Pauline "God was in Christ" (2 Cor. 5:19) and the Johannine "the Word became flesh" (John 1:14). Of the four gospels, Schleiermacher considered John, with its own "mysticism," the gospel most likely to be the composition of an eyewitness.

What did Jesus do? As the Redeemer, Jesus "assumes believers into the power of His God-consciousness."[7] The God-consciousness latent in human nature became activated and made dominant through the influence of Christ; and Christ continued to impart his blessedness by incorporating believers into his fellowship. Schleiermacher referred to this view of redemption as "mystical" and dismissed as "magical" those traditional views of atonement whereby the forgiveness of sins depended upon the sufferings and death of Christ independent of the believer's assumption into his fellowship.

Schleiermacher had already prepared his readers for his relegating to the very end of his work his treatment of the "The Divine Trinity."[8] As in his discussions of the person of Christ and the work of Christ, so here too he shied away from endorsing the traditional formulation of the doctrine. He identified two difficulties that needed future consideration and possible reformulation: the relation of the unity of the divine essence to the trinity of persons; and the designation of the first person as "Father" and the relation of the first person to the other two persons, the Son of God and the Holy Spirit.

The original subtitle of *The Christian Faith* (not indicated on the title page of the English translation), namely *According to the Principles of the Evangelical Church*, clearly identified the context out of which and for which Schleiermacher's masterwork was written: the Protestant church in Prussia, recently formed by the union between the Reformed and the Lutheran churches. Thus the subtitle itself signaled that the work would explore the religious self-consciousness in accordance with the doctrines of the Evangelical church.

Among the last of the nineteenth-century German liberal theologians was Adolf von Harnack (1851–1930).[9] He was born of Prussian Lutheran parents in Dorpat, then in East Prussia, now in

Estonia. His father was a professor of church history and taught preaching at the local Lutheran university. Harnack's own advanced studies carried him to the University of Leipzig, where in 1875 he began his own teaching career before moving to the University of Giessen, then to the University of Marburg, and finally to the University of Berlin, in 1888. Over his lifetime, Harnack received many recognitions: election to the Prussian Academy of Sciences; appointment to the directorship of the Royal Library in Berlin; conferral of a knighthood by Kaiser Wilhelm II; and offers to join the faculty of Harvard University, which he declined.

Church history became Harnack's chosen theological field. He was committed to the historical-critical method and to the academic freedom to pursue what he later called "scientific theology." His monumental three-volume *History of Dogma* (1885, 1887, 1889; seven volumes in English translation) popularized the phrase "the Hellenization of Christianity."[10] He developed the thesis that the simple teaching of Jesus had been transformed into a system of dogma by the emerging church through the influence of the Greek spirit – Greek language and Greek philosophy.

At the turn of the new century, in 1899–1900, at the University of Berlin, he delivered a series of lectures on "The Essence of Christianity." These lectures, published in English under the title *What Is Christianity?*,[11] soon became a publishing phenomenon throughout the Christian world. Harnack considered the core of Christianity to reside in the teachings of Jesus as set forth in the Synoptic Gospels, not in the Gospel of John. Accordingly, Harnack summarized this Gospel of Jesus under three headings: "The Kingdom of God and its coming"; "God the Father and the infinite value of the human soul"; "The higher righteousness and the commandment of love."[12] Although Harnack discussed the question of Christology in the published lectures, he concluded that Jesus understood himself and identified himself as "the Son of God" (appealing to Matthew 11:27, not to passages in John). However, Jesus thereby simply indicated that he as the Son had knowledge of God the Father. Therefore, as discussed in more detail in his history of dogma, Harnack considered the traditional doctrines of the Trinity, the Incarnation, and the Atonement to represent developments along the pathway toward Hellenization.

Throughout his academic career, Harnack was also concerned with defining the social mission of the German Evangelical churches, or the limits of such. However, in the United States, a "social gospel" had flowered in the latter half of the nineteenth century as churches strove to apply the gospel to the changed circumstances of modern, industrial society. The Methodist Episcopal Church, in 1908, became the first Protestant denomination to adopt a "Social Creed."[13] This statement appealed to the "Golden Rule" (from Jesus) and the "mind of Christ" (from Paul) as the bases for social reform in such areas as arbitration in labor disputes, safety in the workplace, and living wages for workers.

A leading advocate of social Christianity was Walter Rauschenbusch (1861–1918), whose father was a German Lutheran pastor who came to the United States to work among German immigrants, taught German at Rochester Theological Seminary, and became a Baptist. The younger Rauschenbusch himself attended Rochester, with intermittent periods of study in Germany where he imbibed the views of such nineteenth-century German theologians as Schleiermacher and Harnack. Rauschenbusch's own awakening to the social ills of modern life occurred during an extended pastorate at the Second German Baptist Church in the "Hell's Kitchen" section of New York City, 1886–97.

Rauschenbusch later joined the faculty at the Rochester Theological Seminary and expressed his advocacy for a social gospel through his many writings. But his *A Theology for the Social Gospel* (1917)[14] reinterpreted traditional theological categories systematically. As with Jesus, his overriding theological category was the "the Kingdom of God," which he interpreted to mean humankind organized in love, under the will of God. As the principal end of God, the kingdom was the purpose for which the church existed.

Christologically, Rauschenbusch acknowledged that the social gospel was less concerned with the metaphysical issues related to the three persons of the Trinity and the relation of the divine and the human natures in the Incarnation than with the progressive social incarnation of God. Thus Rauschenbusch described Jesus as the "Initiator of the Kingdom of God."[15] By virtue of Jesus' personality and through his life, his teachings, and his death, Jesus initiated God's reign. Rauschenbusch also acknowledged that the social gospel was less interested in the traditional ways of explaining Jesus' death as an atonement – whether ransom or satisfaction – than in answering three "how" questions: How did Jesus bear the sins of humans? How did Jesus' death affect God? How did his death affect humans?[16] First, Jesus bore at least six categories of the sins of organized society that were related to the sins of participating individuals: religious bigotry; graft and political power; corruption of justice; mob action; militarism in war; and class contempt. Secondly, the crucifixion of Jesus affected God through God's presence in Jesus' personality, his consciousness, and his experience. Thirdly, therefore, the crucifixion affected humans through its reconciling and redemptive power: by demonstrating the power of sin over humans; by disclosing the power of God's love; and by reinforcing the prophetic religion exhibited in the lives of the prophets and Jesus.

The optimism and sense of cultural progress generated by the technological developments of the nineteenth century died in the trenches on the western front in Europe in World War I (1914–18). The confidence in human progress reflected in and reinforced by liberal theology was also shattered. Within a generation, civilization had experienced a second death epitomized by the genocidal horrors in Europe and Asia associated with World War II (1939–45). But Protestant theology had already begun to speak in multiple voices. No voice has been more influential than the voice of the Swiss theologian Karl Barth. His initial call for theology and the church to recognize God as sovereign resulted in a movement initially identified as "dialectical theology," but later called "neo-orthodoxy."

Modern Protestant Theology: Neo-Orthodoxy (Twentieth Century)

Karl Barth (1886–1968) was born in Basel, Switzerland. His grandfathers and his own father had been Reformed pastors.[17] Barth studied the then fashionable liberal theology in the German universities of Berlin, Tübingen, and Marburg. Subsequently he served ten or so years, 1911–21, as a Reformed pastor in the Swiss parish of Safenvil.

He later recalled how his disillusionment with theological liberalism began in 1914 when he saw on a public statement supporting Germany's war aims the names of theologians among whom were those of his own former teachers, including Adolf von Harnack. As a response, he wrote a commentary on Paul's Epistle to the Romans (1919, revised 1922), wherein he argued that the God revealed in Jesus Christ challenged all attempts to ally God with human culture and human achievement.[18]

Barth returned to academic life in 1921, teaching theology at Göttingen and Münster before moving to Bonn, where he was teaching when Hitler came to power in the early 1930s. Barth joined others in protesting Nazi control over the German Evangelical Church by drafting the so-called "Barmen Declaration," in May 1934, and creating the "Confessing Church." This statement contained uncompromising words about the one to whom the church and Christians owed their allegiance: "Jesus Christ, as he is attested to us in Holy Scripture, is the one Word of God whom we have to hear, and whom we have to trust and obey in life and in death."[19] Shortly thereafter, Barth refused to pledge loyalty to the Führer. He was removed from his academic position and returned to Switzerland, where he taught at the University of Basel from 1935 until his retirement in 1962.

Both Barth's 1922 commentary on Paul's Epistle to the Romans and the 1934 "Barmen Declaration" signaled his opposition to identifying God or Christ with human institutions and culture. He had already published, in 1932, the first half-volume (volume 1, part 1) of his projected multi-volume systematic theology, *Church Dogmatics*.[20] The title itself indicated that he considered theology to be the language of the church, and dogmatics to be the theological discipline by which the church tested her language about God. At Barth's death in 1968 he had completed only four of the projected five volumes, but these four had appeared in thirteen parts, or bindings, which represented nearly 10,000 pages.

Although schooled in nineteenth-century theology, Barth considered the liberal theological tradition to have been too anthropocentric and too willing to accommodate Christian truth to the modern demands of worldly reason. He again emphasized the traditional theological category of the Word of God. Indeed, the first part of volume 1 of his *Church Dogmatics* bore the title *The Doctrine of the Word of God*.[21] For Barth, the Word of God as God's self-communication to humankind comes in threefold form: as preached, within the church; as written, in scripture, and as revealed, in Jesus Christ as God's Son. This last move identifying Jesus Christ as God's self-revelation presupposed by scripture and by the church makes Barth's theology radically Christocentric. For Barth, both natural theology and philosophy were considered inappropriate handmaidens for Christian theology. "Religion" as a word and as a phenomenon became an outcast beyond the pale of God's self-revelation.[22]

Barth's intention to turn nineteenth-century liberal theology on its head also became apparent in his placement and treatment of the doctrine of the Trinity. Whereas Schleiermacher had confined consideration of the Trinity to the concluding pages of *The Christian Faith*, Barth explored the Trinity in the very first half-volume of his *Church Dogmatics*. In characteristic Barthian fashion, this exploration involved his engagement with theologians who had preceded him; but he agreed with the Protestant Reformers that the doctrine was consistent with scripture. For Barth, God is of one essence, but three in one, the Father (Revealer), the Son (Revelation), and the Holy Spirit (Revealedness). However, he preferred to speak of the three not as "persons," but as "modes" or "modes of existence."[23] Thus Barth's systematic theology moved within the framework of traditional orthodox teaching on the Trinity as expressed in the creeds formulated at Nicaea (325) and Constantinople I (381). But his reading of scripture led him to side with Roman Catholicism, not Eastern Orthodoxy, in affirming the procession of the Holy Spirit from the Father and the Son as articulated in the *Filioque* clause.[24]

Barth's treatment of the Incarnation appeared in the second part of the first volume of *Church Dogmatics*: *The Doctrine of the Word of God*. Here Barth provided his answer to the traditional

Christological questions about the person and work of Jesus Christ, although he considered the traditional two questions to be an unnecessary expansion of the single question: Who is Jesus Christ? Barth affirmed that Jesus Christ as "the eternal Word of God chose, sanctified, and assumed human nature and existence into oneness with Himself, in order thus, as very God and very man, to become the Word of reconciliation spoken by God to man."[25] Barth's abbreviated answer to the Christological question became the phrase, "very God and very man," derived from the "two natures" definition formulated at Chalcedon I (451).[26] Barth understood the creedal phrase to be a description of Jesus Christ based on the "incarnation" verse from the Gospel of John: "And the Word was made flesh" (John 1:14).

Barth's more expansive answer to the Christological question above, with its reference to "the Word of reconciliation," anticipated the four parts that constitute the fourth volume of *Church Dogmatics*: *The Doctrine of Reconciliation*. Within this broader context, how did Barth understand the reconciliation between God who so loved the world and the world that was so loved? How did he understand the atonement effected by Jesus Christ who as very God and very man appeared as the sole mediator between God and humankind? Barth can ask these questions using the Latin phrasing popularized by Anselm centuries ago: *Cur Deus Homo?* (Why did God become human?). Although Barth did not develop a satisfaction view of the atonement, he did use substitutionary language to describe what occurred on the cross: "What took place is that the Son of God fulfilled the righteous judgment on us men by Himself taking our place undergoing the judgment under which we had passed."[27]

However, for Barth the atonement presupposed the eternal covenant between God and humankind, once broken by humanity, but now fulfilled by Jesus Christ. In the beginning, God in freedom and love elected humankind for salvation and elected Jesus Christ the Son, the God–Man, to suffer the penalty for all humanity, on behalf of every human transgressor. So Jesus Christ, the Lord as Servant, humbled himself by becoming one with his fellow humans and dying in their place. Then Jesus Christ, the Servant as Lord, was resurrected by God the Father.

Here Barth, as a theologian in the Reformed tradition, provocatively redefined John Calvin's teaching of double predestination whereby God through his absolute decree distinguished between the elect and the reprobate, by consigning the former to eternal blessedness and the latter to eternal damnation. Barth's redefinition has been read by some theologians as implying a doctrine of universal salvation.

Barth also belonged to those theologians, such as Rudolf Bultmann, discussed in the previous chapter, who adopted a no quest attitude toward the historical figure of Jesus. He was committed to the full humanity of Jesus, even as he was to Jesus' full divinity; but the truth of revelation was communicated through scripture, not through critical historical research into the life of Jesus.

Christian theology exhibited greatest ferment among Protestants in the nineteenth and early twentieth centuries. However, in each of these centuries, under the aegis of the Roman Catholic Church, great councils were held bearing the name of its sponsorship and location: Vatican I (1869–70) and Vatican II (1962–5). I now turn to a consideration of Roman Catholic theology during these two centuries.

Modern Roman Catholic Theology: Two Vatican Councils (Nineteenth and Twentieth Centuries)

Protestant theology in the nineteenth century, especially in Europe, had responded to the Enlightenment critique of traditional Christian teaching about Jesus as the Christ by challenging and reformulating the creedal-based doctrines of the Trinity, the Incarnation, and the Atonement. However, the Roman Catholic Church aggressively defended itself and its traditional teaching. Pope Pius IX (1846–78) promulgated *The Syllabus of Errors* (1864), an encyclical that condemned eighty errors of thinking ranging from absolute rationalism to modern liberalism. Pius IX subsequently convened Vatican 1 to address the issue of authority within the Church.[28] On July 18, 1870, the council explicitly confirmed the implicitly held doctrine of papal infallibility. In 1879

Pius' papal successor, Leo XIII (1878–1903), declared Thomas Aquinas to be the official philosopher and theologian of the church. Through such thinkers as the French Catholics Jacques Maritain (1882–1973) and Étienne Gilson (1884–1978) Thomism experienced a revival early in the twentieth century.

Vatican II had a very different agenda than its nineteenth-century predecessor. Called by Pope John XXIII the Second Vatican Council was charged with bringing the Catholic Church into the modern era. The council became the twenty-first ecumenical council, insofar as non-Catholic Christian representatives and representatives of other faiths were welcomed and included as official observers. The most venturesome Catholic theologian of the mid-twentieth century was also the theologian whose influence shines through several conciliar pronouncements: Karl Rahner (1904–84).[29]

Rahner was born into a Catholic family in Freiburg, Germany. He became a Jesuit, and his later writings reflected an Ignatian sensibility in the Jesuit dictum, "Finding God in all things." He was ordained to the priesthood in 1932 and studied for a doctorate in philosophy at Freiburg, where he studied with the German philosopher Martin Heidegger. He wrote his dissertation related to a statement in Thomas Aquinas' *Summa Theologiae* and developed a Christian anthropology using insights from Heidegger and Aquinas, among others. His dissertation was rejected for not being Catholic enough – perhaps too much Heidegger, too little Aquinas. However, his conceptual synthesis became the philosophical framework for how he did theology. In 1937 Rahner began teaching theology at the University of Innsbruck. He spent most of the war years based in Vienna, and after the war rejoined the theological faculty in Innsbruck.

Karl Rahner, the Catholic Jesuit, and Karl Barth, the Reformed Protestant, make for an interesting comparison. Whereas Barth called Protestant Christianity back to its Reformation origins through the threefold Word of God. Rahner challenged Roman Catholicism to confront the changed world by recasting the traditional ways of viewing, approaching, and speaking about Christianity into modern idiom. Whereas Barth limited God's revelation to Jesus Christ, Rahner considered the created world as an arena for God's grace and self-communication with human beings. Whereas Barth became the author of a massive systematic theology, Rahner preferred to tackle individual issues such as those discussed in his extended series of essays published in English as *Theological Investigations* – on such topics as the immaculate conception and the assumption of Mary, the Trinity and the future of Christology.

Because of Rahner's commitment to exploring edgy topics, he stayed in trouble with church authorities throughout the decade of the 1950s. Only Pope John XXIII's appointment of him as a theological "expert" for Vatican II in 1962 resulted in his avoiding being censured. After teaching at Munich and then at M?nster for a decade, he formally retired in 1971.

In 1978 Rahner published his *Foundations of Christian Faith*, which represented his most comprehensive and systematic presentation of his theology. Within the theological and literary setting of this work, chapter 6, titled "Jesus Christ," focused on his own distinctive Christological reflections in dialogue with the traditional teachings of the church.[30]

At the outset of the chapter, he distinguishes between two principal approaches to Christology. First, he says, there have been Christologies, "from above," or descending Christologies. This approach begins in all eternity with the divine Trinity, and the Son descends upon the world as the pre-existent Logos in the person of Jesus. This is the approach of Nicaea and Chalcedon – and Karl Barth. Second, there have been Christologies "from below," or ascending Christologies. This approach begins with the human figure of Jesus and ascends toward God. This is the approach assumed by many participants in the historical quest for Jesus and by representatives of nineteenth-century Protestant theology. This is also the approach taken by representatives of twentieth-century theology such as the Protestants Jürgen Moltmann (b. 1926) and Wolfhart Pannenberg (b. 1928) and the Catholic Edward Schillebeeckx (b. 1914).

Although Rahner's Christological reflections incorporate both descending and ascending approaches, he identified his own distinctive approach as "transcendental Christology." He said that "a transcendental Christology takes its starting point in the experiences which man always and inescapably has."[31] In what follows, I consider a series of questions related to Rahner's Christology. What was his philosophical- theological understanding of the human situation in the world that presupposed his Christology? How did he deal with the doctrine of the Trinity? What about the person and work of Jesus, including the doctrines of the Incarnation and the Atonement?

What was Rahner's philosophical-theological understanding of the human situation in the world that provided the setting for his Christology? For Rahner, humans existentially are "transcendent" beings. They are persons who have the God-given capacity to become more than they are by asking ultimate questions, receiving ultimate answers, and making choices freely in the presence of the Absolute Mystery – experienced and known by Christians as "God." Since all persons are called by God and have been graced by God with the ability to respond to God's self-communication, humans give evidence of hearing and heeding God's call when they live in righteousness and with love of their neighbor. For such a person, Rahner coined the phrase "anonymous Christian." This notion became Catholic teaching through Vatican II declarations that Rahner explained by saying that "someone who has no concrete, historical contact with the explicit preaching of Christianity can nevertheless be a justified person who lives in the grace of Christ."[32]

How does Rahner deal with the Trinity? Even before explicating his transcendental Christology, he reflected on the doctrine of the Trinity.[33] He observed how the words traditionally used are themselves problematical – especially the category of "person," which today designates a center of individual consciousness distinct from others. Rahner also found the psychological theory of the Trinity, first employed by Augustine, to be less than helpful. Nonetheless, he found "real meaning" in the doctrine because it conveyed the sense that God as the incomprehensible ground of human existence was also the God who desired to be close to humans in their spiritual depths. Rahner seemingly preferred to identify the Father, the Son, and the Holy Spirit not as "persons," but as "modes of presence."

How does Rahner deal with the incarnation? In anticipation of his consideration of Jesus as a human figure, he asked the question based on John 1:14: "What does it mean to say, 'God became Man.'?"[34] Rahner also found fault in the wording of the Chalcedonian formula of one person, two natures, because this talk of two natures undercut the claim of Jesus' having been fully human. So Rahner introduced the New Testament notion of the *kenosis*, or self-emptying of God, so that God as Logos – as God's self-revelation – dispossessed himself and became human (see Phil. 2:5–11). As Rahner said, "The man Jesus must be the self-revelation of God through who he is and not only through his words, and this he really cannot be if precisely this humanity were not the expression of God."[35]

The importance for Rahner's tweaking the Chalcedonian formula of the incarnation to underscore Jesus' humanity became apparent in his lengthy discussion of issues related to the historical figure of Jesus – appropriate for a Christology from below.[36] In presenting an overview of what Jesus was like before his resurrection, Rahner acknowledged his indebtedness to the exegetical and historical conclusions of scholars involved in life-of-Jesus research.

Rahner's own stated assumptions reflect those of the new quest: methodological possibility and theological legitimacy. Methodologically, he denied the possibility of writing a biography of Jesus but affirmed the ability to make probable historical judgments about Jesus, his words, his deeds, and his death. Theologically, he considered it not only legitimate but necessary to establish continuity between Jesus as the Christ and Jesus as a historical figure.

But more than this, Rahner boldly claimed that two minimal historical conditions must be met to establish an orthodox Christology. First, Jesus must have understood himself to be not just another prophet but the eschatological prophet, the absolute Savior. Secondly, Jesus' self-claim must have become credible when in faith one looks at the resurrection as that event that mediated the Savior in his total reality. Rahner proceeded to argue that both conditions had been met. Jesus had understood himself to be the eschatological prophet whose message about the imminent Kingdom of God was the definitive proclamation of salvation. In unity with his crucifixion, Jesus' resurrection became the event that validated his life and his death in freedom and obedience. Therefore Rahner's transcendental Christology from below had been demonstrated to be an orthodox Christology. Nonetheless, he concluded his chapter on "Jesus Christ" by reviewing the classical views of Christology and soteriology, by noting certain limits to related dogmatic statements, and by considering new ways to approach an orthodox Christology.

Among the two hundred or so Catholic theologians who served as "experts" at Vatican II was not only Karl Rahner but also his German countryman Joseph Ratzinger, who became Pope Benedict XVI, elected in 2005. Two years later, there appeared in twenty-two languages around the world a book by Benedict that bore the title *Jesus of Nazareth: From the Baptism in the Jordan to the Transfiguration*.[37] This first of a projected two volumes represents the pope's personal retelling of the Jesus story in a harmonizing format, based on the Synoptic Gospels with an occasional chapter devoted to themes from the Gospel of John. Of particular interest was Benedict's foreword to the book, which acknowledges how the Catholic Church in 1943, during the century between the Vatican councils, had finally embraced historical-critical methodology as delineated in the encyclical *Divino Afflante Spiritu*. Thus Karl Rahner could appeal to such exegetical scholarship in doing his theology.

Beyond Liberalism and Neo-Orthodoxy: Process Theology (into the Twenty-First Century)

Although Karl Barth emerged as the dominant Protestant theologian of the first half of the twentieth century, there were other continental theologians associated with him who made their mark contemporaneously with him. Each made his own contribution to theological discourse, including talk about Jesus as the Christ.

Dietrich Bonhoeffer (1906–45), who participated with Barth in the establishment of the Confessing Church, wrote *The Cost of Discipleship* (1937).[38] Based on Jesus' Sermon on the Mount (Matt. 5–7), these reflections popularized succinct phrases for alternative ways of following Jesus: either the disciplined path of "costly grace." or the way of "cheap grace" – forgiveness without sacrifice. After a brief visit to New York City in 1939, Bonhoeffer refused the protective asylum offered by Union Theological Seminary and returned to join his fellow Germans in their opposition to Adolf Hitler and the Third Reich. He was arrested and imprisoned for participation in an assassination plot against the Führer. He was hanged on April 9, 1945. Published after his death, Bonheoffer's *Letters and Papers from Prison* (1953) contained tantalizing statements about a "world come of age," "the suffering God," and Jesus as "the man for others."[39]

Paul Tillich (1886–1965), like Barth, had taught in German universities before losing his teaching post when the Nazis came to power. In 1933 he left Germany for the United States at the urging of theologian Reinhold Niebuhr and joined Niebuhr on the faculty of Union Theological Seminary. Tillich later enjoyed professorial careers at Harvard and the University of Chicago. Among his many writings was his masterful three-volume *Systematic Theology* (1951, 1957, 1963)[40] that correlated existential questions with theological answers. Tillich spoke of God as the "Ground of Being" and Jesus Christ as the bearer of the "New Being."

Rudolf Bultmann (1884–1976), whom we have already considered in the preceding chapter, remained in Germany teaching at the University of Marburg throughout World War II. In 1941, during the early stages of the conflict, he published a provocative essay that after the war set the theological agenda for a generation, "The New Testament and Mythology."[41] As had Tillich, so Bultmann also returned to the nineteenth-century liberal objective of making Christianity understandable for the modern age. Both of them have therefore been described as promoting an agenda beyond liberalism and beyond neo-orthodoxy – sometimes identified as post-liberalism.

What was Bultmann's agenda? He believed that scientific and technological advances had resulted in a dramatic shift to a modern worldview sharply different from the ancient three-story mythological worldview reflected in the New Testament. He claimed that modern people could no longer in good faith accept as credible those mythological details integral to the Jesus story: his virgin birth, his miracles, his substitutionary atonement, his resurrection from the dead, his ascension, and his so-called second coming. Thus the question of Bultmann's agenda gave way to another question: Did the *kerygma*, or proclamation, of salvation through Jesus Christ still have meaning in the modern world? Bultmann claimed that it still had meaning only if the text was demythologized through existential interpretation.

Using the categories of Martin Heidegger's existentialist philosophy, Bultmann understood the human situation to be a matter of either continuing to live inauthentically, based on the ephemeral "stuff" of this world, or realizing authentic existence based upon God through faith in Jesus Christ. Although Bultmann understood "faith" in Jesus Christ to be a person's "original possibility of authentic existence," he claimed that authentic existence was a possibility only through the existential act of responding to the *kerygma* of Jesus Christ. Only Jesus could save! Thus Bultmann had reduced Christology to soteriology, but his soteriology was centered in Jesus Christ.

Bultmann was caught in a pincer between two sets of critics. Many traditional Christians responded to his proposal with outrage because he had denied what they considered to be central elements of Christian belief. Atheists chided him for clinging to the belief that only faith in Jesus Christ enabled one to live authentically. But that was Bultmann's position, and he stuck to it! Not even Bultmann's claim that the New Testament itself, in the writings of Paul and the Gospel of John, gave evidence of the Christ-event's being interpreted existentially was convincing to his conservative critics. Neither was his claim convincing that he was simply being a good Lutheran by affirming justification by faith.[42]

However, among those attracted to Bultmann's demythologizing proposal was the American scholar Schubert M. Ogden (b. 1928), then a recent doctoral graduate of the University of Chicago, and a future long-time member of the faculty at Southern Methodist University. In his *Christ Without Myth* (1961), Ogden identified a basic inconsistency between Bultmann's recognition that "faith" was a person's original possibility for authentic existence and Bultmann's claim that authentic existence, or salvation, was only possible in response to the *kerygma* of Jesus Christ.[43] By contrast, Ogden claimed that the ultimate basis for salvation was not faith in Jesus Christ but "the unconditioned gift and demand of God's love, which is the everlasting ground and end of all created things." Nonetheless, he continued by affirming that "the decisive manifestation of this love, however, is the event of Jesus of Nazareth, which fulfills and corrects all other manifestations and is the originative event of the church and its distinctive word and sacraments."[44] What Ogden intimated but did not elaborate on was his own understanding of God – a model derived from process theology.

Originating with the philosophy of the English mathematician and philosopher Alfred North Whitehead (1861–1947) and elaborated in a theological direction by the American philosopher Charles Hartshorne (1897–2000), this "new theism" emphasized becoming, not being.[45] This view of God came to be identified as pan-en-theism, to be distinguished from the classic Trinitarian monotheism, but not to be confused with pantheism.

Ogden spoke about God, by analogy to the human self, as the eminent Self both socially and temporally.[46] As the human self relates to the body, so God as the eminent Self relates to and interacts with the universe of other beings. But whether Ogden was speaking about God, or about Jesus Christ, or about other religions, the love of God was central to the matter at hand. Theologically, Ogden repeatedly underscored how "God is love" (1 John 4:8, 16), even "boundless love" (with reference to a Charles Wesley hymn).[47] Christologically, Ogden repeatedly declared Jesus to re-present God, to be the love of God made manifest, in other words, "Jesus means love."[48] Ogden supported his Christological claim not by appealing to the historical Jesus – which he considered inaccessible – but to the earliest layers of witness to Jesus embedded in the canonical texts. Ogden also pursues his argument on the centrality of God's love within the pluralistic setting of the world's religions in the title of another of his works: *Is There Only One True Religion or Are There Many?*[49] His answer can be surmised from the logic of his theological reflections: There can be more than one true religion to the extent that religions, including Christianity, reflect the universal love of God re-presented through Jesus Christ.

Liberation Theology: Latin America (into the Twenty-First Century)

On October 12, 1931 the colossal statue of Christ the Redeemer, which stands atop Corcovado Mountain overlooking Rio de Janeiro, was dedicated. With his arms open, but paradoxically cruciform, Jesus rises 120 feet above the 2,300 foot height of the mountain. Jesus as the Christ bears witness not only to Brazil's Christian past but to the Christian heritage of all Latin America – more specifically to the Roman Catholic Church that had historically dominated and culturally shaped the entire continent.

Nearly four decades later, in 1968, following Vatican II, the Latin American Episcopal Conference (CELAM) of the Roman Catholic Church at its meeting in Medellín, Colombia, adopted detailed declarations on justice and peace that called for reform throughout the South American continent politically, socially, and economically. Liberation theology was an answer to this call. The sharp socio-economic division between the haves and the have-nots served as the immediate context for advocating and doing liberation theology.

Gustavo Gutiérrez, OP (b. 1928), a Peruvian priest and university professor from Lima with a life-long commitment to the poor, has often been recognized as the founder of liberation theology and the movement engendered by it. His influential *A Theology of Liberation: History, Politics, and Salvation* appeared in 1971.[50] The subtitle itself indicated the sweeping scope of this volume.

In his book, Gutiérrez defined theology as reflection upon praxis – that is, reflection upon activity, activity lived in solidarity with the poor as summoned by the gospel of Jesus Christ.[51] From this understanding of theology and the theological task came the phrase that served as the watchword for the movement: "the preferential option for the poor." Accordingly, God in the scriptures and Jesus Christ in the New Testament exhibit a predilection for

Figure 8 Statue of Christ the Redeemer, overlooking Rio de Janeiro, Brazil, designed and assembled by Hector da Silva Costa and Paul Landowski (dedicated in 1931). *Reproduced by courtesy of Franck Camhi/ Shutterstock.com*

those who are economically impoverished and thereby often excluded from even the basic necessities of life. It's in the book!

Although a theology, and not specifically a Christology, this volume has at its center a chapter on "Liberation and Salvation" that concludes with a brief section on "Christ the Liberator."[52] What does it mean to be liberated or saved? In responding to this question, Gutiérrez observed that salvation had often been viewed futuristically as a cure for personal sin in this life and thus an assurance for the life beyond. He continued by noting that in recent times the essential meaning of salvation had been recovered with the recognition of salvation as a reality occurring within history now.

As articulated by Vatican II, salvation was acknowledged to be universally present for those beyond the church who had opened themselves to God and to others. Here are Karl Rahner's "anonymous Christians" who unknowingly act in accordance with the requirement of love, such as those depicted in Jesus' parable about the "least of these" (Matt. 25:31–46).

Gutiérrez also underscored how the church had recovered the meaning of salvation by identifying three levels of liberation, or salvation, in Christ.[53] First, there was liberation from situations of socio-economic oppression and marginalization. Secondly, there was an inner transformation of persons who thereby became equipped to live in the midst of great injustice. Thirdly, there was deliverance from sin; for sin separated persons from God and from each other and can only be eradicated by the redemptive love of Jesus Christ received by faith in communion with him and with one another. Thus, liberation theology carried forward not only the sacramental ministry of the church but pastoral care through small, lay-led base communities.

Not long after Gutiérrez's *A Theology of Liberation*, there appeared two volumes, each a Christology from a liberation point of view: *Jesus Christ the Liberator* (1972) by Leonardo Boff, OFM (b. 1938),[54] and *Christology at the Crossroads* (1976) by Jon Sobrino, SJ (b. 1938).[55]

Boff, a native of Brazil, became a Franciscan and a priest, and earned his doctorate in Germany at the University of Munich. He then returned to his homeland, where he committed himself to a life of teaching and work among the poor. The first edition of Boff's *Christology* was published during a period in Brazil's history when the word "liberation" itself was banned from use in communications media.

Sobrino was born in Barcelona, but at an early age entered the Jesuit order. He went to El Salvador, where he has spent most of his life, except for periods of study in the United States and in Frankfurt, where he received a doctorate in theology. Although working among the poor in El Salvador in treacherous times, Sobrino escaped the fate of his Archbishop Oscar Romero and other fellow priests, who were murdered at governmental initiative in the 1980s.

Both Leonardo Boff and Jon Sobrino developed their Christologies "from below." Both considered the historical figure of Jesus to be the appropriate starting point for a Christology of liberation. Each in his own fashion critically retraced Jesus' way to the cross and then continued beyond with his own critical reflections on Jesus as the Christ – including the traditional doctrines of the Incarnation and the Trinity.

Although liberation theology was begotten out of the Roman Catholic Church, the theology itself has been watched very carefully by the Vatican, and its practitioners on occasion have received official inquiries and reprimands. Two of the many areas of concern perceived over the last forty years have been deviations from a robust Christology, and misguided appeals to Marxist socio-economic analysis.

Pope John Paul II gave expression to the issue of Christology in his opening address for the CELAM gathering in Puebla, Mexico, on January 28, 1979.[56] He spoke about the frequent silence with regard to the divinity of Christ, and pointed to characterizations of Jesus considered inconsistent with church teaching – including Jesus as a political activist, as a fighter against Roman domination, and as a subversive from Nazareth.

Subsequently, Cardinal Joseph Ratzinger – then the Prefect of the Congregation for the Doctrine of the Faith, but now Pope Benedict XVI – released at the behest of Pope John Paul II a lengthy communication for pastors, theologians, and the faithful, dated August 6, 1984, on dangerous tendencies evident in a "Theology of Liberation."[57] These tendencies included the acceptance of the Marxist view of history as class conflict without recognizing the atheistic assumptions of Marxist ideology.

Nonetheless, liberation theology – in its many expressions – was no longer confined to Latin America, but was manifesting itself around the globe. A black liberation theology in the United States of America occurred independently of the kindred movement in Latin America. Here too, as with liberation theology in its varied forms, the Christological focus was less on orthodoxy and more on orthopraxis, or right practice, that takes into account the experiences of the oppressed.

Black Theology: The United States and Beyond (into the Twenty-First Century)

On December 1, 1955, with Rosa Parks' refusal to vacate her seat for a white man on a segregated city buses in Montgomery, Alabama, the resulting bus boycott initiated the twentieth-century protest movement for civil rights under the leadership of Martin Luther King, Jr. In June 1966, with the cry of "black power" by Stokely Carmichael in Greenwood, Mississippi, a new militancy both polarized and energized the struggle for black freedom against white racism.

Out of the civil rights and black power movements was begotten black liberation theology. The father was James H. Cone (b. 1938), a native of Arkansas, and a graduate with multiple degrees from Garrett-Evangelical Theological Seminary and Northwestern University. Before joining the faculty of Union Theological Seminary, New York City, Cone had already published *Black Theology and Black Power* (1969),[58] in which he developed the thesis that Christianity and black power were not antithetical, but rather black power was Jesus Christ's central message for twentieth-century America.

The very next year Cone came out with *A Black Theology of Liberation* (1970).[59] This volume represented a systematic theological exposition that followed traditional rubrics or headings including the content, the sources, and the norm of theology. The content was liberation: a biblical theme evident in God's deliverance of the Israel from Egypt (Exod. 19:4–5a) and underscored by Jesus' announced mission to the poor and the oppressed (Luke 4:18–19). Among the sources were dimensions of the community for whom this liberation theology was intended: black experience, black history, and black culture. Therefore, the norm of black theology revolved around the poles of scripture and the black community, at the center of which was Jesus as the black Christ.

However, what was anything but traditional about Cone's exposition was the colorful language whereby "black" became good, and "white" became bad. Sometimes "black" functioned as an ethnic signifier, but at other times it functioned symbolically for the oppressed and those who sided with the oppressed. Correspondingly, "white" sometimes functioned as an ethnic signifier but also functioned as that to be repudiated. It was Cone's uncompromisingly colorful and admittedly passionate language that both expressed his anger throughout the work and often elicited anger from readers in response to it. Throughout Cone attacked the way whites had used God-talk and artistic images of Jesus to obscure the gospel message of Jesus Christ's concern for black liberation – socially, economically, and politically. Cone expressed disdain for all those pictures of Jesus as "a blue-eyed honky" and called for black theologians to "dehonkify him."[60] In other writings, Cone explored the role in the liberation process of characteristically black music, the spirituals and the blues.[61]

More specifically, what does Cone say about God? About Jesus as the Christ? About salvation? Understandably, Cone colored God black insofar as God participates in the liberation of the oppressed. Although Cone referred by name to the doctrine of the Trinity, he identified each person according to function: God as Father identified with the oppressed peoples of Israel; God as Son became the Incarnate and Oppressed One so that all might be liberated; and the Holy Spirit, as the Spirit of the Father and the Son, continues to perform works of liberation today. Cone, of course, colored Jesus as the Christ black.[62]

In his discussion of Christology, Cone sounds like Karl Barth, on whose theology he wrote his doctoral dissertation, by affirming that theology begins and ends with Jesus Christ.[63] However, he went beyond Barth by stressing that black theology took seriously the historical Jesus and followed those new quest scholars like Ernst Käsemann and Günther Bornkamm who sought continuity between the historical Jesus and the Christ of faith. Thus Cone proceeded to demonstrate that the character of Jesus in the New Testament supported the claim that Jesus' entire life was bound up with the lowly through whom God acted for liberation: from his birth, his baptism, his temptation, and his ministry to his death and resurrection.

With his death and resurrection, Jesus the Oppressed One disclosed that God had vindicated him and was present in all dimensions of human liberation. The transition had been made from the historical Jesus to the black Christ. According to Cone, the work of Jesus as the black Christ – or salvation, or the kingdom of God – is still continuing as Christ comes to black people today liberating them from the effects of white racism.

In the midst of the "black power" and "black theology" furor of the early 1970s, two other book-length theological contributions appeared. By comparison to Cone's monographs, these two works reflected a different demeanor – even in their titles. Major J. Jones of Gammon Theological Seminary, in Atlanta, Georgia, published *Black Awareness: A Theology of Hope* (1971),[64] and in the same year J. Deotis Roberts of Howard University, Washington, DC, published *Liberation and Reconciliation: A Black Theology*.[65] But Albert B. Cleage, Jr., a United Church of Christ clergyman and pastor of the shrine of the Black Madonna in Detroit, Michigan, had already released a collection of his sermons. *The Black Messiah* (1969).[66] Cleage characterized Jesus as a black zealot, or revolutionary, seeking to lead a Black Nation to freedom, and contrasted Jesus with the apostle Paul, who pandered to white Gentiles.

Over the decades, African American theologians and proponents of black theology from the United States have interacted with representatives of kindred theologies from around the globe, including Latin America, Asia, and Africa. Along the way, James H. Cone has participated in many of these dialogues.[67] Deserving special notice was the establishment of the Ecumenical Association of Third World Theologians (EATWOT), which organized itself in Dar es Salaam, Tanzania, in 1976. The organization continues to gather regularly in different locales, particularly in Third World countries, and maintains a "Black Theology" link on its website.[68]

Feminist Theology: The United States and Beyond (into the Twenty-First Century)

In 1963 the publication of *The Feminine Mystique* by Betty Friedan became a harbinger of the twentieth-century women's movement, at least in North America.[69] The "mystique" referred to in her title was the spell cast upon women convincing them that their satisfaction in life came through child-bearing and house-keeping. The role of women in all areas of life soon became a subject for public discussion. By the end of 1966, Friedan had spurred the founding of the National Organization for Women (NOW), which would become and remains the largest civil rights organization in the United States, dedicated to equal opportunity and rights for women and equal partnership with men.

What became feminist theology emerged out of this growing concern for women's liberation from social structures and practices that subordinated females (patriarchy) and attitudes that favored males (androcentrism). The church, or churches, came under scrutiny from within with regard to the status and treatment of women – such as their eligibility for leadership and clerical ordination. Feminist theologians brought feminist perspectives to bear on all dimensions of church life, including the Bible, the liturgy, the traditional doctrines, and the language in which the latter were expressed. Of particular interest were those teachings related to Christology: the doctrine of God as Trinity, whereby the "Father" and the "Son" were clearly identified with masculine categories; the doctrine of the Incarnation, whereby God became human in Jesus but as male human by gender; and the doctrine of Salvation, whereby God saved humans through the life, death, and resurrection of the male Jesus.

Among the earliest feminist theologians was Mary Daly (b. 1928), an American Catholic, who earned doctorates in sacred theology and philosophy in Switzerland at the University of Fribourg.[70] She later reported that her study in Europe was necessitated by the fact that no Catholic institution in the United States would allow a woman to take a doctorate in sacred theology. She also reported on a visit she made while in Europe to the Second Vatican Council, on which occasion she was struck by the contrast in attire and demeanor between the brightly clad male prelates and the drably dressed nuns as the latter received Holy Communion in ant-like procession.

Upon Daly's return to the United States in 1966, she began her eccentric and tumultuous teaching and writing career at Boston College, where she completed *The Church and the Second Sex* (1968).[71] In this volume, she acknowledged how Jesus in the New Testament treated women with respect as persons; however, women did not fare so well with Paul and his ecclesiastical successors. Already the church appeared to her to be incorrigibly patriarchal and uncompromisingly androcentric. Her next two books, *Beyond God the Father: Toward a Philosophy of Women's Liberation* (1973) and *Gyn/ecology: The Metaethics of Radical Feminism* (1978) made it clear that she as a feminist had moved beyond the church, beyond God, and beyond Christianity.[72] By contrast, Virginia Ramey Mollenkott (b. 1932) and Letty M. Russell (1929–2007) represent Protestants who expressed their theological feminism in more traditional ways.

Mollenkott was born into a Plymouth Brethren family and, as an adult, joined the Evangelical Women's Caucus. With a doctorate in English literature from New York University, she taught for a number of years at William Patterson University of New Jersey, and used her hermeneutical skills for biblical interpretation. In her *Women, Men, and the Bible* (1977), she identified herself as a "biblical feminist."[73] She understood that each person of the Trinity exhibited masculine and feminine characteristics, and identified mutual submission, or partnership, as the normative pattern for relations between women and men (Eph. 5:21).

Russell was ordained in the United Presbyterian Church and served as a pastor in the East Harlem Protestant parish before earning graduate degrees at Union Theological Seminary and joining the faculty of the Yale Divinity School. In her *Human Liberation in a Feminist Perspective: A Theology* (1974), Russell claimed Jesus to be the representative of true humanity breaking into history. Jesus modeled servanthood, which presents a difficulty for oppressed peoples who have been forced to be servants.[74] Therefore, the problem with which the incarnation confronted women lay not in Jesus' maleness but in his servanthood. Russell conceded that sisterhood might be necessary as a step toward authentic partnership among peoples, but the goal remained being free for others in love and service.

One of the tasks of Christian feminists has been to reread critically the ancient literary sources and to reconstruct the beginnings of earliest Christianity in ways that do not highlight Jesus' "feminism" at the expense of Jewish patriarchal society so as to reinforce Christian anti-Judaism or anti-Semitism. No feminist theologian has made more of a contribution in this regard than Elizabeth Schüssler Fiorenza (b. 1938). She was educated in Germany prior to an academic career at the University of Notre Dame and the Harvard Divinity School. Her foundational historical investigations were: *In Memory of Her: A Feminist Theological Reconstruction of Christian Origins* (1983) and *Jesus: Miriam's Child and Sophia's Prophet: Critical Issues in Feminist Christology* (1994).[75]

Schüssler Fiorenza's reconstruction of Christian origins presupposed her discovery of "a feminist impulse" in pre-70 CE Judaism in the book of Judith and identified the Jesus movement within Judaism as a renewal movement.[76] The Jesus movement constituted a "discipleship of equals" whose praxis, or practice, was based on an understanding and experience of God as "all-inclusive love."[77] Schüssler Fiorenza documented in detail women who figured prominently in this renewal movement, and she even adapted her book title from Jesus' words addressed to the unnamed woman who had anointed him with oil that wherever the gospel was preached in the world what she did would be told "in memory of her" (Mark 14:3–9).[78]

Schüssler Fiorenza's feminist reinterpretation of Jesus not only affirmed him as Miriam's child but also identified him as Sophia's prophet (based on Jesus' words in Luke 7:35). She points out that Sophia, or wisdom, became a personification of the divine as woman. Thus Jesus here spoke of God as a woman whose prophet he was.[79] Although Schüssler Fiorenza disclaimed knowledge of how Jesus understood his impending death, she viewed his execution as "King of the Jews" to be the originating event for how his followers understood his death. Based not on the gospels but on earlier traditions preserved in Paul's letters, she identified the earliest interpretation of Jesus' death to be a confession, such as "God raised Jesus from the dead" (cf. 1 Cor. 6:14, 8:11, etc.). Given the prominence of women in the gospel resurrection stories, their absence in the early Pauline list of those to whom the resurrected Jesus had appeared must have been intentional (1 Cor. 15:3–5).[80]

The feminist theologian whose scholarship has probably represented the broadest range of subjects is Rosemary Radford Ruether (b. 1936). She received her doctorate from Claremont Graduate School in California, and later taught at Howard University, Washington, DC, and at Garrett-Evangelical Seminary, Evanston, Illinois.

Among Ruether's first forays into Christology was her survey of the historical origins of Christian anti-Judaism titled *Faith and Fratricide* (1974).[81] Herein she articulated and developed the thesis that Christian anti-Judaism developed theologically as "the left hand of Christology." That is, as emerging Christianity developed its Christological understanding of Jesus as the messiah who fulfilled Jewish messianic expectations, there also emerged a virulent anti-Judaic polemic that continued in the *adversus Judaeos* tradition of the Church Fathers and, in fact, throughout the subsequent history of the Christian church.

Rosemary Ruether also published possibly the first systematic presentation of a feminist theology, *Sexism and God-Talk: Toward a Feminist Theology* (1983).[82] In it, she follows the traditional theological headings, from creation to eschatology, and midway she introduces the chapter on Christology with a provocative question: "Can a male savior save women?" Ruether begins her exposition by acknowledging that the Christology defined as orthodoxy by the Council of Chalcedon in 451 resulted from and contributed to the patriarchalization of Christology and of Christianity. With the maleness of the historical Jesus exemplifying normative humanity, and with the incarnate maleness of the divine Logos, or Word, women were destined for exclusion from priestly leadership and social subordination. So again: Can a male savior save women?

To begin formulating a response, Ruether turns not to Christological doctrine but to the Jesus of the Synoptic Gospels – to his message and praxis. She discovers a parallel between Jesus' critique of the religious and social hierarchy in his day and the contemporary feminist critique. In prophet-like fashion, this Jesus not only challenged the privileged but also spoke and acted on behalf of the lowly and the marginalized. She refers to this Jesus as "liberator" and claims that his ability to speak as liberator resided not in his maleness but in his repudiation of the domination system. Jesus as the Christ appeared as the embodiment of a "new humanity, female and male," and disclosed the *"kenosis of patriarchy."* And Christ must not be confined to the past but continues in the Christian community in the personhood of the sisters and brothers.

Among Ruether's earliest writings is a perceptive essay that notes the awkward situation of black women who are caught between the racism of white males (and females) and the sexism of black males.[83] To the predicament of black women and their theological response I now turn.

Womanist Theology: The United States and Beyond (into the Twenty-First Century)

Womanist theology has become the designation for the theology about and practiced by African American women, especially in the United States, but by extension applicable to the theology of women of color worldwide.[84] The term "womanist" was taken over from the African American novelist Alice Walker, who reflects on this colloquial turn of phrase at length in her collection of essays, *In Search of Our Mothers' Garden: Womanist Prose* (1983). Walker even uses the expression to distinguish black feminists from other feminists: "Womanist is to feminist as purple is to lavender."[85]

The experiences of the black liberation movement and the women's liberation movement of the 1960s and 1970s created the socio-political context for black women to recognize that they had voices of their own. Although black women had expressed solidarity with their black brothers in opposing racism, and had expressed commonality with white feminists in opposing sexism, black liberationists often acted out the assumptions of male domination, and white feminists generally reflected the middle-class interests of the dominant white society. Therefore, black women had to contend with the triple jeopardy of sexism, racism, and classism. Those black women who assumed the responsibility of speaking theologically on behalf of themselves, the black community, and a common humanity, drew on their experiences as black women as a source for their theologizing and eventually identified themselves as womanists.

Among the first black women to question in print the apparent neglect of black women's concerns in black theology was Jacquelyn Grant (b. 1948). She received graduate degrees from Union Theological Seminary in New York City, was ordained an elder in the African Methodist Episcopal Church, and later taught systematic theology at the Interdenominational Theological Center in Atlanta, Georgia.

In her 1979 article, "Black Theology and the Black Woman," Grant audaciously challenged black theology and the black church to live up to their claim that liberation was the core message of the gospel by extending the liberation principle to include black women.[86] Although Grant also acknowledged in this article her theological differences with white feminism, she deferred to another occasion her views on that subject. That occasion came ten years later with the publication of her *White Women's Christ and Black Women's Jesus: Feminist Christology and Womanist Response* (1989).[87] This tantalizing title recalls the traditional distinction between the Christ of faith and the Jesus of history.

Grant developed a threefold typology of feminist Christologies. In evaluating particular feminist theologies she considered the writings, among others, of the feminist theologians I have already discussed. The first type, biblical feminism, which projected Jesus as the feminist, was exemplified by Virginia Ramey Mollenkott. The second and broadest type, liberation feminism, which projected Jesus as the liberationist, was exemplified by Letty Russell, Rosemary Radford Ruether, and Elisabeth Schüssler Fiorenza. The third type, rejectionist feminism, which repudiated Jesus as being unusable for feminist theology, was exemplified by Mary Daly. In Grant's own reflections, Grant observed that the greater the role scripture played in the construction of a feminist Christology, the greater the likelihood the theologian would affirm the traditional Christological definition of Chalcedon that Jesus was both divine and human.

Nonetheless, for Grant, the bottom-line inadequacy of feminist theology was that it was white and racist. She documented at length how the experience of black women in America has differed from the experience of white woman, both before and after slavery. Although Grant acknowledged that being white does not necessarily mean to be a racist, she affirmed that the feminist movement took on a racist character from the surrounding white racist society. Grant suggested that feminists should more accurately call themselves white feminists and that black feminists should, as was already being done, identify themselves as black womanists.

Whither womanist theology and Christology? From her perspective in the late 1980s, Grant made several points. First, she noted the pervasive use of the Bible by Christian black women who read the book out of their own experiences. Secondly, she highlighted the role and significance of Jesus as black women identified with him because he had identified with them, especially in their suffering. Thirdly, she understood black women, by and large, to believe Jesus to have been God incarnate, and that what mattered to them was not his maleness but his humanity. Therefore, for her it meant that Jesus as the Christ discovered in the experiences of black women was a black woman. Fourthly, Grant challenged womanist theologians to do constructive and liberating Christology.

In addition to Grant herself, other womanists who have engaged in significant Christological reflection include Delores S. Williams, *Sisters in the Wilderness: The Challenge of Womanist God-Talk* (1993),[88] and Kelly Brown Douglas, *The Black Christ* (1994).[89] Williams considers the traditional views on redemption and the atonement, all of which center on the cross of Jesus, but suggests that such theological views may be problematical due to the African American woman's lifelong experiences with "surrogacy" – taking on, or being forced to take on, tasks for others. Williams finds in the Synoptic Gospels, in Jesus' liberating words and liberating deeds (especially in Luke 4), how Jesus came to show the way to redemption based on a "ministerial vision" of wholeness among peoples, including women and men, and wholeness of body, mind, and spirit.[90] Similarly, Kelly Brown Douglas refers to the basic Christological statements of Nicaea and Chalcedon and notes how these creeds focus so on the incarnation that they diminish Jesus' ministry – his words and deeds during his lifetime.[91]

Before leaving our consideration of black, feminist, and womanist theologies, it must be noted that during the ten-year interval between 1979 and 1989 James H. Cone acknowledged in several settings his own failure to recognize early in his career the problem of sexism in church and society. Among these settings was the preface to the 1986 edition of his *Black Theology of Liberation*, which was reprinted in the twentieth anniversary commemorative edition in 1990. The latter edition also includes written responses to this formative work, two of which bear the names of Rosemary Radford Ruether and Delores S. Williams.

Theology in the Third World: Latin America, Africa, Asia (into the Twenty-First Century)

As Jesus was carried into the twenty-first century, Christianity itself was experiencing a significant shift geographically and demographically. Although originating in Asia near the intersections of Asia with Africa and Europe, Christianity has historically been identified with Europe and later with North America. However, in recent times, the center of gravity for Christianity as a world religion has increasingly moved southward – toward Latin America, Africa, and parts of Asia.

After World War II, countries on these three continents came to be called the Third World. This designation originally identified them as being economically underdeveloped or developing and as being politically non-aligned with either the First World bloc of capitalist nations led by the United States or the Second World bloc of communist countries under the Soviet Union. Although the political world has changed and the economic status of some countries has improved, the phrase "the Third World" continues as a way of indicating the poorer areas still recovering from colonial domination, although the expressions "two-thirds world" and "post-colonial world" have also been used. What has been going on in these countries theologically and Christologically?[92]

Latin America had been conquered and settled in the seventeenth century by Spain and Portugal with a division of territory sanctioned by the Roman Catholic Church. The Protestant nineteenth-century missionary movement that accompanied colonization by the European powers, especially in Africa and Asia, also produced an era of co-operation among competing Protestant denominations and missionary societies.

The World Missionary Conference, held in Edinburgh in 1910, has often been identified as the beginning of the ecumenical movement that eventuated in the creation of the World Council of Churches (WCC), which first met in Amsterdam in 1948. The WCC today describes itself as "a fellowship of churches which confess the Lord Jesus Christ as God and Savior, according to the scriptures, and therefore seek to fulfill together that common calling to the glory of the one God, Father, Son and Holy Spirit."[93]

The WCC, with its headquarters in Geneva, brings together more than 340 denominational bodies, from more than a hundred countries, representing some 560 million Christians. Whereas many Orthodox churches are included among the participants, Catholic ecclesiology has not allowed the Roman Catholic Church to belong to the WCC or other ecumenical organizations mentioned here.

In the years before and since the creation of the World Council of Churches, families of Reformation-era Protestant churches have organized themselves with periodic gatherings, including the Lutheran World Federation (1947), the Worldwide Association of Reformed Churches (1875), the Anglican Communion (nineteenth century) and the World Methodist Council (1881). In addition, continents also have umbrella organizations for national councils and churches in their areas, including the All-Africa Conference of Churches (1957), the Christian Conference of Asia (1959), and the Latin American Council of Churches (1982).

Insofar as the Christological statements hammered out by the fourth- and fifth-century Councils of Nicaea I, Constantinople I, Ephesus, and Chalcedon were adapted by and incorporated into the articles of belief developed by the Protestant churches, the traditional formulations of the Triune God, Jesus the Son of God as divine and human, and the salvific effect of his death have found their way into post-colonial, global Christianity. Although Jesus as the Christ of creedal Christianity does not in itself represent post-Enlightenment theologizing, Jesus does offer different "faces" within the cultural and confessional contexts of Latin America, Africa, and Asia.

Established in 1911, the Catholic Foreign Mission Society of America – the Maryknoll Fathers, Brothers, Sisters, and lay Missioners – also focuses upon missionary work in Latin America, Africa, and Asia. The society, through its publishing venture Orbis Books, encourages dialogue and makes available literature related to Christian belief and practice on these continents. The editors of and contributors to these publications on the "faces" of Jesus represent an ecumenical spectrum.

José Miguez Bonino, a Methodist from Argentina, has edited a diverse collection of essays on the "faces of Jesus" in Latin America.[94] The emergence of "Christ the liberator," who sides with the poor, whom I have already discussed, receives due recognition. This Christ stands over against two classic visual images of Christ, described as images of oppression and evident throughout Latin America. These two representations are the "conquered Christ," who passively suffers, and the "celestial Christ," or the Pantocrator, who rules from on high. The observation is also made about the inseparable presence and pervasiveness in Catholic churches of visual images of Christ, the Son, and his mother, the Blessed Virgin. By contrast, Protestant preaching holds out a personal Christ that one gets to know as a presence and a friend. Pentecostals, in particular, call upon this Jesus by personal name as one who heals and confers power through the Spirit. Nonetheless, there are also operative so-called "defective" Christological models such as "the Santa Claus Christ," who brings presents, and the "passport Christ," who punches your ticket to heaven.

Robert J. Schreiter, CPPS, although an American Catholic, has edited the volume of essays on the "faces of Jesus" in Africa.[95] Because of its Catholicization centuries ago, Latin America displays a homogeneity alien to African Christianity. The contributors to this volume on African Christianity, male and female, come primarily from French-speaking West Africa and English-speaking East Africa. In addition to Catholic and Protestant churches that carry forward their European-derived traditions, there are many, many independent churches and church movements in Africa that have broken away from their European roots. But whatever the origin, African theology today reflects two orientations. The first is enculturation – expressing Christian thought and practice in and through distinctively African culture. A number of Christological profiles present themselves that reflect African values: "Jesus as ancestor"; "Jesus as elder brother"; "Jesus as chief"; "Jesus as master of initiation"; and "Jesus as healer." The second theme in African theology today is liberation. Therefore, once again, there surfaces the Christological model of "Jesus as liberator." In the African setting, a distinction is made between South African black theology and simply African liberation theology. The former, centered around race and apartheid, has kinship with North American black theology. The latter, with broader interests of gender and class, has kinship with Latin American liberation theology and provides more of a Christological basis for women who are calling for emancipation.

R. S. Sugirtharajah, a Sri Lankan theologian who teaches in England at the University of Birmingham, has edited a volume on the "faces of Jesus" in Asia.[96] These essays are written for Asian Christians, to assist them in understanding the significance and relevance of Jesus within the Asian context of religious pluralism and debilitating poverty. Jesus is often compared to Krishna and the Buddha. Within this Asian setting, Jesus is once again considered as "liberator," with concern for the poor; but now "the Buddha and the Christ" are also profiled together as "mediators of liberation." Jesus is also considered in relation to the yin/yang of Chinese thought and also examined within an Islamic context. Several contributors challenge the exclusivist claim that salvation comes only through Jesus as the Christ. One of the women theologians contributing to the volume includes among the more recent images of Jesus emerging from the Asian women's movement "Jesus as mother," "Jesus as woman," and "Jesus as shaman."

Just as theology and biblical scholarship have made a distinction between the Jesus of history and the Christ of faith, so film study – in various ways – has made a distinction between the cinematic Jesus and the cinematic Christ. I have already considered in the previous chapter how the Jesus story was adapted to film, thereby initiating an ever-lengthening tradition of movies depicting the life of Jesus. These films retold the story of Jesus, as narrated in the gospels, with an actor playing Jesus.

However, alongside the tradition of Jesus-story films there has flourished a tradition of Christ-figure films. These films tell stories in which characters, events, and details substantially recall, or resemble, the story of Jesus. The character whose life and death mirror those of Jesus represents "the Christ-figure."[97]

Christ-figures have appeared in movies representing most genres or types: drama and action, western and comedy, historical epic and science fiction. Understandably, Christian priests – or preachers – and Jewish characters lend themselves to be projected as Christ-figures. All Christians are called upon to imitate Christ in their living, and priests, with their clerical attire, are easily identifiable as persons with a commitment to Jesus as the Christ. Since Jesus was a Jew, a persecuted Jew, contemporary Jewish characters have sometimes been portrayed as embodying suffering similar to his. Social misfits, alienated individuals, also lend themselves to be portrayed as Christ-figures. Among these outcasts have been inmates of prisons and others kinds of asylums.

In this connection, I consider films whose stories formally recall the Jesus story to be Christ-figure films, whatever the intention of the filmmaker and whatever the message communicated. The Christ-figure need not be "a saint" and the message need not be "Christian." However, some Christ-figure films have a character who explicitly identifies himself, or herself, as Jesus, or who is explicitly identified with Jesus or a particular dimension of the Jesus story. Sometimes these films revolve around a specific gospel text that is cited, verbally or visually, within the story itself.[98]

No twentieth-century filmmaker drew more extensively on theological and biblical themes than the Swedish pastor's son Ingmar Bergman. His *Winter Light* (1963, English) represents a profound commentary on Jesus' words of dereliction from the cross that appear in the film on the lips of the church sexton, "My God, my God ..." (Mark 15:34 and Matt. 27:46). Like Jesus on the cross, the church pastor Tomas Ericsson (a "doubting" Tomas) has agonizingly experienced the absence of God.

The film comedy *Heavens Above!* (1963), by the Boulting brothers, satirically shows what would happen if Jesus' message about wealth were actually implemented in an industrial society. Along the way, the viewer sees Jesus' words to the rich young ruler highlighted in an open Bible, "If you would be perfect, go, sell what you have and give to the poor ..." (Matt. 19:21). The story revolves around the Anglican parson of Holy Trinity church in a small English town, and concludes with an ending in which the parson literally ascends into the heavens with the aid of modern rocket technology.

In John Frankenheimer's *The Fixer* (1968), set in tsarist Russia, the Christ-figure appears in the personage of Jacob Bok, a Jewish fixer, or carpenter, who becomes the object of blood-libel – the false accusation that he has killed a Christian child to obtain blood for religious purposes. During his captivity, Bok identifies personally with the Jewish carpenter of ages past by reading the story of Jesus in a New Testament given to him by his captors. Later Bok tells the jailer: "I understand something. He who hates a Jew, or any other man, hates Jesus. To be anti-Semitic you've first got to be anti-Christian. It's in the book."

In addition to films that openly identify the lead character with Jesus and the Jesus story, there are others that exhibit greater subtlety. One of the most widely discussed Christ-figure films is Stuart Rosenberg's *Cool Hand Luke* (1967). The film tells the story of Luke Jackson, a loner and nonconformist, who has done time on a southern prison farm for petty theft. He does not survive what proves to be his final escape attempt, but stories about him live on among his fellow inmates after his death. Parallels between Luke's story and Jesus' story abound. Allusions and images are obvious. Nonetheless, there is no indication on the screen that

Luke or his friends view him as a Christ-figure. Such an identification potentially occurs through the eyes and in the minds of the viewer.

The production of Christ-figure films is not confined to the 1960s nor has the subject matter always been reflective of time past. With their science fiction trilogy *Matrix* (1999–2003), the Wachowski brothers tell a story set in the future, around the year 2199. Thomas A. Anderson, or Neo, becomes a computer hacker called to the redemptive mission of sacrificing life to save humanity. The film recalls a plethora of religious traditions and raises a myriad of philosophical questions appropriate for a beyond-postmodern world. However, in the sequence that introduces Neo, he is acclaimed with "Hallelujah! You're my savior man, my own personal Jesus Christ."

The list of Christ-figure films goes on and on. But this sampling does not divulge the principal source of the screenplays underlying many of these films – works of literary fiction, novels.[99] The movies *The Fixer* and *Cool Hand Luke* are based on earlier novels by Bernard Malamud and Donn Pearce respectively, which were published in the mid-1960s. Many well-known modern novels featuring Christ-figures, have also been adapted for the screen, often retaining the title of the book. These include Stephen Crane's *The Red Badge of Courage* (1895), Benito Pérez Galdós' *Nazarín* (1895), Herman Melville's *Billy Budd* (1924, published posthumously), John Steinbeck's *The Grapes of Wrath* (1939), Howard Fast's *Spartacus* (1951), Ernest Hemingway's *The Old Man and the Sea* (1952), and Ken Kesey's *One Flew Over the Cuckoo's Nest* (1962). Isak Dinesen's work of short fiction *Babette's Feast* (1985) and Stephen King's serialized novel *The Green Mile* (1996) have also provided the basis for popular movies. The Christ-figure in the former is female; the Christ character in the latter is African American.

The western literary tradition continues to transfigure the Jesus of old into fictional characters of a much later time. But like the modern novel itself, the Christ-figure seems to be the product primarily of the modern literary imagination, although there may be antecedents in allegorical works such Edmund Spenser's *The Faerie Queene* (1596) and John Bunyan's *The Pilgrim's Progress*

(1684). In the twentieth century, the literary use of fantasy, possibly even allegory, in the service of Christian thought and practice, reasserted itself in the writings of J. R. R. Tolkien and C. S. Lewis, who for decades were colleagues and friends at the University of Oxford. Tolkien's *Ring* trilogy has already found its way, with great popular success, into motion picture theaters (2001, 2002, 2003). C. S. Lewis' seven-part *The Chronicles of Narnia* has begun its serial cinematic debut with *The Lion, The Witch, and the Wardrobe* (2005) and *Prince Caspian* (2008).

Notes

1 Keith W. Clements, ed., *Friedrich Schleiermacher: Pioneer of Modern Theology*, The Making of Modern Theology (Minneapolis: Fortress Press, 1991).

2 Friedrich Schleiermacher, *On Religion: Speeches to its Cultured Despisers*, trans. John Oman (New York: Harper & Row, 1958).

3 Friedrich Schleiermacher, *The Christian Faith*, ed. H. R. McIntosh and James S. Stewart (Edinburgh: T. & T. Clark, 1928).

4 Schleiermacher, *Christian Faith*, 5–16.

5 Schleiermacher, *Christian Faith*, 52.

6 Schleiermacher, *Christian Faith*, 385.

7 Schleiermacher, *Christian Faith*, 425.

8 Schleiermacher, *Christian Faith*, 738–51.

9 Martin Rumscheidt, ed., *Adolf von Harnack: Liberal Theology at its Height*, The Making of Modern Theology (Minneapolis: Fortress Press, 1991).

10 Adolf Harnack, *History of Christian Dogma*, trans. Neil Buchanan, 7 vols. (New York: Russell & Russell, 1958).

11 Adolf Harnack, *What Is Christianity?*, trans. Bailey Saunders (New York: Harper & Row, 1967).

12 Harnack, *What Is Christianity?*, 51.

13 For the text of the Social Creed, see Richard M. Cameron, *Methodism and Society in Historical Perspective*, Methodism and Society, vol. 1 (Nashville, TN: Abingdon Press, 1961), 323–8.

14 Rauschenbusch, *A Theology for the Social Gospel* (Nashville, TN: Abingdon Press, 1946).

15 Rauschenbusch, *Social Gospel*, 146.

16 Rauschenbusch, *Social Gospel*, 240–79.

17 Clifford Green, *Karl Barth: Theologian of Freedom*, The Making of Modern Theology (Minneapolis, Fortress Press, 1991).

18 Karl Barth, *The Epistle to the Romans*, trans. E. C. Hoskyns, 6th edn. (New York: Oxford University Press, 1968).

19 Arthur C. Cochrane, *The Church's Confessions Under Hitler* (Philadelphia: Westminster Press, 1962), 237–42.

20 The complete set of volumes in English is published as *Church Dogmatics*, ed. G. W. Bromley and T. F. Torrance (Edinburgh: T. & T. Clark, 1956–62).

21 *The Doctrine of the Word of God, Church Dogmatics*, vol. 1, pt. 1, 98, 111, 124.

22 *The Doctrine of the Word of God*, ibid., vol. 1, pt. 2, 297–325.

23 *The Doctrine of the Word of God*, ibid., vol. 1, pt. 1, 406–13.

24 *The Doctrine of the Word of God*, ibid., vol. 1, pt. 1, 541, 548.

25 *The Doctrine of the Word of God*, ibid., vol. 1, pt. 2, 122.

26 *The Doctrine of the Word of God*, ibid., vol. 2, pt. 2, 132–71.

27 *The Doctrine of Reconciliation*, ibid., vol. 4, pt. 1, 222.

28 <www.piar.hu/councils/ecum20.htm>, *Decrees of the Ecumenical Councils*, trans. Norman P. Tanner.

29 Geffrey B. Kelly, *Karl Rahner: Theologian of the Graced Search for Meaning*, The Making of Modern Theology (Minneapolis: Fortress Press, 1992).

30 Karl Rahner, *Foundations of Christian Faith: An Introduction to the Idea of Christianity*, trans. William V. Dych (New York: Crossroad, 2000), 176–321.

31 Rahner, *Foundations*, 208.

32 Rahner, *Foundations*, 176.

33 Rahner, *Foundations*, 133–7.

34 Rahner, *Foundations*, 212–28.

35 Rahner, *Foundations*, 224

36 Rahner, *Foundations*, 228–85.

37 Pope Benedict XVI, *Jesus of Nazareth: From the Baptism in the Jordan to the Transfiguration*, trans. Adrian J. Walker (New York: Doubleday, 2007).

38 Dietrich Bonhoeffer, *The Cost of Discipleship*, trans. R. H. Fuller, rev. edn. (London: SCM Press, 1959).

39 Dietrich Bonhoeffer, *Letters and Papers from Prison*, trans. R. H. Fuller (London: SCM Press, 1953).

40 Paul Tillich, *Systematic Theology*, 3 vols. (Chicago: University of Chicago Press, 1951, 1957, 1963).

41 Rudolf Bultmann, "The New Testament and Mythology," in Hans Werner Bartsch, ed., *Kerygma and Myth*: *Rudolf Bultmann and Five Critics* (New York: Harper & Brothers, 1961), 1–44.

42 Consult Bartsch, ed., *Kerygma and Myth*, for critical assessments of Bultmann's proposal.

43 Schubert M. Ogden, *Christ Without Myth: A Study Based on the Theology of Rudolf Bultmann* (New York: Harper & Row, 1961), 117.

44 Ogden, *Christ Without Myth*, 153.

45 Alfred North Whitehead, *Process and Reality: An Essay in Cosmology* (New York: Macmillan, 1929), and Charles Hartshorne, *The Divine Relativity: A Social Conception of God* (New Haven: Yale University Press, 1948).

46 Schubert M. Ogden, *The Reality of God and Other Essays* (New York: Harper & Row, 1964), 57–61.

47 Ogden, *Reality of God*, 68, 177.

48 Schubert M. Ogden, *The Point of Christology* (Dallas: Southern Methodist University Press, 1982), 122, 97–105.

49 Schubert M. Ogden, *Is There Only One Religion or Are There Many?* (Dallas: Southern Methodist University Press, 1992), 79–104.

50 Gustavo Gutiérrez, *A Theology of Liberation: History, Politics, and Salvation*, trans. and ed. Sister Carida Inda and John Eagleston, 2nd, revised, edn. (Maryknoll, NY: Orbis, 1988).

51 Gutiérrez, *Theology*, 6.

52 Gutiérrez, *Theology*, 83–105.

53 Gutiérrez, *Theology*, pp. xxxviii, xl, 103.

54 Leonardo Boff, OFM, *Jesus Christ the Liberator: A Critical Christology for Our Time*, trans. Patrick Hughs (Maryknoll, NY: Orbis, 1978).

55 Jon Sobrino, SJ, *Christology at the Crossroads: A Latin American Approach*, trans. John Drury (Maryknoll, NY: Orbis, 1978).

56 Pope John Paul II, "Opening Address at the Puebla Conference," January 28, 1979, <www.ewtn.com/library/PAPALDOC/JP791228.htm>, June 13, 2008.

57 Joseph Paul Ratzinger, "Liberation Theology," a "private document" which preceded the *Instruction of Fall* (1984), from Cardinal Ratzinger's homepage, <www.Christendom-awake.org/pages/ratzinger/liberationtheol.htm>.

58 James H. Cone, *Black Theology and Black Power* (New York: Seabury, 1969).

59 James H. Cone, *A Black Theology of Liberation* (Philadelphia: J. B. Lippincott, 1970).

60 Cone, *Black Theology of Liberation*, 61.

61 James H. Cone, *The Spirituals and the Blues: An Interpretation* (New York: Seabury, 1972).

62 Cone, *Black Theology of Liberation*, 120, 121–2, 212, 215.

63 Cone, *Black Theology of Liberation*, 197–227.
64 Major J. Jones, *Black Awareness: A Theology of Hope* (Nashville, TN: Abingdon Press, 1971).
65 J. Deotis Roberts, *Liberation and Reconciliation: A Black Theology*. (Philadelphia: Westminster Press, 1971).
66 Albert B. Cleage, *The Black Messiah* (New York: Sheed & Ward, 1968).
67 Dwight N. Hopkins, *Introducing Black Theology of Liberation* (Maryknoll, NY: Orbis, 1999), 157–80.
68 EATWOT website, <www.eatwot.org>.
69 Betty Friedan, *The Feminist Mystique* (New York: W. W. Norton, 1963).
70 Mary Daly, "Autobiographical Preface to the 1975 Edition," *The Church and the Second Sex: With the Feminist Postchristian Introduction and the New Archaic Afterwards by the Author* (Boston: Beacon Press, 1985), 5–14.
71 Mary Daly, *The Church and the Second Sex* (1968; 1975 edn.; Boston: Beacon Press, 1985).
72 Mary Daly, *Beyond God the Father: Toward a Philosophy of Women's Liberation* (New York: Harper & Row, 1977); *Gyn/ecology: The Metaethics of Radical Feminism* (Boston: Beacon Press, 1978).
73 Virginia Ramey Mollenkott, *Women, Men, and the Bible* (Nashville, TN: Abingdon Press, 1977).
74 Letty Russell, *Human Liberation in Feminist Perspective: A Theology* (Philadelphia: Westminster Press, 1974).
75 Elisabeth Shüssler Fiorenza, *In Memory of Her: A Feminist Theological Reconstruction of Christian Origins* (New York: Crossroad, 1986), and *Jesus: Miriam's Child and Sophia's Prophet: Critical Issues in Feminist Christology* (New York: Continuum, 1995).
76 Schüssler Fiorenza, *In Memory*, 106–7.
77 Schüssler Fiorenza, *In Memory*, 130–54.
78 Schüssler Fiorenza, *In Memory*, 128.
79 Schüssler Fiorenza, *Jesus*, 157.
80 Schüssler Fiorenza, *Jesus*, 109–11, 111–28.
81 Rosemary Radford Ruether, *Faith and Fratricide: The Theological Roots of Anti-Semitism* (New York: Seabury, 1974), 116.
82 Rosemary Radford Ruether, *Sexism and God-Talk: Toward a Feminist Theology* (Boston: Beacon Press, 1983).
83 Rosemary Radford Ruether, "Between the Sons of White and the Sons of Blackness," in *Racism and Sexism in America* (New York: Seabury, 1975), 115–33.

84 Stephanie Y. Mitchem, *Introducing Womanist Theology* (Maryknoll, NY: Orbis, 2002).

85 Alice Walker, *In Search of Our Mothers' Garden: Womanist Prose* (San Diego: Harcourt Brace Jovanovich, 1983), p. xii.

86 Jacquelyn Grant, "Black Theology and the Black Woman," in Gayraud Wilmore and James H. Cone, eds., *Black Theology: A Documentary History*, (Maryknoll, NY: Orbis, 1979), 2:323–38.

87 Jacquelyn Grant, *White Women's Christ and Black Women's Jesus: Feminist Christology and Womanist Response*, AAR Academy Series 64 (Atlanta, GA: Scholars Press, 1989).

88 Delores S. Williams, *Sisters in the Wilderness: The Challenge of Womanist God-Talk* (Maryknoll, NY: Orbis, 1993).

89 Kelly Brown Douglas, *The Black Christ*, ed. James H. Cone, Bishop Henry McNeal Turner Studies in North American Black Religion 9 (Maryknoll, NY: Orbis, l993).

90 Williams, *Sisters in the Wilderness*, 161–7, 167–70.

91 Douglas, *Black Christ*, 111–13.

92 Priscilla Pope-Levison and John R. Levison, *Jesus in Global Contexts* (Louisville, KY: Westminster/John Knox Press, 1992). This well-researched and helpful volume surveys and analyzes understandings of Jesus in Latin America, Asia, Africa, and North America.

93 World Council of Churches (WCC), <www.oikoumene>. Other worldwide and regional church organizations mentioned in this chapter also have their own individual websites.

94 José Bonino Miguez, ed., *Faces of Jesus: Latin American Christologies,*, trans. Robert R. Burt (1984; repr. Eugene, OR: Wipf & Stock, 1998).

95 Robert J. Schreiter, CPPS, ed., *Faces of Jesus in Africa*, Faith and Cultures Series (Maryknoll NY: Orbis, 1991).

96 R. S. Sugirtharajah, ed., *Asian Faces of Jesus*, Faith and Cultures Series (Maryknoll, NY: Orbis, 1993).

97 W. Barnes Tatum, "Jesus-Story Films and Christ-Figure Films," in *Jesus at the Movies: A Guide to the First Hundred Years*, revised and expanded edn. (Santa Rosa, CA: Polebridge Press, 2004), 245–51.

98 Lloyd Baugh, SJ, *Images of the Divine* (Sheed & Ward, 1997).

99 Theodore Ziolkowski, *Fictional Transfigurations of Jesus* (Princeton: Princeton University Press, 1972).

Chapter 7

Jesus and World Religions
(Since the First Century)

Jesus as the Christ, through Christianity, has experienced a long and varied relationship to those traditions long recognized as major religions of the world. In addition to Christianity, these religions include Judaism, Islam, Hinduism, Buddhism and other traditions indigenous to China, specifically Taoism and Confucianism. Like Christianity, each of these religions has had a complicated history, with diversity of thought and practice. Each has responded to Jesus in different ways.

Christianity has experienced longstanding reciprocal relationships with Judaism and Islam, as I have occasionally noted. Not only did these three religions originate in western Asia, where the continent abuts Europe and Africa, they also constitute a monotheistic tradition by affirming that God is one. However, Judaism and Islam have often viewed Christianity's Trinitarian definition of oneness and the Christological claims on behalf of Jesus as problematical. By contrast, Hinduism and Buddhism also originated in Asia, but in southern Asia, on the Indian subcontinent. Buddhism relocated by moving northward into central and eastern Asia, where it became associated with Taoism and Confucianism in China and Shinto in Japan.

What can be said about the occasion for and the nature of Jesus' relationship to these religions? How have these religions responded to Jesus – to the traditional Christian claims that Jesus was the Christ, the Son of the Triune God, the Savior of the world?

Judaism: Jesus, a Jew, but no Messiah

Jesus of Nazareth was a Jew. Both the Judaism into which Jesus was born, lived, and died and the Christianity centered in Jesus as the Christ that emerged out of Judaism looked back to ancient Israel as their time of family beginnings, and ultimately to Abraham as their common ancestor. Judaism and Christianity were, in a sense, siblings. Referring to the story of Abraham's son Isaac, who had twin sons by his wife Rebecca (Gen. 25:19–26). Alan F. Segal speaks of Judaism and Christianity during the Roman period as "Rebecca's children."[1] The subsequent two thousand-year saga of the entangled relationship between Judaism and Christianity becomes in this view an account not simply of sibling rivalry but one where the younger child repeatedly victimizes the elder.

A synopsis of this tragic domestic dispute goes something like this. Jesus' relationship to Judaism involved his being born, living, and dying as a Jew under Roman rule. There resulted an in-house struggle between those who claimed Jesus to be God's messiah and those who disputed the claim. Both sides appealed to the same scriptures to support their point of view. After the apostolic conference in Jerusalem (ca. 49 CE) and the Roman destruction of Jerusalem and the Second Temple (70 CE), the circumstances increasingly pointed toward a division between church and synagogue, between Gentiles and Jews.

Toward the end of the fist century, the New Testament writings – especially the gospels of Matthew and John – reflect the harsh rhetoric of sibling rivalry used by those Jews who had accepted Jesus as the Christ against those Jews who did not believe. The Gospel of Matthew portrays Jesus as attacking the religious leaders of the people, "scribes" and "Pharisees," and calling them "hypocrites" (Matt. 5:20, 23:1–26). But Matthew places the most damning statement against Jesus' contemporaries on the lips of the crowd before Pontius Pilate after the latter had declared his own innocence in the Jesus matter by washing his hands. The crowd shouts: "His blood be on us and on our children" (Matt. 27:25). The Gospel of John later broadens Jesus' attack by referring to the

"Jews" more than sixty times, often pejoratively, thereby leaving the impression that Jesus was not a Jew. The de-Judaizing of Jesus has begun in earnest. Jesus allegedly declared to his Jewish opponents that Abraham was not their father but rather, "You are from your father the devil ..." (John 8:44). These statements in Matthew and John continued to feed the growing theological anti-Judaism of scholars, and the more general racist anti-Semitism of later centuries.

However, early rabbinic Judaism had already launched attacks of its own. Evidence comes from a rare passage in the Gospel of Matthew itself, where the collective word "Jews" appears. The passage intends to rebut the claim circulating among non-believing Jews in Matthew's day that Jesus' disciples had stolen Jesus' body from the tomb, contrary to the Christian claim that he had been resurrected by God (Matt. 28:11–15). Evidence also comes from an addition by the rabbis to the *Shemoneh Esrei* ("Eighteen Benedictions"), the central prayer for Jewish devotion. Possibly formulated around the turn of the second century, the addition constituted a nineteenth benediction, or malediction, directed against *ha-minim*, variously translated "slanderers" or "apostates." The precise origin, object, forms, and force of these words have been much debated, but those condemned probably included those fellow Jews who had accepted Jesus as messiah.[2]

In 313 Christianity received recognition as a licit religion in the Roman empire, primarily through the agency of Constantine. Shortly thereafter, in 395, the Emperor Theodosius I declared Christianity to be the established religion of the Roman empire. After Constantine, and during the Middle Ages, the civil codes joined the ecclesiastical laws passed by local, regional, and even ecumenical councils that mandated the religious and social separation of Christians from Jews thus assuring the increased marginalization of Jews. The Fourth Lateran Council of 1215, at the height of the Roman Catholic Church's power, even prescribed that Jews and Muslims be readily identified by their distinctive dress – a foreshadowing of the yellow stars used to identify Jews under the Third Reich in the twentieth century.[3]

Central to the defamation of Jews in Europe was the Christian theological assertion and accusation that they were responsible for the death of Jesus. Jews were labeled "Christ-killers." They had committed deicide. They had killed God. The cross, which had become the public symbol for Christianity and the object of personal devotion for Christians, correspondingly became for Jews a sign of loathing and fear.

A Jewish view of Jesus appears in the Talmud – that massive collection of materials, transmitted and edited by the rabbis. The Talmud finally appeared in two versions: the Palestinian or Jerusalem Talmud was finalized in Palestine in the fifth century, and the Babylonian Talmud was finalized in Babylonia, in the seventh century. Who was the Jesus of the rabbis?

The answer is hard to come by for two reasons. First, the Talmud(s) initially printed in the sixteenth century had been expurgated upon the order of church authorities and references to Jesus were possibly excised by Jews themselves to avoid further church reprisals. Secondly, even in the earlier scribal editions by the rabbis, references to Jesus were scattered about and pseudonyms, or false names, were often used to disguise Jesus' identity in the text. A recent answer to the question of the rabbinic view of Jesus comes from Peter Schäfer and his *Jesus in the Talmud* (2007).[4] Schäfer broadens the category "Talmud" to encompass all surviving literary evidence from the rabbis, but builds his case primarily on the Babylonian Talmud, since the rabbis in Babylonia early on had the relative freedom to articulate in writing their understanding of Jesus. Although the evidence evaluated is garnered from passages that are themselves scattered, Schäfer reports his findings in the format of a "counter-gospel." He assumes that the rabbis knew gospel literature – specifically the Gospel of John, or at least Tatian's *Diatessaron*. The Jesus of the rabbis, of course, was not the Jesus of the Christian church. Their Jesus was a figure who parodied and subverted the Christian story. Here I will only mention how the rabbis viewed the beginning and the end of Jesus' life.

In the Talmud, a figure presumed to be Jesus – called Ben Stada or Ben Pandera/Pantera – is the illegitimate offspring of his whorish mother and her lover. (BT *Shab.* 104b; BT *Sanh.* 67a).[5] These accounts echo the tradition reported by the philosopher Celsus that Jesus was begotten of his adulterous mother by a soldier named Pantera. In the Talmud there appears one brief passage about the trial and execution of one Jesus, wherein this Jesus is identified by a word meaning Nazarene (BT *Sanh.* 43a–b).[6] Here in the text are multiple surprises for those familiar with the gospel accounts! Contrary to the Synoptics, but consistent with John, Jesus was executed on the eve of Passover. Contrary to the four gospels, Jesus was executed by the Jewish method of stoning, after which his body was hung on public display – not by the Roman method of crucifixion. Jesus was also executed on the Torah-based charges of sorcery and instigating and seducing Israel to idolatry – not on a political charge of sedition or treason. The charges seem consistent with the characterization of Jesus in the gospels, where Jesus discloses who he is through his miraculous "signs" and his God-like "I am" sayings.

According to Schäfer's interpretation, the rabbis of the Talmud had boldly claimed – in an intentional reversal of the church's imputation of shame and guilt to the Jews – that the Jews were indeed responsible for the death of Jesus. But the Jewish leaders themselves had nothing to be ashamed of or to feel guilty about since Jesus was obviously not the messiah or the Son of God. Thus the Jews had lawfully and responsibly executed Jesus as a blasphemer and idolater. Remember how Matthew and John shift the responsibility for Jesus' crucifixion away from the Roman authorities and placed it squarely on the Jews; but here the Jewish authorities boldly claim responsibility.

The Middle Ages brought escalating pain and suffering upon the Jews. The crusades against the Muslims often resulted in the slaughter of Jews, who also rejected the claims made by Christendom on behalf of Jesus Christ. The Inquisition, with its concern for Christian deviants or heretics, often confronted Jews with a stark choice: conversion or death. Then there was the emergence of the ghettos, as Jews were forced to live in restricted areas, as well as mass expulsions – from England in 1290, from France in 1394, and from Spain in 1492.

Against this backdrop, another approach appeared by which Jews challenged the veracity of Christian claims about Jesus as the Christ, the Son of God. If the rabbis responsible for the Talmud subverted the gospel story of Jesus by telling a counter-narrative, this new approach involved publicly staged disputations between Jews and Christians that more directly addressed issues of Christian doctrine and the interpretation of Scripture. Jewish leaders were called upon to explain and defend their rejection of Jesus as the Christ, the Son of God. The Christian goal, of course, was the conviction and conversion of Jews. Memorable disputations were held in Paris in 1240, in Barcelona in 1263, and in Tortosa, Spain, in 1413–14.[7]

This socio-religious custom generated a market for handbooks to be used by disputants. A Jewish disputant during this period was the chief rabbi of Saragossa, Hasdai Crescas (ca. 1340–1411). One of his more philosophical works, which has survived, has come to be known as *The Refutation of the Christian Principles*.[8] Crescas identifies and discusses ten basic Christian doctrines, each of which – as he says – "the Jew denies." These doctrines (in order) are: the punishment of Adam's sin; the redemption from Adam's original sin; the Trinity, the incarnation, the virgin birth, transubstantiation, baptism, the coming of the messiah, the New Torah, and demons. However, the coming Reformation and the advent of Protestantism did not improve the lot of the Jews.

In 1517, only twenty-five years after the expulsion of the Jews from Spain, Martin Luther ushered in the Protestant Reformation by posting on the door of the cathedral church at Wittenberg his Ninety-Five Theses. In 1523, Luther wrote a pamphlet with the intriguing title, *That Jesus Was Born a Jew*. If Jews were enticed into reading Luther's words, they would have probably found its kindly sentiment toward them betrayed by its stated goal – conversion. But after the Jews in subsequent years failed to meet his expectations, Luther unleashed his outrageous 1543 treatise, *On the Jews and their Lies*.

When the United States Holocaust Memorial Museum, in Washington, DC, opened its doors in the mid-1990s, there was available for visitors a brief movie on "Anti-Semitism." This fast-paced film flashed on the screen two thousand years of images in fourteen minutes. Toward its conclusion, the film cited Adolf Hitler's claim that his actions against the Jews were intended to finish what the church had begun.[9]

However, even before the nadir of the Holocaust, before the founding of the state of Israel in 1948, and before the move by the Roman Catholic Church, at the Second Vatican Council, and by other churches as well, to address and redress Christianity's unrighteous past against the Jews, a momentous event had already occurred. For the very first time, a Jewish scholar had written a book about Jesus in Hebrew, for Jewish readers of Hebrew, which was intended to be neither polemical nor satirical.

The scholar was Joseph Klausner (1874–1958).[10] Born in Russia and educated in Germany at the University of Heidelberg, he was well versed in historical-critical scholarship and investigations into the life Jesus. After World War I, Klausner followed the Zionist path to Palestine in 1919, and for years he taught Hebrew literature at the Hebrew University of Jerusalem. His Hebrew book was *Jesus of Nazareth*, first published in 1922; it first appeared in English translation in 1925.

After nearly four hundred pages, Klausner provides a succinct summary of his conclusion: "Jesus was a Jew and a Jew he remained until his last breath. His one idea was to implant within his nation the idea of the coming of the Messiah and, by repentance and good works, hasten the 'end.'"[11] According to Josef Imbach, this publication by Klausner, after eighteen centuries, began a new era of engagement with Jesus as a subject by Jewish writers in various fields. Jews had begun welcoming Jesus home.[12] For centuries Christians had suffered amnesia about Jesus' Jewishness because the church had transformed him into a Gentile Christian, particularly with the aid of pictorial representations, which often portrayed him as a Nordic Gentile – not with the look of a Mediterranean Jew. For centuries, Jews also had amnesia about Jesus' Jewishness, perhaps because the trauma of even mentioning the name was too great. As we have seen, the emphasis on Jesus as a Jew in the most recent phase of the historical quest scholarship has also contributed to a recovery of memory for Christians and Jews.

Islam: Jesus, a Prophet, but no Son of God

Just as Christianity claimed to have superseded Judaism, so Islam claimed to have superseded Judaism and Christianity. All three monotheistic religions reflect a linear worldview according to which the God who created the heavens and the earth will at some future day render judgment on creation and humankind. Many of the same characters appear in the sacred writings of these three religions. Whereas Judaism and Christianity have, according to the biblical scenario, historically traced their descent from Abraham by way of his wife Sarah, so Islam has also traced its lineage from Abraham/Ibrahim by way of his banished maid-servant Hagar and their son Ishmael/Ismail.

As with Christianity and Judaism, so with Christianity and Islam, the relationship has often been akin to a family feud. Over the centuries, it has been marked by two principal confrontations and their related events. I have already noted the medieval crusades when Christians in the name of Christ assaulted the Holy Land. More recently, there occurred the events of September 11, 2001, when Muslims in the name of Allah attacked the United States as an unholy land. This most recent confrontation, with its antecedents and its continuing effects, has been interpreted by some to represent "a clash of civilizations."[13] Certainly, more has been involved in the recent conflict than the relationship between Jesus and Islam, but Christians, in particular, are often unaware of the importance of Jesus to Muslims.

The relationship of Jesus to Islam (meaning, "submission") began with the appearance of Islam, in Arabia, in the seventh century CE by Christian reckoning. When Muhammad (570–632) was born in Mecca, the city had already become an important destination for religious pilgrimages because of the Ka'ba ("cube") – a shrine that honors a black stone that fell from the heavens in the distant past. By Muhammad's day, religious images had also been placed in the Ka'ba, with statues located around the city square. Although there was belief in a supreme deity referred to as Allah (meaning "the God"), Allah was associated with three goddesses, and religious practices involved the veneration of varied tribal gods and local spirits.

The reverence shown to Jesus by Muslims (meaning, "those who submit" to Allah) stems from Jesus' prominence in the revelations of Allah to Muhammad that eventually constituted Islam's sacred book – the Qur'an (meaning "recitation").[14] Muhammad was a religious person and periodically withdrew for prayer into the caves on Mount Hira, north of Mecca On one such occasion, in the year 610, he had an inaugural experience of revelations that continued throughout his lifetime. Out of Muhammad's experiences, about which he spoke to friends, came the Muslim movement that faced and overcame two challenges in its early years. In 622 occurred the migration (*hijra*) of Muslims from Mecca to Yathrib (later known as Medina) to escape hostility – an event by which the beginning of the Islamic calendar is reckoned. In 630 occurred the victorious return of Muhammad and his forces from Medina to Mecca – an event that resulted in the rededication of the *Ka'ba* to Allah and the purification of the city from all idols. As the basic creed, or witness (*Shahadah*), of Islam declares: "There is no god but Allah, and Muhammad is the messenger of Allah." These words, in Arabic, continue to call Muslims to prayer from the minarets, or towers, of mosques around the world.

According to the Qur'an, who was Jesus? The Qur'an itself, written in Arabic, was finalized after Muhammad's death in 632, and divided into 114 chapters, or suras, with each chapter further divided into verses, or ayas. Following the brief opening sura, the subsequent suras are arranged in a descending order according to length, from the longest to the shortest – not in a chronological nor in a thematic sequence. Therefore, the references and allusions to Jesus in the Qur'an, of which there are many, are scattered throughout the sacred text. Longer passages in the Qur'an recall details that appear in the Christian gospels and even in non-canonical Christian writings.

Here I will concentrate principally on the way the Qur'an views the beginning and the end of Jesus' life. Two passages tell about the circumstances related to Jesus' birth (3:35–51 and 19:16–26). Both passages share common features: how the aged Zecharias' prayer for a son was answered by the birth of John (the Baptist); the unexpected annunciation to Mary that she would bear a child; her quizzical response that she had never been touched by a man; the identification of the miraculously conceived babe as Jesus, the Son of Mary; the claim that the babe speaks from the cradle; and a concluding exhortation that Allah be served.

Consequently, the Qur'an affirms and defends what Christianity refers to as the virgin birth of Jesus. The title of honor bestowed upon Jesus in both stories, "Son of Mary," becomes a common ascription associated with Jesus' personal name more than thirty times in the Qur'an and constantly reminds readers and hearers of his miraculous origin and his special status within Islam – but not as "Son of God."

The first passage (3:35–51) begins with a brief notation about Mary's own divinely sanctioned birth, recalling the Infancy Gospel of James. The narrative also refers to Jesus' miracle of giving life to a pigeon of clay, which recalls an incident in the Infancy Gospel of Thomas, and anticipates Jesus' acts of healing the blind and the leper and of raising the dead, all of which recall moments in the four gospels. Within this literary setting, Jesus is identified as an apostle or messenger sent specifically to the Israelites.

In the second passage (19:16–26), Jesus speaks of himself in categories more characteristic of Islam, but categories not foreign to Judaism and Christianity. He is a servant of Allah, who has appointed him as a prophet and charged him to remain steadfast in prayer and to be generous in alms-giving. He speaks of his blessedness on the day of his birth, his blessedness on the coming day of his death, and invokes peace upon himself on the day of his being raised to life. Whenever referring to Jesus by name, Muslims traditionally express their respect for him, as for other prophets, with words of blessing, such as, "Peace be upon him."

In the Qur'an, one brief and enigmatic statement mentions circumstances related to Jesus' death (4:156–8; see also 3:55). This passage says that the Jews speak falsely against Mary, and that they then boastfully declare: "We have put to death the Messiah, Jesus the Son of Mary, the apostle of Allah." The narrator immediately refutes this claim: "They did not kill him, nor did they crucify him, but they thought they did." Much debate has centered around the meaning of this passage. It should be noted here that the claim by Jews that they killed Jesus coincides with both the Christian anti-Judaic accusation that the Jews had killed Jesus and the account by the Jews themselves in the Babylonian Talmud that they had acted appropriately and legally in executing him. It should also be said that the stated denial that Jesus actually died on the cross is consistent with the Gnostic, or docetic, view in the Apocalypse of Peter, that Jesus' spirit had already left his body before his crucifixion. Nonetheless, the dominant Muslim view has been that Jesus did not die on the cross. Passages in the Qur'an that speak about Allah's taking Jesus up give support to this view (3:55, 4:158).

Therefore, Jesus in the Qur'an is an honored prophet who stands in the prophetic tradition from Abraham, to Moses, to himself, and finally to Mohammad, "the Seal of the Prophets" (33:40). Allah – The God – is one and has no son. A protective defense of Allah's oneness and the denial of Christian claims for God's three-in-oneness and Jesus' divine Sonship runs through the entire Qur'an. Jesus, the Son of Mary, is not truly God and truly human, only fully human. Whether or not Jesus actually died on the cross, according to the Qur'an, he was certainly no vicarious sacrifice on behalf of the sins of humankind. Allah saves those who submit to the will of Allah.

Because Jesus was received into the Qur'an, he has gone wherever Muslims have gone, geographically and chronologically. The Islamic theocratic ideal had been established by Muhammad in Medina before his return to Mecca. After his death, the leadership of the Islamic community passed to four of his closest associates: Abu Bakr (632–4), Umar (634–44), Uthman (644–56), and Ali (656–61). These early decades brought to the Islamic community both consolidation and a lasting division between the minority Shi'as (party of Ali) and the majority Sunnis. These years also witnessed the beginning of rapid expansion.

The Muslim move eastward resulted in immediate military victories over the Syrians in 635, the Persians in 636, and, in subsequent centuries, occasioned the spread of Islam into central Asia, the Indian subcontinent, southeast Asia, and across to the Indonesian archipelago and even into the southern Philippines.

Early Muslim ruling dynasties were the Umayyad, center Damascus (661–750), and the Abbasid, centered in Bagh (750–1258.). Abbasid rule ended with the marauding invasion the Mongols. In 1453, after centuries of pressure from and fights with various Muslim peoples, Constantinople and the Byzantine empire itself finally fell to the Ottoman Turks. The Ottoman empire, centered in Turkey, with Istanbul (formerly Constantinople) as its capital, flourished and then endured until after World War I (ca. 1300–1922). The Jesus of the Qur'an had indeed traveled far from his place of origin.

The Muslim move westward saw the arrival of Muslim armies in Palestine by 638 and in Egypt by 640. Arab and Berber Muslims in 711 completed the sweep across northern Africa and crossed the straits to the Iberian peninsula. Only their military defeat by the Franks under Charles Martel at the battle of Tours in France, in 735, turned the Muslim forces back to the Iberian peninsula. Al-Andalus was the Arabic name given to those areas of Spain occupied by the Muslims, or Moors, who lived in Spain for seven hundred years with varying experiences of harmony, accommodation, and conflict with Christians and Jews. However, Roman Catholic Christianity represented by King Ferdinand and Queen Isabella finally completed the reconquest of Spain when, in 1492, they expelled the Muslims – and the Jews. The Jesus of the Qur'an had also traveled far to the west of his place of origin.

However, there was more to Jesus than the figure portrayed in the Qu'ran. By the ninth century, traditions about what Muhammad said and did during his lifetime had been collected, evaluated for authenticity, and produced in the volumes known as the Hadith ("remembrance") – the most important of which was compiled by Muhammad al-Bukhari (810–70).[15] These collections also contain materials pertaining to Jesus, the Son of Mary. From the Hadith of al-Bukhari, for example, we learn that Jesus had curly hair and a reddish complexion (vol. 4, no. 648).

Moreover, apart from the Qur'an and the Hadith, several hundred stories and sayings about and by Jesus appear in Arabic Islamic literature. The Sufis, those Islamic mystics who emphasized the importance of personal experience of the divine, had a great fondness for Jesus, both because of his ascetic lifestyle and

se of his teaching. The Qur'an itself barely mentions the
ching dimension of Jesus' activity, but the writings of al-Ghazali
058–1111), a respected teacher in Baghdad who adopted Sufi
ways, provide a number of examples from this popular tradition.
As a teacher himself, al-Ghazali often cites sayings attributed to
Jesus that scoff at those who are pretentiously learned.

The Sufi poet Rumi (1207–73), a native of Afghanistan whose
family fled to Konya in Turkey to avoid the Mongols, also had a
deep affection for Jesus as expressed in his own poetic lines of
subversive wit. A few tantalizing lines go like this:

> I called through your door.
> "The mystics are gathering
> in the street. Come out!"
>
> "Leave me alone.
> I'm sick."
>
> "I don't care if you are dead!
> Jesus is here, and he wants
> To resurrect somebody."[16]

The Mughal dynasty ruled northern India for several centuries
(1526–1857), and Akbar was the third emperor in the succession
(1556–1605). He had a passion for religious matters. But his most
lasting accomplishment was the new city he built for his capital –
Fatehpur Sikri, a striking ensemble of buildings, which still stand,
although they were abandoned not long after their completion.
On the magnificent city gate has been inscribed a saying attributed
to Jesus, Son of Mary, that includes this line: "This world is a
bridge, pass over it, but build no houses on it."[17]

A recent collection of 303 sayings and stories associated with
Jesus from Arabic Islamic literature represents what Tarif Khalid
calls, "the Muslim Jesus," to differentiate this characterization of
Jesus from the presentation of Jesus in the Qur'an.[18] This collection of 303 literary units contains a saying (number 99) with a
line similar to that inscribed on the gate at Fatehpur Sikri: "Christ
said, 'The world is a bridge. Cross this bridge but do not build
upon it.'" Of the literary units in his collection, Khalid has identified eighty-five or so units as the oldest. He divides the units from

this core material into four basic groups.[19] Those in the large group emphasize Jesus' asceticism. Those in a second group are more eschatological and emphasize Jesus' role in the judgment of the last day. Those in still another group reflect intra-Muslim polemics in which Jesus is used against this or that Muslim faction. A final group seems to be adapted from sayings of Jesus known from the Christian gospels.

Thus, wherever Muslims go, the Qur'anic Jesus and the Muslim Jesus seemingly go with them. The Qur'anic Jesus, fashioned in Islam's earliest years, appears as one who readily acknowledges his own submission to Allah, standing in the prophetic succession, and rejecting the Christian notion that he is the Son of God. After all, Jesus is the Son of Mary. But the Muslim Jesus has a more diverse repertory of words and deeds.

Now we return to Islam's beginnings in the seventh century and then fast-forward to our own day. The ancient city of Jerusalem not only had longstanding ties to Judaism and Christianity, but already in Muhammad's lifetime had joined Mecca and Medina among the three holiest cities in Islam. According to the Qur'an (17:1), it was from Jerusalem that the Prophet made his Night Journey through the seven heavens to meet Allah in paradise. The details of this event, only hinted at in the Qur'an, vary in the Hadith. Nonetheless, in the year 620 – or thereabouts – on a night when he was still in Mecca, the Prophet was approached by the angel Gabriel and taken on the back of a winged steed named Buraq, first to Jerusalem, and then upward through the heavens, where he surpassed other great prophets from the past, including Jesus, before being ushered into the presence of Allah. Allah spoke to the Prophet unutterable words, but words of encouragement indicating that he belonged in the company of those whom he had seen. The final stage of Muhammad's Night Journey took flight from the mount where the Second Temple, destroyed by the Romans in 70 CE, had stood.

After the Muslims gained control over Jerusalem, they built a shrine on the Temple Mount, between 685 and 691, to mark the spot, or the rock from which Muhammad had ascended on his Night Journey, namely the Dome of the Rock. Reflecting Islam's aversion to images, but also exemplifying its ornamental use of lligraphy, verses from the Qur'an are beautifully inscribed on the exterior and the interior of the dome. Among the Arabic letters, words, and lines on the interior appears at least three times the phrase, "Jesus, Son of Mary."[20] Except for the name of the Prophet himself, the only personal name to appear in the decorative patterns on the structure is that of Jesus. The inclusion of his name serves the polemical function of putting him in his place as a prophet, by denying that Allah has a son. However, through Muslim eyes, Jesus' name appears there because he is a holy person to be respected ("Peace be upon him").

The gleaming golden Dome of the Rock remains the most recognizable structure in the city considered holy by all three of the monotheistic faiths. Nearby, also on the Temple Mount, stands the Al Aqsa mosque. The exterior of the western wall of the Temple Mount has become a place of veneration and prayer for Jews. Not too great a distance away appears the church of the Holy Sepulcher.

That the Dome of the Rock remains at all defies the odds. In the Christian taking of Jerusalem in 1099, the crusaders – who were merciless in their treatment of Muslims and Jews – did not destroy the Dome of the Rock.[21] The shrine was indeed profaned in the eyes of the Muslims. The space was transformed into a place of Christian worship with a cross on the dome and an altar on the rock. However, the Dome of the Rock survived, and was reconsecrated as a Muslim site by Saladin in 1287. In the Six-Day War of 1967 between Israel and her Muslim Arab adversaries Jordan, Syria, and Egypt, the Israeli armed forces seized the Temple Mount, but did not lay waste the Dome of the Rock. Although the Dome of the Rock may not yet represent the peace of Jerusalem, perhaps it can serve as a reminder that restraint can be exercised by these kindred religions, which have so much in common, including their progenitor Abraham.

Religions of South and East Asia: Jesus, the Outsider

Jesus was a stranger and an outsider to many of the lands of Asia for years. Whenever he came to be known in particular areas it

may have been initially through Jewish scribes or even M.
not through those who confessed him to be the Chris.
whenever Christians first appeared, Jesus through them w.
have encountered adherents of Hinduism, Buddhism, Taois.
and Confucianism among the religions of the Asian continent.

Jesus as the Christ may even have appeared through the
preaching of Thomas, the doubting disciple, in southwestern
India before Peter and Paul carried him to Rome. In an early tradition in the third-century Acts of Thomas the apostle came to
India to preach the gospel.[22] In our day, Thomas is remembered in
India by Christians who claim that Thomas arrived in the year 52
on the Malabar coast in the vicinity of Cranganore in the state of
Kerala, where he established churches that continue to bear his
name.[23]

The Roman Catholic mission to India began much later, in
1542. Jesuits including Francis Xavier (1506–52) came to Goa, a
Portuguese enclave, which was also located on the west coast.
British imperialism began asserting itself in India through the
East India Company in the seventeenth century, but not until
1793 did William Carey, the celebrated Baptist missionary, begin
his work in the vicinity of Calcutta. But whether Catholic or
Baptist, missionaries would have faced similar challenges.

Hinduism is the name given to the ancient religion and traditional culture of India. Just as the growing awareness of the oneness of God among the Israelites served as a source for the
monotheistic worldviews of Judaism, Christianity, and Islam, so
the developing monistic worldview, evident in such Hindu classics as the Upanishads, became the matrix for the rich diversity of
the religious views of India.

Dating from before the Common Era, the Upanishads are collections of treatises, usually in the form of dialogues between
teachers and students on philosophical issues such as the relationship between Ultimate Reality and the individual self.[24]
According to the *Chandogya Upanishad*, the Reality that pervades
the universe (*Brahman*) and the reality of the particular soul
(*atman*) are one. So in this treatise, when the student peels away
layers from a common fruit, his guru asks, "What do you see?"
When the student claims not to see anything, his teacher declares

on refrain "That art thou."[25] You are that subtle essence
∖annot perceive! *Brahman* = *atman*. Ultimately, all is one.
∖e, a monistic worldview!

Within the framework of this worldview, Hindus themselves
∖ave claimed that Hinduism has 330 million gods. According to
this view, gods are not Ultimate Reality, but simply mediators of
that Reality. However, over the centuries, Hinduism came to focus
on three principal gods known as the Trimurti: Brahma, the creator, Shiva, the destroyer, and Vishnu, the preserver. Vishnu periodically expresses himself in the form of avatars, or incarnations,
who appear on earth to maintain the moral order.

Perhaps the most celebrated avatar through the ages has been
Krishna – that playful cavorter with young milkmaids and the
charioteer for Arjuna in the dramatically powerful *Bhagavad-Gita*
("Song of the Lord").[26] (It was also for Lord Krishna in the late
1960s that George Harrison of Beatles fame wrote the popular
song, "My Sweet Lord.") Since Jesus became a presence through
his followers in India, and Krishna became better known in the
west, there have been comparative studies of Lord Krishna and
Lord Jesus, both as savior figures and as subjects of devotion.
Each in his own way was indeed understood to be an avatar and
adored by his devotees.[27]

Whatever the similarities between Krishna and Jesus, however,
there are striking differences between Christianity and Hinduism.
Within the context of the Hindu monistic worldview, other beliefs
also give expression to Hinduism's distinctiveness. There is the
belief in the continuing cycle among living things of birth, death,
rebirth (*samsara*); there is also the related notion that at death
individual souls, which are imperishable, can transmigrate from
one life-form to another. Moreover, in Hinduism, salvation
(*moksha*) means to be liberated from the cycle of birth, death, and
rebirth and to be united in oneness with the Ultimate. That which
determines whether or not one achieves liberation is the law of
cause and effect (*karma*, whether good or bad).

Also within Hinduism, this understanding of the human situation is contextualized socially within a hierarchical and inflexible
caste system so that good *karma* produced by performing duties of
caste, family, and gender determines one's destiny. The traditional

castes range downward from the three upper castes of Brah[...] (priests), Kshatriyas (warriors), and Vaisyas (merchants), to [...] fourth caste, the Shudras (laborers and farmers). Beyond th[...] social pale are the untouchables, ritually unclean themselves, who perform the most menial and impure tasks. The constitution of the modern state of India, adopted after independence from British rule in 1947, forbids discrimination based on caste; but caste remains an important feature in some social relations, especially marriage.

It was Mohandas Gandhi (1869–1948), the leader of the campaign to free India from British rule, who dignified the untouchables by calling them *harijans*, "children of God," although the term *dalits* has become more acceptable. Among the influences on Gandhi as he developed his own non-violent philosophy of *satyagraha*, "truth force," was Jesus' teaching on love and non-retaliation in the Sermon on the Mount (Matt. 5–7). Gandhi was following the path of other Hindu social and religious reformers who had found direction and inspiration from the Jesus story.

Among the many Hindu leaders attracted to Jesus in India were such nineteenth-century social reformers as Ram Mohan Roy and Keshub Chunder Sen, and the twentieth-century Nobel Laureate in literature, Rabindranath Tagore. In fact, R. S. Sugirtharajah has claimed that "among other faith traditions only Hindus have worked out such elaborate and varied images of Jesus."[28] Sugirtharajah epitomized the images projected by the aforementioned as follows:

> Ram Mohun Roy, "Jesus as Supreme Guide to human happiness"
> Keshub Chunder Sen, "Jesus as true Yogi and Divine Humanity"
> Rabindranath Tagore, "Jesus as the Son of Man, seeking the last, the least, and the lost"
> Mohandas Gandhi, "Jesus as the Supreme Satyagrahi (lover and fighter for truth)"

As Christianity was to Judaism, so Buddhism was to Hinduism. That is, Buddhism began within Hinduism as a reform movement, inspired by a charismatic leader, which eventually discovered its own identity and strength outside the homeland – outside India.

e Buddha ("awakened" or "enlightened one") was born in thern India, actually in the Himalayan foothills of Nepal, as ddhartha Gautama (ca. 563–483 BCE). He received his honorific name while meditating, from the primal experience of being awakened to a deeper understanding of existence. He formalized his insight into the Four Noble Truths and the Noble Eightfold Path:

> Life is suffering;
> Suffering comes from desire;
> Desire can be ended;
> Desire can be ended by following the Noble Eightfold Path:
>   Right understanding
>   Right intention
>   Right speech
>   Right action
>   Right work
>   Right effort
>   Right meditation
>   Right contemplation.

Thus the Buddha's approach to life was "the middle way" – between extreme self-denial and extreme self-indulgence. By contrast to the conventional Hindu view, the Buddha did not believe in an individual soul (*atman*) that could merge with the One Soul (*Brahman*). His view was that of no soul (*anatta*). Thus the goal of *nirvana*, the state of peace and release from the cycle of birth, death, and rebirth, was described as extinction – like snuffing out a flame. After setting in motion the wheel of *dharma* (teaching) in the Deer Park, near the holy city of Benares on the river Ganges, the Buddha spent his long life as an itinerant teacher sharing his wisdom and gathering followers, male and female, for whom caste distinctions mattered not and respect for all life became paramount (*ahimsa*).

After the Buddha's death, the movement bearing his name spread beyond India: to Sri Lanka and China, by the first century; into southeast Asia by the fourth century; then from China into Korea and Japan by the sixth century; and into Tibet by the seventh century. Along the way, Buddhism transformed itself into

an increasingly complex and diverse religion variously re.
the Buddha and Buddhist teaching. The outcome has be
threefold distinction: Theravada or Hinayana Buddhism, loce
primarily in southeastern Asia; Mahayana Buddhism; in the
north; and Vajrayana Buddhism, in Tibet.

Out of Tibet, late in the nineteenth century, came a claim that
will seemingly be an attention-getter forever: that Jesus spent his
so-called "missing years" in Tibet – although historical scholarship has repeatedly examined the evidence and found the claim
wanting.[29] The claim involved a Russian named Nicholas
Notovitch, who in 1887 visited the Hemis monastery of Buddhist
monks, near the city of Leh, the capital of the Ladakh district, on
the border between India and Tibet. Allegedly based on what
Notovitch had heard being read to him, he eventually published
a volume titled *The Unknown Life of Jesus Christ* (1894).Originally
published in French, this volume contained the text – based on
his notes – of his newly recovered story of Jesus in Tibet, "The
Life of Saint Issa." Much of the critical commentary on Notovitch's
life of Jesus (or Issa) involves an analysis of the modern story
presupposed by it. But what is the shape of the Jesus story itself?
And how is Jesus portrayed in it?[30]

The story opens with a brief prologue that laments the execution of Issa, in whom the "soul of the universe" had become
incarnate, and then discloses that certain merchants from Israel
are the narrators of what follows. The story of Issa proper begins
with an account of his miraculous birth, although the names of
his parents are not given. But at age 13 he runs away from home
and sets out to the east with these merchants. He returns to his
native land of Israel at age 29.

The story concludes after Issa's crucifixion, after his soul has
left his body, after the burial of his body, and after the tomb is
discovered to be empty. A striking feature of the preceding trial
scene is the cry by the Jews present that they do accept responsibility for Issa's execution and that they proclaim him to have been
a just man.

The account of Issa's sixteen years in the east is described with
much local color, as appropriate for good fiction as for accurate
history. Issa spends six years in holy cities, such as Benares, before

the birthplace of the Buddha in Nepal, where Issa learns
ali language and studies the sacred sutras. Issa denies the
du Trimurti of Brahma, Shiva, and Vishnu. An interesting
eme throughout the story is Issa's verbal attack on idolatry and
his own acts of iconoclasm. He also contends with representatives
of the high-caste Brahmins and the Kshatriya and sides with the
lower-caste Vaisayas and Shudras. On his way home, Issa visits
Persia, the home of Zoroaster, where Issa is accused of blasphem-
ing their god. But he does get home. Three years later, his growing popularity with the people prompts Pontius Pilate to have
him arrested, which leads to his crucifixion with Pilate's full
responsibility and approval.

Out of Tibet, in years more recent than Notovitch's life of Jesus,
has also come Tenzin Gyatso, the fourteenth Dalai Lama, who
was forced to leave his native land by the Chinese government in
1959. During his long exile, the Dalai Lama has expounded on
not only traditional Buddhist texts, but even the Christian gospels.[31] When asked how he views Jesus, he often gives this answer,
"Jesus was a fully enlightened being." There's something Buddhist
about that! But the Dalai Lama does not mean that Jesus became
enlightened during his sixteen years in Tibet.

Certainly the plight of the Dalai Lama and the Chinese threat
to traditional Tibetan culture have contributed greatly to an
increased familiarity with Buddhism by Christians in the west
over the past century. Among other contributors to an apprecia-
tion of Buddhist teaching has been the Vietnamese monk Thich
Nhat Hanh, whose writings, such as *Living Buddha, Living Christ*
(1995), correlate Buddhist understandings and devotional practices with those of Christianity.[32] Many Christian scholars and
theologians have been participants in a Christian–Buddhist dialogue in different settings and on varied levels. The Sri Lankan
Jesuit Aloysius Pieris has articulated a theology of liberation
appropriate for the Asian setting.[33] The American Protestant
scholar Marcus Borg has focused on a comparison between the
historical Jesus and the Buddha.[34]

In recent years, a report has been published about discoveries
made not in Tibet but in China, in the vicinity of the modern city
of Xian. That report is Martin Palmer's *The Jesus Sutras*.[35] Some of

the finds to which Palmer had access and which he inte
have been known for years.[36] But these finds are more interest
and credible – than the phantom documents presupposed
Notovitch's book. These discoveries represent different kinds c
evidence that reinforce each other. Taken together, the evidence
tells the story of the first Christian mission to China from Persia
that arrived at the imperial capital of Chang-an (modern Xian) in
635 during the Tang dynasty (618–906).

By the seventh century, the three religious traditions characteristic of Chinese thought and life were well established. Taoism
and Confucianism, the two indigenous traditions, were associated with the sages Lao Zi (ca. 600 BCE) and Confucius (551–478
BCE). The Tao, or the Way, is the mysterious power that pervades
the universe, symbolized by the yin/yang -- the circle of light and
darkness, the two complementary forces of the universe that gen-
erate the varied forms of reality. Taoism stresses that humans
should live in harmony with nature. Confucianism, with its
emphasis on a hierarchy of relationships, emphasizes how
humans should live in harmony within the established social
order. The veneration of ancestors also became an important
dimension of Chinese religion.

By the first century, Buddhism had entered China and brought
with it a concern for the ultimate issues of death, *karma*, and reincarnation. Theravada or Hinayana Buddhism had looked upon
the Buddha as a teacher who enabled one to achieve *nirvana*
through disciplined practices. But the dominant Buddhism in
China represented Mahayana Buddhism, which had become a
salvation religion whereby the divinized Buddha beckoned individuals to seek aid from a plethora of Bodhisattvas. Bodhisattvas
are enlightened beings whose exemplary past lives had freed
them from rebirth, but who had compassionately delayed realizing *nirvana* in order to save others. Bodhisattvas are a lot like the
Dalai Lama's view of Jesus.

Lao Zi, Confucius, and Buddha, these three, were often pic-
tured harmoniously together as a religious threesome representing the best of Chinese wisdom. What about the discoveries
related to the first Christian mission to China? Who was the Jesus
of the sutras? There are three kinds of evidence that have enabled

n Palmer and his collaborators to reconstruct this period of
t he has called Taoist Christianity.

First, there is a large stone stele, or inscribed monument. Now
displayed in the Forest of Stone Steles Museum, in Xian, this stele
tells the story of the first Christian mission to China that arrived
at the imperial court in 635 under the leadership of a person
named Aluoben. The stele dates from 751 and was rediscovered
in 1625 by diggers working near Xian.[37]

Second, there is the surviving pagoda of the long-lost Da Qin
monastery, the name given to the Christian monastery on the
stele. Palmer's identification of a known Buddhist pagoda, that
had previously been Taoist, and before that an eighth-century
Christian structure, enabled him to confirm the old site of the Da
Qin monastery.[38]

Third, there are the scrolls themselves. Of the eight sutras published in this collection are four theological texts and four liturgical texts. These texts have previously been translated twice, once
in 1930 and later in 1937; but the current translations represent
a collaborative enterprise. The scrolls were most likely among
those discovered early in the twentieth century in a cave near
Duhuang – a town on the old Silk Road, connecting China to the
west and the west to China. Evidence at the discovery site indicated that the cave had been sealed around the year 1005.[39]

Who is the Jesus of these sutras? The place to begin answering
this question is with the stele, which constitutes a stone sutra.
Furthermore, the monk Jingjing, from the Da Qin monastery, is
named as the source of the instruction on the stone and identified
in one of the sutras as a key figure in life of the church.[40]

Jingjing begins the story of the church with a prologue reminiscent of the Gospel of John but with a Taoist twist: "In the
beginning was the natural constant, the true stillness of the Origin
and the primordial void of the Most High." Readers will recognize, beneath the turns of phrase and concepts on the stone –
whether Taoist, Buddhist, or even Confucian – details from the
familiar gospel narratives. Up front, there is Trinitarian-sounding
talk with references to "Joshua" who was crucified, and to "my
Lord Ye Su," who became incarnate through a virgin and was
visited by gift-bearing, light-following "Persians." As Jingjing

continues his story of the "religion of light," images anc from Buddhism and Taoism recur: "the raft of salvation an passion," "subdue thoughts of desire," "stillness to build our dations," and a marvelous play on that multivalent concept of Tao – the Way.[41]

In the four theological sutras, references to familiar materials from the gospels continue to appear. "The Sutra of the Teachings of the World-Honored One," an honorific name for the Buddha, but here for Jesus.[42] This sutra represents a conventional appropriation of gospel materials, possibly based on Tatian's *Diatessaron*. The sutra begins abruptly with a block of Jesus' teachings and continues haphazardly through his trial, his death, his resurrection, his post-resurrection appearances, his ascension, and the gift of the "Pure Wind" (at an unnamed Pentecost). But the text paraphrases the closing words from the Gospel of Matthew, including the Trinitarian baptismal formula (Matt. 28:16–20) – although the English translation here too is jarring, "in the name of the Father, the Son, and the Pure Wind."

"The Sutra of Jesus Christ" introduces the messiah as a teacher of the laws of God -- of Yahweh.[43] Within the text, there is a list of precepts that recall not only the ten Judeo-Christian commandments but the Confucian hierarchy of relationships and includes the Buddhist respect for all living beings. Strikingly, these teachings are set within a magical universe of Buddhas and associated with the messiah, whose compassionate suffering and death free living beings from *karma*. Both Chi-Chu (Golgotha) and Pilate are mentioned by name. More abstractly, but more directly, the "Sutra of Cause, Effect, and Salvation" addresses the foundational Buddhist issue of *karma* and reincarnation.[44] This sutra obliquely describes Jesus as "a Visitor" who came into this world and suffered, thereby enabling those in this world, in the knowledge of his suffering, to do good and be freed from the cycle of birth, death, and rebirth.

Therefore, in the theological sutras, which presuppose competing worldviews, Jesus clearly appears as a savior figure. Within the liturgical sutras, we see this understanding of Jesus as savior in the context of worshiping communities. The sutras "Taking Refuge in the Trinity" and "Let Us Praise" reflect Trinitarian

. The former Trinity, less traditional than the latter, con-
.he Father of All Things, the Jade-Faced One, and the Holy
and Dharma Lords.[45] The latter three in one consist of the
.itional Father, Son, and Holy Spirit.[46] The liturgical sutra,
.eturning to Your Original Nature," cast as a dialogue between
the messiah and his disciple Simon, articulates a common Taoist
notion that sharply contrasts with the Christian doctrine of original sin. Persons have innate goodness that may be obscured by
negativity, but remains waiting to be recovered.[47]

The Christianity that arrived in China in 635, during the rule of
the Tang dynasty, did not last. After the state adoption of an anti-
religion edict in 845, Christian mission that began with promise
eventually faded away. Although there were brief reappearances
of Christianity in China during the Middle Ages, it was not until
the arrival in the Far East of Jesuit missionaries from the west,
such as Matteo Ricci (1552–1610), that the story of Christian mission in China began anew. Debate resumed about how Jesus
through the church should relate to the surrounding culture and
the limits, if any, of enculturation. Whether or not traditional
Chinese rites related to the veneration of ancestors constituted
idolatry was among the concerns.

Material Culture: From Stone to Celluloid

Around the time Aluoben and his companions from the west
arrived in the ancient city of Chang-an, the Tang dynasty began
pursuing the Chinese custom of recording literary works and historical events by carving them on massive stones. Several thousand steles are preserved today in the Forest of Stone Steles
Museum in the modern city of Xian.

I have already commented on the text of the stone sutra that
celebrated the coming of Ye Su into the world and the story of
how the religion of light was transmitted in China. But I have not
yet mentioned the symbol carved near the top of the stele: a cross
rising out of a lotus. What a perfect union between two powerful
symbols. The cross had finally established itself as the symbol for
Christianity. The lotus had become an important symbol for

Figure 9 Scene of Jesus and a young girl from *Dayasagar* (*Oceans of Mercy*, ca. 1978), a film produced in India about the life of Jesus. *Reproduced by courtesy of Dayspring International*

eastern religions, particularly Buddhism. The white lotus represented the Buddha and the purity of perfect enlightenment; its petals, generally eight in number, suggested the Noble Eightfold Path as the self unfolds toward enlightenment.

It is a long stretch from eighth-century China to the world of the twenty-first century – from stone to celluloid. In the final sections on material culture of the previous two chapters, I highlighted the contemporary medium of film, and implicitly the stuff of which film is made, namely celluloid. The Jesus films and the Christ-figure films featured in those chapters, although having theological and religious meaning, were for the most part created for commercial audiences.

However, early in the development of moving pictures there were those who immediately recognized the potential of film as a communications medium that could be used for evangelistic purposes – intending to bring non-believers to belief in Jesus as the st. Cecil B. DeMille, the great Hollywood impresario who ated that Jesus spectacle known as *The King of Kings* (1927), rote in his 1959 autobiography that he supposed more people had been introduced to the Jesus story through *The King of Kings* than through any other means, except for the Bible itself. He even calculated the total number of viewers to have been more than 800 million people; and he noted how the film had been used in faraway jungles by Catholic and Protestant missionaries. Obviously DeMille's silent film had enjoyed a long post-theatrical life.[48]

Certainly the best-known film produced for evangelistic use is the movie simply called *Jesus* (1979). I have previously observed how this film, which for thirty years has been "in the fields," intended to be a faithful rendering of the Jesus story according to the Gospel of Luke. Although this *Jesus* can be heard on screen in more than a thousand languages, the look of Jesus – played by Brian Deacon – remains unchanged. He still looks northern European. However, there is another Jesus film, from the same film era, that was adopted for evangelistic use. This Jesus projects a persona quite different from the Jesus in most other films.

The film *Dayasagar*, meaning "Oceans of Mercy," first appeared in theaters in India in 1978.[49] The worldwide rights were secured by the evangelistic organization known as Dayspring International, whose founder and president is John Gilman. The film itself was produced by Indian filmmaker Vijay Chandar, who also plays the role of Jesus. Both the production crew and the cast are said to have been Indian Christians. Jesus wears a white garment that highlights his dark complexion and has long, black hair and a beard. Reportedly, the script includes many of the familiar stories and sayings from the canonical gospels. But there is also the convention, characteristic of Bollywood or Indian filmmaking, of having occasional song-and-dance numbers. The auspicious moments for such musical outbursts in *Dayasagar* are the sequences related to the Jesus' birth and his entry into Jerusalem.

Dayspring maintains more than two hundred mobile teams crisscrossing India, showing this life of Jesus in fourteen languages, native to India, to audiences that average around four hundred people. With movies of all kinds, statistics are important, certainly no less so for evangelistic films – although box-office

statistics are not the determining measure of success. D[...]
reports that *Dayasagar* has been shown in more than 250,0[...]
lages to 240 million people, of whom 10 million experienced[...]
version – or a coming to Christ.

Northern India, the Kashmir region, provides the setting fo[...]
another Jesus-related movie. This film is more Hollywood than
Bollywood, and already has its own many-layered website. On
the site, there appears the title in English with eye-catching flour-
ishes: *Jesus in India*.[50] Instead of a narrative retelling of the Jesus
story, *Jesus in India* follows the American adventurer Edward
T. Martin, from Lampasas, Texas, as he searches for the manuscript claimed long ago to have been seen by Nicholas Notovitch
at the Hemis monastery, near Tibet. The film represents a cinematic
quest for Jesus' missing years. Experts, one of whom is the Dalai
Lama, representing a variety of religious and scholarly viewpoints
provide appropriate commentary. The viewers visit the tomb in
Srinagar, Kashmir, where Jesus was buried, according to the
Ahmadiyya Islamic sect.

Still further north, but beyond India, we come to the Islamic
Republic of Iran where we have our third encounter with a cinematic Jesus in Asia. We have already met this so-called Qur'anic
Jesus. In October of 2007, during the holy month of Ramadan,
there appeared on the screen in Tehran a film called *Jesus, the
Spirit of God*.[51] The expression "Spirit of God" is a common name
of honor for Jesus in the Qur'an, although like "Son of Mary" it
is used polemically to deny that Jesus was in any sense one of a
divine Trinity. Funded by state broadcasting, the film was directed
by Nader Talebzadeh, and stars Soleimani-Nia in the title role.
Surprisingly, the actor has a light complexion with lightly dyed
long hair and beard, both somewhat knotted. As expected, this
Islamic Jesus is neither crucified nor resurrected. Instead, he is
taken up directly to Allah. As acknowledged by Talebzadeh, the
film represents a Muslim answer to Mel Gibson's *The Passion of the
Christ* (2004), which specialized in the brutality inflicted on Jesus
even before he was nailed to the cross.

Thus I conclude my consideration of how Jesus has been
received over the last two millennia, and end up at last in the
neighborhood of where it all began.

Alan F. Segal, *Rebecca's Children: Judaism and Christianity in the Roman World* (Cambridge, MA: Harvard University Press, 1986).

2   David Klinghoffer, *Why the Jews Rejected Jesus: The Turning Point in Western History* (New York: Doubleday, 2005), 116.

3   Clark M. Williamson, *Has God Rejected his People? Anti-Judaism in the Christian Church* (Nashville, TN: Abingdon Press, 1982), 107–12.

4   Peter Shäfer, *Jesus in the Talmud* (Princeton: Princeton University Press, 2007).

5   Shäfer, *Jesus*, 15–23

6   Shäfer, *Jesus*, 63–74.

7   Klinghoffer, *Why the Jews Rejected Jesus*, 150–81.

8   *The Refutation of the Christian Principles by Hasdai Crescas*, trans. Daniel J. Lasker (Albany: State University of New York Press, 1992), 23–7.

9   W. Barnes Tatum, "The Christian Origins of Anti-Semitism," *The Fourth R*, 8/3–4 (May/Aug. 1995), 15–17.

10   Joseph Klausner, *Jesus of Nazareth*, trans. Herbert Danby (New York: Macmillan, 1957).

11   Klausner, *Jesus*, 368.

12   Josef Imbach, *Three Faces of Jesus: How Jews, Christians, and Muslims See Him* (Springfield, IL: Templegate, 1992), 28–45. For a collection of writings by Jewish scholars from the mid-twentieth century, on the topics of Jesus' Jewishness and his trial and death on a Roman cross, see Trude Weiss-Rosmarin, ed., *Jewish Expressions on Jesus: An Anthology* (New York: KTAV Publishing House, 1977).

13   See the much-discussed book by Samuel P. Huntingdon, *The Clash of Civilizations and the Remaking of World Order* (New York: Simon & Schuster, 1996).

14   The English translation of the Qur'an used herein is N. J. Dawood, *The Koran*, 5th, revised, edn. (London, 1993). For a bilingual Arabic–English edition, see Abdullah Yusuf Ali, *The Holy Qur'an: Text, Translation and Commentary*, new revised edn (Brentwood, MD: Amana, 1409; AH 1989).

15   <http://www.sacred-texts.com/isl/bukhari/bh4/bh4-651.htm>. For examples of Jesus' parables that appear on the lips of the Prophet, see Alfred Guillaume, "Borrowing from Christian Documents and Tradition," in *The Traditions of Islam: An Introduction to the Study of the Hadith Literature* (Beirut: Khayats, 1966), 132–49.

16 Coleman Barks, *The Essential Rumi*, trans. with John Moyne, Arberry, and Reynold Nicholson (HarperSanFrancisco, 19. 201–5.

17 Akbar S. Ahmed, *Islam Today: A Short History of the Muslim World* (London: I. B. Tauris, 1999), 89.

18 Tarif Khalid, *The Muslim Jesus: Sayings and Stories In Islamic Literature* (Cambridge, MA: Harvard University Press, 2001).

19 Khalid, *The Muslim Jesus*, 32–8.

20 Islamic Awareness website: "The Arabic Inscriptions on the Dome of the Rock in Jerusalem, 72 AH: 692 CE," <http://www.Islamic-awareness.org/History/Inscriptions/DoTR.html>.

21 Carole Hillenbrand, *The Crusades: Islamic Perspectives* (Chicago: Fitzroy Dearborn, 1999), 298, 301, 316, 506.

22 The Acts of Thomas are available in English translation: E. Hennecke, *New Testament Apocrypha*, ed. W. Schneemelcher, trans. and ed. R. McL. Wilson, 2 vols. (London: Lutterworth Press, 1965), 2:423–531.

23 For a critical assessment of the Acts of Thomas and the beginnings of Christianity in India, see Samuel Hugh Moffett, *A History of Christianity in Asia*, vol. 1: *Beginnings to 1500* (HarperSanFrancisco, 1992), 24–44, 498–505.

24 *The Upanishads*, trans. Swami Prabhavananda and Frederick Manchester (Hollywood, CA: Vedanta, 1948).

25 *The Upanishads*, 68–9.

26 *The Song of God: Bhagavad Gita*, trans. Swami Prabhavananda and Christopher Isherwood (Hollywood, CA: Vedanta, 1944).

27 Ovey D. Mohammed, "Jesus and Krishna," in R. S. Sugirtharajah, ed., *Asian Faces of Jesus*, Faith and Cultures Series (Maryknoll, NY: Orbis, 1993), 9–24.

28 Sugirtharajah, "An Interpretive Forward," in id., ed., *Asian Faces of Jesus*, 3–4.

29 For a brief history and critique of the claim that Jesus was in Tibet, see Robert M. Price, "Jesus in Tibet, A Modern Myth," *The Fourth R*, 14/3 (May/June 2001).<http://www.westarinstitute.org/Periodicals/4R/Articles/Tibet/html>.

30 Elizabeth Clare Prophet, *The Lost Years of Jesus: On the Discoveries of Notovitch, Abhedananda, Roerich, and Caspari* (Malibu, CA: Summit University Press, 1984). This volume contains the text of the initial translation into English of Notovitch's "The Life of Saint Issa," on which my brief summary and analysis are based.

31 Dalai Lama, *The Good Heart: Buddhist Perspectives on the Teachings of Jesus* (Somerville, MA: Wisdom, 1996).

.hich Nhat Hanh, *Living Buddha, Living Christ* (New York: Riverhead Books, 1995).

Aloysius Pieris, S.J., *Asian Theology of Liberation*, Faith Meets Faith Series (Maryknoll, NY: Orbis, 1988).

34 Marcus J. Borg, "Jesus and Buddhism: A Christian View," *Buddhist-Christian Studies*, 19/1 (1999), 93–7.

35 Martin Palmer. *The Jesus Sutras: Rediscovering the Lost Scrolls of Taoist Christianity* (New York: Ballantine, 2001).

36 A. C. Moule, *Christians in China: Before the Year 550* (New York: Octagon Books, 1930; repr. 1977).

37 Palmer, *Jesus Sutras*, 224–34.

38 Palmer, *Jesus Sutras*, 11–25.

39 Palmer, *Jesus Sutras*, 1–10.

40 Palmer, *Jesus Sutras*, 40.

41 Palmer, *Jesus Sutras*, 225–32.

42 Palmer, *Jesus Sutras*, 60–9.

43 Palmer, *Jesus Sutras*, 159–68.

44 Palmer, *Jesus Sutras*, 139–46.

45 Palmer, *Jesus Sutras*, 180–1.

46 Palmer, *Jesus Sutras*, 183–5.

47 Palmer, *Jesus Sutras*, 189–204.

48 *Autobiography of Cecil B. DeMille*, ed. Donald Hayne (Englewood Cliffs, NJ: Prentice-Hall, 1959), 274–87.

49 John Gilman, "*Dayasagar* and the Life of Christ in India," <http://www.lausanneworldpulse.com/worldreports/470/09-2006?pg=all>. A critical assessment of the film known in the Hindi language as *Dayasagar* has recently appeared under the film's title in Telugu. See Dwight H. Friesen, "*Karunamayudu*: Seeing Christ Anew in Indian Cinema," in David Shepherd, ed., *Images of the Word: Hollywood's Bible and Beyond*, Semeia Studies. (Atlanta: Society of Biblical Literature, 2008), 165–88.

50 A Paul Davids Film – *Jesus in India*, <http://www.jesus-in-india-the-movie.com/>.

51 Art and Culture Team, "*Jesus, the Spirit of God*, Iranian Movie Hits the Screens," May 12, 2008, <http://www.islamonline.net>.

Epilogue

Jesus, a Global Christ

At the outset of the third millennium CE, Jesus the Christ elicits the allegiance of more than 2 billion people around the globe – approximately one-third of the earth's population. Jesus the Jew from Galilee has come a long way. Among the world's religions, Christianity ranks as having the most adherents, with Islam second, with 1.5 billion acknowledged believers. Judaism is the source from which sprang the religions of Jesus the Christ and Muhammad the Prophet has adherents scattered around the globe but there are far fewer – some 15 million or so. As we have discovered, Jesus, in different capacities, has been claimed by all three of the great monotheistic faiths and has received honors from the followers of other religions as well. Jesus has indeed become a global Christ.

The image on the cover of this brief history, *Jesus of the People*, painted by the American artist Janet McKenzie, has imaginatively captured the universality in the particularity of the first-century Jew who has become known by people around the world. As the world was anticipating the shift from one millennium to the other, *The National Catholic Reporter* sponsored an art competition called simply "Jesus 2000." Nearly 1,700 entries from 1,000 artists representing 19 countries were submitted. The striking painting by McKenzie received the top prize. Her work was chosen from 10 finalists by Sister Wendy Beckett, a South African-born Edinburgh-reared Oxford-educated nun and art connoisseur, who came to public notice in the 1990s through her writings and television programs.

How have Jesus as the Christ and the religion associated with him negotiated their way across these centuries to achieve such prominence? The intention of this brief history of Jesus has been to tell his story and the story of how his followers carried him with them as they spread across and around the globe. We have observed how he has been received, how he has transformed lives, and how he became a shaper of culture. In these concluding words to his brief history, I will recall in broad strokes the path taken and consider where his journey has situated him as he faces his third millennium.

As the religion of Jesus the Christ, Christianity began as a first-century Jewish movement in the Jewish homeland, but within a decade it had established itself among the Gentiles in the cities of the eastern Mediterranean world. The first three centuries constituted a period of increasing diversity among those devoted to Jesus as the Christ. Institutionally, Christianity defined itself over against both the Greco-Roman world and Judaism, and, on its own terms, created bishops, scripture, and creed. Early Christological diversity proceeded along two trajectories: proto-orthodoxy, which would become normative Christianity; and heterodoxy, such as Gnosticism – to use that disreputable name. The end of the beginning for Christianity came with the Roman Emperor Constantine, who led the way toward making the religion of Jesus Christ the official religion of the empire: one God, one emperor, and one church.

The period of the four ecumenical councils – Nicaea I (325), Constantinople I (381), Ephesus (431), and Chalcedon I (451) – represented the triumph of Christological orthodoxy with its prescribed uniformity. God was affirmed as one essence or substance, but triune, Father, Son, Holy Spirit, three co-eternal and co-equal persons. The Son, with two natures, divine and human, became incarnate through the Virgin Mary for the salvation of humankind. This winnowing process left beside the road both Arius and Nestorius, among others. While Christianity was spreading into Europe and across North Africa, some churches to the east, beyond the boundaries of the Roman empire, were dissenting from the Christological formulations of the ecumenical councils.

The next thousand years was the period of Christendom, medieval orthodoxy, when the papacy ruled and even emperors and kings had to jostle for some kind of shared authority. Along the way – in 1054 – Christianity divided into the western Catholic Church and the Eastern Orthodox churches. Although the Trinitarian, incarnational, and soteriological claims on behalf of Jesus as the Christ remained similar, there were the matters of the *Filioque* addition to the Nicene Creed in the west and the diverging patterns of liturgical and devotional practices, especially the veneration of icons, in the east. Crusade, Inquisition, heresy, and the variety of religious orders that furthered the work of Jesus Christ are associated more with Rome than with Constantinople. The latter finally fell to the Muslim Ottoman Turks in 1453. Meanwhile, over these centuries Christianity continued its expansion across Europe and into Asia.

The great intellectual and cultural revolution that effected the transition from the Middle Ages to modernity, from a worldview informed by belief in the Triune God to a scientifically based worldview, resulted from three great challenges to Christological orthodoxy. The Renaissance emphasized humanistic learning and human achievement in this world. The Reformation, with an appeal to the authority of scripture and the repudiation of the pope, contributed to the fragmentation of the western church – although the main Protestant bodies reaffirmed traditional understandings of the Trinity, the Incarnation, and the Atonement. But the eighteenth-century Enlightenment tore asunder the medieval synthesis of reason and revelation by elevating reason over faith as the determinant of truth. Jesus, who had reigned as the divine–human Savior and whose salvific work was centered in the cross, seemed to be threatened by the rise of Unitarianism and Deism. But the threat did not limit geographical expansion since Christianity had staked out North and South America as prime property and established plots in Asia.

Nineteenth-century European colonizers and missionaries carried Christianity into sub-Saharan Africa and to eastern Asia. At home, European Protestantism followed the way of critical historiography by seeking the historical figure of Jesus behind the creeds. Indeed, many a Jesus was found, as the continuing

rical quest attests. The past two centuries of the historical
~st have been paralleled both by reaffirmations and by refor-
~ulations of what it means to confess Jesus as the Christ.

Along with historical diversity has come Christological diversity. Nineteenth-century Protestant liberal theology challenged
the traditional orthodoxies at many points and emphasized the
ethical application of Jesus' teaching. Thus Jesus as the Christ has
occasioned much discussion within Protestant and increasingly
within Roman Catholic circles. The ecumenical councils of Trent
(1545–63), Vatican I (1869–70), and, more recently, Vatican II
(1962–5) have profiled the Catholic Church's responses to the
changing cultural forces abroad in the world. Perhaps the theological and ecclesiastical diversity of the first three centuries has
been surpassed by the diversity of recent generations.

Liberation theologies in the twentieth and twenty-first centuries, both Protestant and Catholic, have shifted the emphasis
away from Christological orthodoxy to orthopraxis – to issues of
love and justice. In the name of Jesus Christ, preference has been
shown not just for the poor, but for those who are dehumanized
for whatever reason – whether for class, for race, for ethnicity, for
gender, for sexual identity, or even for religion.

Retrospectively, from Christianity's earliest beginnings, Jesus
was confessed to be the Christ in the face of alien gods and other
religious claims. Judaism, and later Islam, were kindred monotheistic faiths whose own destinies were inextricably bound up
with Christianity. Although Jesus Christ had occasionally
confronted other religions and other gods represented by such
time-honored belief systems as Hinduism, Buddhism, Taoism,
Confucianism, and Shinto, not until global exploration by sea
and global missionary outreach beginning in the late fifteenth
century did the relationship between Christianity and these other
religions become an issue of growing importance.

Several factors have converged to place the issue of Jesus
Christ's relationship to the world's religions increasingly on
Christianity's agenda and on the agendas of many theologians
and believers. In our day, the world's religions are no longer over
there somewhere, but everywhere. Globalization no longer
pertains only to the exchange of goods and services but also to

peoples; and where people are so are their traditions, th practices, and their beliefs.

Already in our brief history of Jesus, we have encountered theologians who have extended the boundaries of belief beyond those of previous generations. When I began this history I articulated three basic Christological questions to be considered throughout with reference to Jesus. Who was he? What did he do? Whose was he? Given the diversity within Christianity, among Christian churches, and between believers, perhaps I must leave Jesus as the Christ facing his third millennium with a series of questions to be pondered by you, the reader.

- Is Jesus unique?
- Wherein lies his uniqueness?
- Is Jesus the only way to salvation?
- What does salvation mean?
- Is there only one true religion?
- Are there many true religions?

Select Bibliography
and Further Reading

This bibliography is not intended to be a comprehensive list of every source cited in the text or in the notes. It is intended to be more conceptual, by identifying a few sources grouped under subheadings that relate to ways in which Jesus has been received within the historical context of the time and place. The bibliography also includes a few items not cited in the text or the notes appropriate for further reading.

General Historical Surveys

Corey, Catherine A., and David T. Landry, gen. eds. *The Christian Theological Tradition*, 2nd edn. Upper Saddle River, NJ: Prentice Hall, 2003.

Ehrman, Bart D., and Andrew S. Jacobs. *Christianity in Late Antiquity: 300–450, C.E.: A Reader*. Oxford: Oxford University Press, 2004.

Holder, Arthur, ed. *The Blackwell Companion to Christian Spirituality*. Oxford: Blackwell Publishing, 2005.

Mursell, Gordon, gen. ed. *The Story of Christian Spirituality: Two Thousand Years, from East to West*. Minneapolis: Fortress Press, 2001.

Pelikan, Jaroslav. *Jesus through the Centuries: His Place in the History of Culture*. New Haven: Yale University Press, 1985.

Pelikan, Jaroslav. *The Illustrated Jesus through the Centuries*. New Haven: Yale University Press, 1997.

Walker, Williston, et al., *A History of the Christian Church*, 4th edn. New York: Charles Scribner's Sons, 1985.

Creeds and Councils

Kelly, J. N. D. *Early Christian Creeds*, 3rd edn. New York: David McKay, 1972.

Leith, John. *Creeds of the Churches*, 3rd edn. Atlanta, GA: John Knox Press, 1982.

Tanner, Norman P. *Decrees of the Ecumenical Councils*, 2 vols. London: Sheed & Ward, 1990.

Ancient Jesus Books and their Interpreters

Ehrman, Bart D. *After the New Testament: A Reader in Early Christianity*. Oxford: Oxford University Press, 1999.

Ehrman, Bart D. *Lost Christianities: The Battle for Scripture and the Faiths We Never Knew*. Oxford: Oxford University Press, 2003.

Kasser, Rodolphe, Marvin Meyer, and George Wurst. *The Gospel of Judas*. Washington, DC, National Geographic Society, 2006.

King, Karen L. *The Gospel of Mary of Magdala: Jesus and the First Woman Apostle*. Santa Rosa, CA: Polebridge Press, 2003.

Layton, Bentley. *The Gnostic Scriptures*. Anchor Bible Reference Library. New York: Doubleday, 1987.

Miller, Robert J., ed. *The Complete Gospels: Annotated Scholars Version*, revised and expanded edn. Santa Rosa, CA: Polebridge, Press, 1994.

Robinson, James M., gen ed. *The Nag Hammadi Library in English*. New York: Harper & Row 1977.

Schneemelcher, W., gen ed. *New Testament Apocrypha*, 2 vols. London: Lutterworth Press, 1963.

Valantasis, Richard, *The Beliefnet Guide to Gnosticism and Other Vanished Christianities*. New York: Doubleday, 2006.

Historical Quest and the Historical Jesus

Powell, Mark Allan. *Jesus as a Figure in History: How Modern Historians View the Man from Galilee*. Louisville, KY: Westminster John Knox Press, 1998.

Robinson, James M. *A New Quest of the Historical Jesus*, Studies in Biblical Theology. London: SCM Press, 1959.

Schweitzer, Albert. *The Quest of the Historical Jesus: A Critical Study of its Progress from Reimarus to Wrede*. Baltimore: Johns Hopkins University Press, 1998. First published in German 1906, and in English translation 1910.

m, W. Barnes. *In Quest of Jesus*, revised and expanded edn. Nashville: Abingdon Press, 1999.

Theology and Christology

Aulén, Gustaf. *Christus Victor: An Historical Study of the Three Main Types of the Idea of the Atonement*, trans. A. G. Hebert. New York: Macmillan, 1967.

Clements, Keith W., ed. *Friedrich Schleiermacher: Pioneer of Modern Theology*. The Making of Modern Theology. Minneapolis: Fortress Press, 1991.

Green, Clifford, ed. *Karl Barth: Theologian of Freedom*. The Making of Modern Theology. Minneapolis: Fortress Press, 1991.

Hopkins, Dwight N. *Introducing Black Theology of Liberation*. Maryknoll, NY, 1999.

Kelly, Geoffrey B. *Karl Rahner: Theologian of the Graced Search for Meaning*. The Making of Modern Theology. Minneapolis: Fortress Press, 1992.

King, Ursula, ed. *Feminist Theology from the Third World: A Reader*. London: SPCK, 1994.

LaDue, William J. *Jesus among the Theologians: Contemporary Interpretations of Jesus*. Harrisburg, PA: Trinity Press International, 2001.

LaDue, William J. *The Trinity Guide to the Trinity*. Harrisburg, PA: Trinity Press International, 2003.

Mitchem, Stephanie. *Introducing Womanist Theology*. Maryknoll, NY: Orbis Books, 2002.

Pui-lan, Kwok. *Post-Colonial Imagination and Feminist Theology*. Louisville, KY: Westminster John Knox Press, 2005.

Rumscheidt, Martin, ed. *Adolf von Harnack: Liberal Theology at its Height*. The Making of Modern Theology. Minneapolis: Fortress Press, 1991.

Sundry Faces of Christ

Bonino, José Miguez, ed. *Faces of Jesus: Latin American Christologies*, trans. Robert R. Barr. Eugene, OR: Wipf & Stock, 1998.

Ford, David F., and Mike Hughes, eds. *Jesus*. Oxford Readers Series. Oxford: Oxford University Press, 2002.

Fox, Richard Wightman. *Jesus in America: Personal Savior, Cultural Hero, National Obsession*. HarperSanFrancisco, 2004.

Imbach, Josef. *Three Faces of Jesus: How Jews, Christians and Muslims See Him*. Springfield, IL: Templegate, 1992.

Küster, Volker. *The Many Faces of Jesus Christ: Intercultural Christology*, trans. John Bowden. Maryknoll, NY: Orbis Books, 1999.

Loughlin, Gerard, ed. *Queer Theology: Rethinking the Western Body*. Oxford: Blackwell Publishing, 2007.

Porter, Stanley, Michael Hayes, and David Tombs, eds. *Images of Christ Ancient and Modern*. Roehampton Institute, London Papers, 2. Sheffield Academic Press, 1997.

Prothero, Stephen. *How the Son of God became a National Icon*: New York: Farrar, Straus & Giroux, 2003.

Schreiter, Robert J., ed. *Faces of Jesus in Africa*. Faith and Cultures Series. Maryknoll, NY: Orbis Books, 1991.

Sugirtharajah, R. S., ed. *Asian Faces of Jesus*. Faith and Cultures Series. Maryknoll, NY: Orbis Books, 1993.

Material Culture

Favier, Jean. *The World of Chartres*. Appendices by John James and Yves Flamand; photography by Jean Bernard. New York: Harry N. Abrams, 1990.

Hurtado, Larry W. *The Earliest Christian Artifacts: Manuscripts and Christian Origins*. Grand Rapids, MI: William B. Eerdmans, 2006.

Jensen, Robin Margaret. *Understanding Early Christian Art*. London: Routledge, 2000.

Jensen, Robin Margaret. *Face to Face: Portraits of the Divine in Early Christianity*. Minneapolis: Fortress Press, 2005.

Metzger, Bruce M., and Bart D. Ehrman. *The Text of the New Testament: Its Transmission, Corruption, and Restoration*, 4th edn. New York: Oxford University Press, 2005.

Snyder, Graydon F. *Ante-Pacem: Archaeological Evidence of Church Life Before Constantine*. Macon, GA: Mercer University Press, 2003.

Snyder, Graydon F. *Irish Jesus, Roman Jesus: The Formation of Early Irish Christianity*. Harrisburg, PA: Trinity Press International, 2002.

Tatum, W. Barnes. *Jesus at the Movies: A Guide to the First Hundred Years*, revised and expanded edn. Santa Rosa, CA: Polebridge Press, 2004.

White, L. Michael. *Building God's House in the Roman World: Architectural Adaptation among Pagans, Jews, and Christians*. ASOR Library of Bible and Near Eastern Archaeology. Baltimore: Johns Hopkins University Press, 1990.

Ziolkowski, Theodore. *Fictional Transfigurations of Jesus*. Princeton: Princeton University Press, 1972.

Index